Lobsang Rampa, mystic, sage
and student of the Astral, offers
another of his profound
dissertations on the progress of
the psychic world.

Here he foretells the disasters
and happenings of the future,
the events to come that will
purify and evolve a new cycle
of life.

Also by LOBSANG RAMPA

THE THIRD EYE
DOCTOR FROM LHASA
THE RAMPA STORY
THE CAVE OF THE ANCIENTS
LIVING WITH THE LAMA
YOU—FOREVER
WISDOM OF THE ANCIENTS
THE SAFFRON ROBE
BEYOND THE TENTH

and published by CORGI BOOKS

LOBSANG RAMPA
CHAPTERS OF LIFE

CORGI BOOKS
TRANSWORLD PUBLISHERS LTD
A National General Company

CHAPTERS OF LIFE

A CORGI BOOK   552 07652 X

First publication in Great Britain

PRINTING HISTORY

Corgi Edition published 1967
Corgi Edition reprinted 1968
Corgi Edition reprinted 1969
Corgi Edition reprinted 1970
Corgi Edition reprinted 1971

Illustrated by Victoria Harvey

This book is set in 10 pt. Plantin

Corgi Books are published by Transworld Publishers, Ltd.,
Cavendish House, 57–59 Uxbridge Road, Ealing,
London, W.5

Made and printed in Great Britain by
Richard Clay (The Chaucer Press), Ltd., Bungay, Suffolk

TO THANK . . .

Mrs. Valeria Sorock (a language purist!) for her noble action in typing extra copies of this manuscript, bravely ignoring and unaltering fractured English and graceless grammar.

Victoria Harvey of Brighton, Sussex, England, for the delicate feeling and understanding so adequately displayed in these illustrations by her.

'Ma' for reading and criticising (always kindly) my first thoughts, and 'Buttercup' for such hard work in typing from my dictation.

The Misses Tadalinka and Cleopatra Rampa, the Representatives on Earth of the Lady Ku'ei and Mrs. Fifi Greywhiskers who, in spite of being only six months old, NOBLY entertained and sometimes tore up the pages before they were finished with.

Ladies—good gracious! They are ALL ladies!—THANK YOU!

T. LOBSANG RAMPA

CONTENTS

To Mariechen
A Lady of Germany
A Light in the Darkness,
A friend throughout the years.

CHAPTER ONE

A COMING WORLD LEADER

THE tall, rank weeds at the edge of the unkempt vacant lot stirred slightly. The broad leaves of the ragged old dock plant waved sideways, and the two unwinking green eyes stared out into the gloom of the dismal street. Slowly, and with considerable caution, a gaunt yellow tomcat emerged on to the uneven sidewalk. Carefully he stopped to sniff the night air for signs of enemies. Friends—he had none, for cats in THIS street lived a near-jungle existence, with every man's hand against them.

Satisfied at last that all was clear, he sauntered across to the centre of the roadway and there, sitting, he commenced a meticulous toilet. First the ears, then the back of the neck with a well-moistened paw. Finally, with the left leg pointed skywards, he continued his careful grooming. Pausing for a moment to draw breath, he looked about him, looked at the dreary street.

Dirty brick houses of another era. Tattered curtains at soot-smeared windows, with paint peeling from the rotting window frames. Occasionally there came the loud blare from some discordant radio, to be quickly turned down as a screamed curse testified to some other occupant's disapproval.

Yellow glimmers of light came from such street lamps as had escaped being broken by the local children. Great patches of black shadow sprawled across the area of the broken lamps. The yellow tomcat turned again to his toilet, unmoved by the garbage littering the sidewalks. From far away, from the 'better' area, came the muted roar of the traffic and reflected from the sky came the glow of many neon signs. But here, in this street, all was desolate, a street of the hopeless.

Suddenly the yellow tomcat was all alert, ears erect, eyes staring into the gloom, muscles ready for instant flight. SOMETHING had impinged upon his awareness. Springing to his feet, he gave a warning HISS before merging into the gloom between two houses. For a moment all was normal in the street, the fretful wail of a sick baby, a man and woman quarrelling with lurid anatomical overtones, and the distant screech of brakes suddenly applied in an adjacent street.

At last, there came the faintest of unusual sounds, slow, shuffling footsteps—not a drunk, that was normal here!—but aged, halting footsteps, the footsteps of one who was tired of life, who was hanging on by the merest thread to a miserable and uncertain existence. The shuffling came nearer, like the slow grating of sand beneath sandalled feet. The dark chasm of the gloomy street, but poorly relieved by the infrequent street lamps, made seeing difficult. A vague shadow moved feebly across a lighted patch and was swallowed up again by the darkness.

The sound of wheezing, asthmatic breath smote harshly on the ears as the shrouded figure approached. Suddenly the steps halted, and there came the raucous noise of harsh expectoration, followed by a painfully hissing intake of breath. A heavy sigh, and the tottering steps resumed their weary cadence.

Dimly a whitish shadow materialised out of the semi-darkness of the street and came to a halt beneath a feebly flickering street lamp. An aged man clad in dirty white robes and with tattered sandals upon his feet peered near-sightedly at the ground before him. Stooping, he fumbled to pick up a discarded cigarette end lying in the gutter. As he bent the burden he carried reflected the light; a placard on a pole, with the crudely printed words: 'Repent, Repent, for the Second Coming of the Lord is at hand. Repent.' Straightening, he moved a few steps farther, and then climbed painfully down some stone steps to a basement apartment.

'Don't know why ye do it, Bert, that's a fact I don't. Ye only get's laughed at by the kids. Give it up, will ya?'

'Ah, Maudie, we all got our job to do. Guess I might plant a seed of thought somewhere, you know. I'll keep at it a while longer.'

'A while is all it'll be, Bert, ye'r eighty-one now, time you give it up I say, afore you drop dead on the street.'

. . . . .

The old lych-gate was gleamingly resplendent under the weak afternoon sun. The fresh varnish brought new life to the age-old wood. Farther along the path the ancient grey stone church of St. Mary's looked mellow and benevolent. The great iron-studded doors were open now, waiting for worshippers to the Eventide Service. High above the bells clanged their

eternal message, 'Hurry now, hurry now, or you'll be late.' A thousand years of history was locked in the old churchyard. Great stone tombs of bygone days, with their archaic spellings, vast stone angels with wide-spread wings. Here and there broken marble columns signified a life 'broken' in its prime.

A vagrant shaft of light, bursting unexpectedly from suddenly parted clouds, shot through the old church and threw the stained-glass windows into vivid life, laying the shadow of the castellated tower across the graves of those who were buried so long ago.

People were converging on the church now, coming from all directions, talking animatedly, dressed in their Sunday best. Young children, self-conscious in their finery, and embarrassed by freshly scrubbed faces, tagged along behind their parents. An old Verger appeared briefly and gazed worriedly down the path before retiring into the dim coolness of the church.

From over the stone wall came a burst of laughter, followed by the Rector and a clerical friend. Skirting the old tombstones, they followed a private path leading to the vestry. Soon the wife and children of the Rector appeared, making their way to the main entrance so they could mingle with the incoming throng.

Above, in the bell tower, the clang-clang, clang-clang continued, urging on the tardy, reproaching the churchless. The crowd thinned to a trickle, and came to a stop as the verger peered out once more, and, seeing no one, closed the main door.

Inside there was the hallowed atmosphere so common to old churches of any Faith. The great stone walls soared upwards, to give way at last to massive rafters. The sunlight shone through the stained-glass windows, throwing shifting patterns across the pale faces of the congregation. From the organ loft came the lulling strains of a hymn whose history was lost in the mists of antiquity. A last peal from the bells, and as their echoes were still dying away a door creaked faintly, and the bell-ringers came into the nave to find seats at the back.

Suddenly the organ changed its music. People stiffened with an air of expectancy and there was subdued commotion at the rear of the church. The tread of many feet, the rustle of vestments, and soon the first choirboys were filing up the aisle, to take their places in the choir stalls. There came the fidgeting

14

and murmuring so common to such occasions as the congregation prepared for the service to start.

The Reader droned on, reading the Lessons as he had done for years past, reading automatically—without a thought. Behind him a bored choirboy with a rubber band and some pellets of paper proceeded to find amusement. 'Ouch!' said the first victim, involuntarily. Slowly the organist–choirmaster turned on the organ stool and fixed the culprit with such a ferocious glare that he dropped the rubber band and shuffled uneasily.

The Guest Cleric, ready to give the sermon, slowly mounted the steps of the pulpit. At the top he leaned against the wooden ledge and gazed out complacently at the congregation. Tall, he was, with wavy brown hair, and with eyes of that shade of blue which so appeals to elderly spinsters. The Rector's wife, sitting in the first pew, gazed up and permitted herself to wish her husband could have such an appearance. Slowly, taking his time, the Preacher gave as his text THE SECOND COMING OF THE LORD.

He droned on, and on, and on. In a far-back pew an old retired farmer found it too much for him. Slowly he lapsed into slumber. Soon snores resounded throughout the church. Hastily a sidesman moved towards him and shook him awake before leading him outside. At last the Visiting Cleric finished his Address. After giving the Blessing he turned and made his way down the pulpit steps.

There was a shuffling and stirring of feet as the organist commenced to play the closing hymn. Sidesmen moved along the aisles passing the collection plates and shaking a reproving head at those who did not give enough. Soon they formed into a group of four and marched up the centre aisle to give the plates to the waiting Rector. Later, in the vestry, the Rector turned to his guest and said: 'The Take, nineteen pounds, three shillings, and eleven-pence halfpenny, one Chinese tael, one French franc, and two trouser buttons. Now, I am very concerned about the poor fellow who has lost two trouser buttons, we must hope that he reaches home without untoward event.'

Together, Rector and Guest wended their way along the little path between the age-old tombstones, with the shadows lengthening and pointing to the East. Silently they crossed the little stile set into the wall between churchyard and Rectory

15

grounds. The Rector broke the silence: 'Did I show you my petunia beds?' he asked. 'They are doing well—I planted them myself. We shouldn't talk shop, but I rather liked your sermon.'

'Seemed to me appropriate, with all this talk about God being dead,' replied the Guest.

'Let us look at the croft,' remarked the Rector, 'I must get some of the apple trees pruned. Do you obtain your sermons from the same Agency as I? I just recently started with them —saves a lot of trouble.'

'Rather a large acreage you have here,' responded the Guest. 'No, I do not deal with the Agency now—they let me down twice and I am not going to risk a third time. Do you dig the garden yourself?'

'Oh!' said the Rector's wife, as they were drinking a mild sherry before supper. 'Do you REALLY believe in a Second Coming as you said in your sermon?'

'Now! Now! Margaret!' interposed the Rector. 'That is very much of a leading question. You know as well as I that we cannot preach nor say all that we believe—or disbelieve. We have subscribed to the Articles and we must preach according to the Rules of the Church and the dictates of the Bishop of the See.'

The Rector's wife sighed, and said, 'If ONLY we knew the truth, if ONLY we had SOMEONE who could tell us what to expect, what to believe, what to hope for.'

'Tell me,' said the Guest, turning to the Rector, 'do you use natural manure or chemical fertiliser on your strawberry beds?'

.   .   .   .   .

The grey, shifty-eyed old man sidled ingratiatingly towards the thin-faced man sitting uncomfortably on the battered park bench. 'Wha' time does dey give da 'andouts, Mate?' he enquired anxiously, in a hoarse voice. 'I gotta get da food inside me quick, or I croak, see. Does ye 'av ter do them yimns first, eh?'

The thin-faced man turned and yawned elaborately as he eyed the other from head to foot. Carefully manicuring his nails with a broken tooth-pick, he replied languidly, 'Jolly old Oxford accent, you have, old boy. Old Borstalian myself, Feltham House. So you want to EAT, eh? So do I—so do I.

16

Often! But it is not THAT easy; the Johnnies make us work for it, you know. Hymns, prayers, and then the jolly old rock pile, or wood to saw or split.'

The evening shadows lengthened as they stole across the little park, lending a welcome privacy to young couples who strolled wistfully among the trees. Minutes ago the shops had closed for the night, and now the grotesque and improbable male and female mannikins were left to display their clothing as figures forever frozen into immobility. The lights were on at the Salvation Army headquarters just down the road. From somewhere afar off came the 'bumm bumm bumm' of a heavy drum being pounded with more vigour than skill. Soon there came the sound of marching feet, and the beating of the drum grew louder and louder.

Round the corner came a group of men and women, all dressed in dark blue serge. The men with peaked caps, and the women with old-fashioned poke bonnets. Now in the main street, the band, which before had been just bright reflections under the street lamps, came into action. The bugler expanded his puny chest and blew a mighty blast through his cornet. The drummer enthusiastically whacked the Big Bass Drum, while one of the Salvation Lassies—not to be outdone, clashed her cymbals as if her place in the Hereafter depended upon it.

Just opposite the park gates they stopped and the flag-carrier grounded the butt of the staff with a happy sigh. The lady with the old accordion got into her stride as she squeezed off the opening bars of a hymn. 'Lah-de-da-da, lah-de-da-da, brumm brumm brumm,' quavered the old grey, shifty-eyed man. The little band of Salvation Army men and women formed a circle, and their captain adjusted his glasses and waited hopefully for a crowd to collect. Along the edge of the sidewalk volunteer workers held out copies of the *War Cry*, while other Salvation Army Lassies walked into a public house energetically shaking their collection boxes. Over on the park bench, the two men—now joined by a third—watched the proceedings with interest.

'You gotta confess yer sins if you want a double helpin',' said the newcomer.

'Sins? Ain't got none!' said the shifty-eyed man.

'Aincha?' said the first. 'Then you'd better invent some quick. Reformed drunkard goes over well. Yer can't 'av that—

17

that's mine. Tell ya, yer better be a wife beater wot seed th' light.'

'Ain't got no wife, don't 'av nuthin' to do with THAT truck!' said the shifty-eyed man.

'Gor bless yer, man,' snorted the other in annoyance, 'yer can INVENT a wife, can't yer? Say as 'ow she run off 'cause you threatened ter knock 'er block off. Yer gotta say it OUT LOUD, though!'

'Do you fellows believe in God?' asked the Old Borstalian, as he turned his idle gaze towards the Salvation Army group.

'Gawd?' asked the shifty-eyed man. 'Gawd no! Never 'ad time fer Gawds nor fer wimmin neither!' He turned and spat contemptuously over the back of the seat.

'How come you interested in Gawd?' asked the newcomer of the Old Borstalian. 'I knewed ye was an old con soon as I seed ye.'

'One has to keep one's faith in SOMETHING,' gently replied the Old Borstalian, 'in order to keep one's sanity—such as it is. So many people nowadays say that God is dead. I don't know what to believe!'

A sudden outburst of music made them look towards the park gates. The hymn had just ended, and now the band was playing louder to attract attention for the Captain. Looking about him, stepping a few paces apart from the others, he said, loudly, 'God is NOT dead, let us prepare for the Second Coming of the Lord. Let us prepare for the Golden Age which is so close upon us but which will be ushered in by toil and suffering. Let us know the TRUTH.'

'All right fer HIM,' said the shifty-eyed man in surly tones. ' 'Ee don't know about hunger, 'ee don't 'av ter sleep in doorways and under benches and git some cop come and say, "Move along, there, move along." '

'You fellows give me the creeps,' said the Old Borstalian. 'Remember we are PERFORMING DOGS—we must do tricks before we get our food.'

Shrugging his shoulders and nodding to the two other men, the Old Borstalian graduate shambled off towards the park gates. Soon he was in the midst of the Salvation group, confessing his sins out loud to an uncaring world.

A fat old woman, watching the proceedings from a care-taker's apartment window, shook her head dubiously. 'I don't know, I just don't know,' she muttered to her tabby cat. 'THAT

18

don't seem to be the answer; I wish SOMEONE would tell us the TRUTH of it all!'

. . . .

In little tin-roofed mission huts, in prayer-meeting groups held in the open, and in great cathedrals, men of 'the Cloth' were preaching of the Second Coming of the Lord. Many of them had not the slightest idea that it was not a SECOND coming, but just one of many.

Far away in a distant land beyond the burning sands of a grim and arid desert, where the West was not yet the East, but where the East had not quite thrown off the shackles of the West, a baby boy was resting on his back, gurgling, and sucking his thumb. A baby who was to become a Great Disciple of the soon-to-be Leader of Man. Yet again in another city where East meets West, and both are soiled thereby, a two-year-old baby boy solemnly fingered the yellowed leaves of an ancient book. Gazing round-eyed at the strange writings, perhaps even then he subconsciously knew that he, too, was to become one of the new Disciples.

Yet farther into the East a small group of old Astrologers—like the Three Wise Men of old—consulted the stars and marvelled at what they saw. 'Here,' said the eldest, pointing a gnarled finger at a chart, 'the Sun, the Moon, and Jupiter will conjoin under the Pushya star which then will be in the Sign of Cancer. It shall be in the second or third new Moon.' Gravely they looked at each other, and bent again to check and recheck their figures. Obtaining the hoped-for confirmation, they called in responsible men, messengers——

Throughout history there have been reports of a Second Coming. Actually the One to Come is the TENTH to come in this Round of Existence!

Heedlessly, in the sprawling lands of this world, people went about their mundane occupations, quarrelling, bickering, swindling, always trying to get 'one over' a neighbour—quite uncaring that not so far away two babies, first and second assistants to the Leader of Destiny soon to be born, crowed and crooned in their cradles.

The Wise Men of the East, well knowing of the immature West, gave their edicts that westerners be not told of the dates and places of these Events. For, if the information had spread, maddened hordes of frenetic pressmen would have swooped

19

across the world on jet-propelled wings, to scoff, deny, and misreport. Yammering feature-writers and undisciplined television crews would have invaded the sacred places, bringing dismay and harm wherever they trod. But only those with special knowledge know where these sacred places are. In good time, in a few years, the world will hear more of these things, and by then the Young Ones will be adequately protected. In good time these Young Ones, under a brilliant Leader, will show the Way into the Golden Age at the end of this cycle of Kali, the Age of Destruction.

.   .   .   .

Many people have the quite mistaken idea that this world was but recently populated and history is complete. That is far from being accurate.

For millions of years there have been different civilisations upon this Earth. This Earth is like a school building to which various classes come. As in the case of classes, one can be exceptionally good, another can be exceptionally bad.

Presumably the same thing happens in the case of wines where wines of a certain 'vintage' are especially prized. In the case of the Earth crop, which, of course, is humans, there are fairly set cycles. For example: The Hindus believe that each world period is divided into four classes, or stages, or cycles, each of which is 864,000 years. The first cycle of 864,000 years is a very good one, people try, people have faith in each other and in the essential goodness of mankind. They try to help and there are no wars, not even rumours of wars. But unalloyed bliss is not a good thing because people 'go to seed'. An example of that can be found in the great civilisations of India, China, and Egypt; these were great civilisations indeed, but through excess power, through lack of suitable opposition and competition the civilisations degenerated. One can see the same thing in the history of Rome of many years ago.

The second cycle is that in which people, or rather, the rulers of the world, realise that they have to introduce a 'snake' into 'Eden', and so the second cycle has some difficulties and controversies in order that it may be ascertained how much people can think for themselves and overcome opposition.

Presumably at the close of the second cycle the 'school reports' of those who have taken part in that particular class is not considered very satisfactory, and so the third class, or period, of 864,000 years which is then starting is a bit more severe. People have wars, they go out to conquer others, but even so their particular wars are not the sadistic, barbarous affairs which are present in this cycle. People were not treacherous in the third cycle, they had wars certainly, but it was more in the way of a game in the same way as two small boys will get busy with their fists and each try to alter the features of the other, but that does not mean to say that either would want to kill the other—just make a few structural alterations! However, wars are infectious and it was found that by introducing a few judicious stabs in the back and assorted treachery, one could win a battle before it really started.

Things in the third cycle go from bad to worse, and get very much out of hand. It is like a forest fire which is not checked in time. If some moron drops a lighted cigarette end and sets the undergrowth on fire an observant person can soon extinguish the conflagration. But if the fire is not noticed in time it will really get a hold, and get out of hand, and then many lives will be lost, much property will be ruined before the fire can be brought under control. Life is like that; if evil be allowed to grow and flourish unchecked, it will become more and more, and become stronger and stronger, and like weeds choking the life out of a beautiful cultivated flower, evil will crush out what faint instincts for good Man originally had.

At the end of the third cycle conditions were very much out of hand. One can say that the rowdy elements in the classrooms which were the countries of the Earth stood up to the teachers, and abused them and would not obey their orders. So the fourth cycle came into being, the fourth cycle which is known (from the Hindu) as the Age of Kali.

The Age of Kali is that in which people suffer. If you wish you can think of it as the Age when men and women are tortured in the fires of war that they may be purified, and so that the dross may be burned out to prepare them for the next and better Round, for life goes on and on, people grow better in the natural course of evolution, they get more experience, and if they do not make a success of their life in one stage of evolution they come back to that stage as a schoolboy who cannot pass the end-of-term exam often has to go back to the same classroom, or same grade, instead of being promoted.

In *You—Forever!*, which certainly has gone around a bit, I

refer to the Jews on page 109 of that book. I said, 'The Jewish people are a race who, in a previous existence, could not make progress at all.' This has produced some very friendly correspondence with Jewish readers throughout the world, and in particular some very erudite ladies in Tel Aviv have asked me to give more details about Jews. This request has been supported by Jewish people in Argentina, Mexico, Australia, and Germany. So, let us go a little more deeply into 'the Jewish question'. May I at this stage say that I have quite a number of friends who are Jewish and I have a sincere admiration for them, for they are an old, old race who have knowledge which is the envy of those less gifted.

First of all we might ask, 'What are Jews?' The general idea is a complete misconception, for 'Jew' in its present form is a misnomer. Actually, this word 'Jew' has not been in use for very long.

If you asked the average person who was the Father of the Jews, you would undoubtedly be told, 'Why, Abraham of course!' But as history proves conclusively, this just is not so because in the true sense of the word Abraham was not a Jew!

If you study your ancient history, either by going to a public library, or, more conveniently, by getting at the Akashic Record, you will find that Abraham was actually a native of the place called Ur of the Chaldees. Many places have two names nowadays, so if it will help you, Ur was also known as Ur Kasdim which was in Babylonia. That brings us to the interesting point that Abraham, far from being a Jew, was a Babylonian, and his actual name had no corresponding name or counterpart in Hebrew. The original name of Abraham was Abram.

Abraham lived 2,300 years before the birth of Christ, at a time when the word 'Jew' was not even thought of, but about 1,800 years after Abraham had gone to his 'just reward' the word 'Jew' referred to people who lived in the Kingdom of Juda, and that was in the South of Palestine.

Those of you who are sufficiently interested can look in your Bible, in Kings 11.16.6. Here you will find words written 600 years before Christ, and the word for Jew in those days was Jahudi.

Back to your Bible again, this time to Ester 11.5. Here you will find that Jew is mentioned for the first time, and remember, also, that the Book of Ester was not written until some 2,400 years after the death of Abraham, that is, in the first century A.D. So—we find that Jahudi is that which we now call 'Jew'.

In each cycle there have been twelve 'Saviours' or 'Messiahs' or 'World Leaders'. So when we refer to 'The Second Coming' we are rather behind the times; we can refer to Abraham, Moses, Buddha, Christ, and many others, but the whole point is that in every cycle of world existence there has to be a World Leader of a different Zodiacal sign. There are twelve signs of the Zodiac, and a Leader comes first in one sign, then another, then another, until in all there have been twelve Leaders. On this particular cycle of Kali we are now approaching the eleventh, and after—there will be one more before this actual Age ends and we are really into the Golden Age.

Naturally, with each World Leader there have to be those who can support Him—disciples, if you like, or assistants, or ministers, call them what you like. But there have to be these men who are born specially to be of service to the world.

In 1941 the first of the disciples was born, and others have been born since. The actual 'Saviour' will be born early in 1985, and in the interim the disciples will be preparing the Way.

The 'Saviour' or 'World Leader'—whichever you prefer—will have very special education and training, and in the year 2005, when he is twenty years of age, he will do much to confound godless people who do not believe in Gods, Saviours, etc., etc.

Again, there will be a case of transmigration. If those of you who know the Bible well will study it with an open mind you will find that the body of Jesus was taken over by 'the Spirit of God—the Christ'. In much the same way, the body of the new World Leader will be taken over by a very high Personage indeed, and during the few years after that there will be remarkable events, and the world will be led along those essential steps which will prepare it for the start of a new cycle.

For some 2,000 years the world will make progress by following the precepts of the church to be founded by the new Leader, but at the end of that 2,000 years yet another Leader shall arise—the twelfth of the cycle, completing the destiny of the Zodiac traversal. Conditions shall improve, and so, gently,

23

in the due course of time, people shall be led into a new Age where they have different abilities from those now existing. There shall be clairvoyance and telepathy as there was before the so-called, mis-called, Tower of Babel, in which through abuse of special powers mankind lost their telepathic abilities for the time being. The whole story is given in the Bible, but it is in the form of a story. Actually, Man was able to communicate with fellow Man and with the animals, too, but through treachery to the animal world mankind was deprived of telepathic communication and so there was the utter confusion of people trying to converse in what were local dialects, and which in time became the languages of the world.

This world can now be likened to a train. The train has been going through various stages of scenery, it has been traversing pleasant sunlit lands which can correspond to stage 1, lands in which there was beautiful scenery and amiable fellow passengers. But then we come to stage 2, when the passengers all changed, and this new lot were not so friendly, nor was the journey so pleasant because there was an uneven track with many clattering switchpoints, and the journey continued through depressingly gloomy terrain where the smoke of various factories belched vile chemicals into the atmosphere. Here the passengers were quarrelling and almost coming to blows, but worse was to come. At the third stage the passengers changed again and a lot of bandits got aboard, bandits who tried to rob other passengers, there was much stabbing, much sadistic action. The train, too, rocked along the edge of narrow gorges where landslides made travel precarious. All the time there was discordant noise and the continual quarrelling of the unhappy passengers.

Again the train stopped and took on fresh passengers. This time conditions were even worse, the new passengers were almost wrecking their train, damaging the fittings, torturing, swindling, and engaging in all those activities which the decent person finds abominable.

The train went through increasingly difficult land, with badly laid rails, with many detours and obstructions. At last there came a long and gloomy tunnel; the train plunged in and there appeared to be no lights anywhere in the train. The passengers were in darkness, like the people of the world itself, leaderless. The gloom became gloomier, and the atmosphere more dismal, until the train was pitching and tossing in absolute darkness, with a darkness that comes in a passage through the heart of a mountain. But our train is now in its darkest phase, it cannot get darker, therefore it must get lighter.

As the train goes rocketing along it will get lighter and lighter, and eventually, as a New Age approaches, the train will burst forth from the mountainside, and below the passengers will see a fair and pleasant land with sparkling waters, herds of cattle grazing peacefully. The sun will be shining, and as the train goes on and on, ever changing passengers, they will find that conditions become better and better, where men respect the rights of others, where there is no longer terrorism, sadism, and torture. But much has to be done at the present time because before the Golden Age shall come there will be much more hardship and suffering on this world. Prediction is dealt with in another Chapter of this book, but possibly it would not be amiss to say something here.

According to the age-old art of astrology many sad events are going to take place on this Earth. Round about the year 1981 there will be a very substantial and unexpected increase in the world's heat, with a reduction in rainfall and a drying up of crops, and fruit and other plants will wither up before they can be gathered. This great heatwave could easily be the result of an atom bomb dropped by the Chinese; the Chinese are making haste to develop a super bomb, and the present-day Chinese are like mad dogs, without thought for the rest of the world, because the rest of the world keeps them in virtual seclusion and they do not know what is happening elsewhere, and it is a sad fact that one always fears the person one does not know. Thus, the Chinese, in their xenophobic state of mind, are ready to lash out at that which they do not understand.

One also has to bear in mind that it was bad enough when only the United States had the atom bomb, but now the Russians, the French, the Chinese, and perhaps others have this device. Conditions have reached a most precarious pass.

Much preliminary work has to be done before the advent of the New Leader. Certain people have to be given hints of what is happening, when, and how. But certain other people have to be excluded from getting much knowledge.

In addition to the disciples who are now born and who are still but children, there are those much older people with special knowledge who have to write about such things so that the knowledge will be disseminated, and who will thus 'pave the way'. These older people will not, of course, be upon the Earth at the time of the New Coming, but like those who are to come after, these forerunners will have done their task by taking upon themselves the hatred and the suspicions which always come to the innovator.

People fear that which they do not understand, and so if it is said that a person has changed bodies with another, then he is automatically the subject of much persecution. But it is necessary that there be incidents of changing bodies to bring it into the public consciousness so that when the New Leader comes people will be able to accept the truth of transmigration of souls and the changing of bodies. Thus, while those who are undergoing the scorn and ridicule and active persecution of an ill-informed Press at present, they will know in the fullness of time that their suffering and misery has been justified.

Often people will say, 'Oh, but if these people have such great powers why do they live in poverty? If they were truly what they say they are, they would have all the money they wanted.' This is utterly ridiculous because a person who comes to this Earth under different conditions is something like a splinter in the body of the world, and if you have a splinter in your thumb you agitate, and fidget, and you mess about until eventually you get that splinter dislodged, and you spare no liking for that splinter! In the same way, people who come to this world, and change bodies, and try to prepare a way for another, they too are like a splinter, the world finds them strange, people may be uncomfortable in the presence of such a being. Rather than blame their own lack of development they always try to put the blame on the other person—'Oh, he is queer, he makes me have such an uncanny feeling when he touches me.'

So, the old world goes rolling along full of trouble, but the darkest hour is before the dawn, and when things are at their blackest there is the happy thought that any change can be for the better. And this world and the peoples of this world, after their blackest hour, will go on and on into the light when mankind shall be tolerant of mankind, and when the little people of the animal world shall be understood instead of misunderstood, feared, and tormented as they are at present. So, beginning with the year 2000, the world shall have pleasures, and a Golden Age shall dawn.

CHAPTER TWO

MANY MANSIONS

ALONE he was, alone in the old rambling house in the heart of the Moor. Far off at the end of the long, cultivated garden, a noisy brook went tumbling over the rocks and hissing across the stony stretches. On a warm day he was wont to stand by that babbling brook, or perch on one of the large rocks overhanging the tumultuous torrent. Farther along there was the little wooden bridge with the shaky handrail by which he crossed on his way to the small hamlet for his mail and shopping.

It had been pleasant here, he and his wife. Together they had tried to make a home, tried to keep 'body and soul together' while he painted and waited for recognition. But, as usual, the Press had not understood—nor tried to understand—his art, and so the critics had damned his work with faint praise; recognition was as far off as ever. And now he was alone in the old, old house, his mind and mood in a turmoil matched by the gale outside.

Across the moorland heather the gale screeched in unbridled fury, lashing the yellow gorse, making it bow to the mighty wind. The distant sea was a boiling white mass of foam, with mighty waves breaking in thunder on the great granite shore, dragging back the pebbles with a nerve-jarring scream. A lone gull soared backwards overhead, blowing helplessly inland, powerless in the grip of the storm.

The old house shook and shuddered to the ceaseless pounding of the elements. Flecks of cloud, driven low, whipped by the windows like ghosts seeking entry. A sudden metallic clatter and rumble, and a sheet of corrugated metal went spinning across the garden, to strike the bridge and shear through the old timbers. For a time the broken ends vibrated like an overtaxed violin string, then, one after the other, they shuddered and tumbled into the brook.

Inside the house, oblivious of the turmoil, the man paced back and forth, back and forth. Seeing again and again, the moment when he had returned from the hamlet and found his wife gone. Re-reading the bitter note in which she told him that he was a failure—and she was going elsewhere. Grimly—as a sudden thought struck him—he strode to the battered old desk and wrenched open the centre drawer. Rooting in the back, he dragged out the cigar box in which he kept the rent and living money. Even before he opened it he knew that it was empty, the money, his ONLY money, gone. Groping his way to a chair he sat down and buried his head in his hands.

'Before!' he whispered. 'Before, this has happened to me before!' Lifting his head he stared unseeingly through the window against which torrential rain was beating in an unceasing stream, forcing its way through a loose-fitting window and collecting in a spreading pool on the carpet. 'I've lived through all this before!' he whispered. 'Have I gone INSANE? How could I have known about this?' High up among the eaves the wind shrieked in derision and gave the old house an extra shake and judder.

Against the ancient stone hedge the little moorland ponies huddled head to wind in abject misery, trying to get even slight shelter for stinging eyes. Away in the hall the telephone rang and rang, jarring him from his lethargy. Slowly he made his way to the jangling instrument, which ceased its clanging even as he stretched out his hand to lift it. 'The same, the same,' he murmured to the uncaring walls. 'IT HAS ALL HAPPENED BEFORE!'

.   .   .   .   .

The old Professor plodded wearily across the quadrangle on his way to the Lecture Hall. The years had been hard ones indeed. Born in very humble circumstances he had been the 'bright boy' who had slaved and earned that he could put himself through college. It had been almost a lifetime of clawing his way up against the opposition of those who resented his humble origin. Now in the evening of his life the weight of Time was showing in his white hair, lined face, and feeble step. As he stumbled slowly along, oblivious of the greetings of undergraduates, he pondered on many obscure facets of his speciality, Ancient History.

Completely the model of the Absent-minded Professor, he fumbled for the door-knob of a door already open, and not finding it, turned away, muttering, 'Dear dear! Most strange, MOST strange—there used to be a door here. I must be in the wrong building.' An understanding student—one who had profited from the old man's brilliant Lectures, took his arm and gently turned him round. 'Here, sir,' he said. 'I have opened the door for you. In here.' Gratefully the Professor turned and mumbled his thanks. Entering the Lecture Hall he became a man transformed; HERE was his life, here he expounded upon Ancient History.

Moving like a man rejuvenated, he crossed to the rostrum and smiled benignly upon the assembled undergraduates. They smiled respectfully at him, for even though they did at times make fun of his forgetfulness, yet they still had a genuine liking for the Lecturer who was so willing to help them to the full extent of his power. Remembering his own struggles, he took pleasure in HELPING the student in difficulties, instead of flunking him as was so often the case with other Professors.

Glancing about him to see that his class was complete, and all were ready, he said, 'We are going to continue with our discussion about one of the great enigmas of History, the Sumerian civilisation. Here was a mighty civilisation which seems to have appeared in a most mysterious manner and disappeared in an equally mysterious manner. We have tantalising fragments, but no clear picture. We know, for example, that three thousand and five hundred years B.C. the Sumerians were preparing beautifully written manuscripts. We have fragments of them. Always fragments, and no more. We know also that the Sumerians had a musical system which differed from any other system of musical notation throughout the old or new worlds. There has been discovered a clay tablet which by scientific methods indicates an age of some three thousand years. The tablet has engraved upon it musical symbols which lead us to suppose that it was a hymn, but it has defied musical interpretation.'

The old man paused, his eyes opened wide as if seeing something beyond the normal vision of Man. For a minute he stood thus, gazing into the Infinite, then, with a strangled groan, he dropped to the floor. Stunned amazement held the class motionless for a moment, then two students rushed to his side, while another hurried out in search of medical assistance.

A hushed assembly stood respectfully aside as two stretcher-bearers carefully lifted the unconscious man, placed him upon the opened stretcher, and bore him away to the waiting ambulance. The Head who had been called, appeared full of bustle and dismissed the class for the afternoon.

Away in the cool hospital room the old Professor, now regained consciousness, muttered to his doctor, 'Strange! Strange! I had the distinct impression that I had lived through this incident before, that I KNEW the origin of the Sumerians. I must have been working too hard. But I KNEW the answer, and now it has faded. Strange, strange!'

.   .   .   .   .

The middle-aged man squirmed uncomfortably upon the hard wooden bench, crossing first one leg then the other. From time to time he lifted half-frightened eyes to gaze about him. From the end of the room came the harsh, impersonal voice of the nurse grating out her monotonous orders: 'Garland, you are to see Dr. Northey. Here are your cards. Take them in THAT door, and wait until the Doctor speaks to you. Rogers, you go to Therapy, they want to do some test. Here are your cards. Go down the corridor THERE.' The voice continued like the voice of a bored Announcer quoting the Fat-Stock prices.

The middle-aged man shuddered at the rows and rows of people before him. Patients unaccompanied, new patients with relatives with them, and some with burly Attendants waiting near by. The hours dragged on. Here and there a man or woman screamed in the grip of some mental fantasy. Nearer, a man shouted, 'I gotta, and when you gotta you gotta.' Jumping up, he rushed across the room, scattering people right and left, elbowing aside a clutching Attendant, tripping a clerk, before diving headlong through an open window. Throughout the ensuing commotion the nurse's voice droned on imperturbably.

Outside, the dull red-brick buildings shimmered in the increasing heat. The glass of the many windows threw back the sun's reflection, and showed the thousands of bars across the windows. Scores of blank-eyed men stooped and shuffled as they grubbed among the gravel of the paths in search of weeds. Attendants loitered alertly in any available shade as they supervised the toiling men. Farther along, where the grassy slopes met the main drive, lines of dowdy women bent to the task of picking litter and stones from the grass before the mowers could do their work. Beneath a spreading tree a gaunt woman stood in the pose of utter majesty as she scornfully surveyed the two watchful women Attendants who were poised in anxious expectancy.

At the main gates two Attendants stopped cars entering that the occupants might be directed. An inmate, appearing casual, tried to slip out behind an Attendant's back, but was soon stopped. 'Now, Alf!' the Attendant admonished. 'Back in you go—none of your tricks, I'm busy.' Beyond the high stone walls and heavily barred gates pedestrians peered in curiously, getting a thrill out of a forbidden peep at Life Inside the Walls.

In Admittance the middle-aged man stood up uncertainly as his name was eventually called. Rising to his feet he walked to the Nurse at the desk and said, 'It is all a mistake, I——'

'Yes, yes, I know, you are as sane as can be,' interrupted the Nurse. 'They all say the same.' Sighing, she picked up a card and some papers and signalled to a waiting Attendant. 'You had better take this one to Dr. Hollis,' she said, when the Attendant appeared. 'He says it is all a mistake and he is sane. Mind he doesn't get away.'

'Come on, fella,' said the Attendant, grasping the middle-aged man by the arm and leading him through a small door. Together they trudged along a corridor lined with doors. From behind some came sighs, from others screams, and from yet another a queer bubbling sound which made the Attendant jump to an alarm and energetically summon assistance to one whose life was bubbling away through a cut throat. The middle-aged man shivered and seemed to shrink. 'Scared, eh?' asked the Attendant. 'You ain't seen nuthing yet. YOU WILL!'

At last they stopped before a door, the Attendant knocked and a distant voice called, 'Come in.' Pushing the middle-aged man before him, he entered and placed the card and papers on the desk. 'Another one for you, Doctor,' said the Attendant as he turned and withdrew. The Doctor slowly reached out a languid hand and picked up the papers and compared them with the card. Then, without paying the slightest attention to the middle-aged man he settled back in his swivel chair and began to read. Not until he had read every word, and made notes, did he look up and utter a terse, 'SIT!'

'Now!' said the Doctor as his patient sat shakily before him. 'What's all this about? How d'ye think you can be in two places at once? Tell me all about it.' He sat back with an air of bored resignation and lit a cigarette.

'Well, Doctor,' said the middle-aged man, 'for some time I have had the strangest feeling that another part of me is living in some other part of the world. I feel as if I were one of identical twins sometimes almost completely in rapport with the other.'

The Doctor grunted and knocked the ash off his cigarette. 'Any brothers or sisters?' he asked. 'The report says none, but it could be wrong.'

'No, Doctor, no brothers, no sisters, and no one with whom I am sufficiently friendly to account for this feeling. It is exactly as if I sometimes get in touch with another "me" somewhere else, someone who also is aware of this feeling.'

The Doctor stubbed out his cigarette and said, 'How frequently do you have these remarkable occurrences? Can you predict their onset?'

'No, sir,' the middle-aged man replied. 'I may be doing something quite ordinary, then I will experience a tingling in the navel, and after that I feel as if I were two telephone lines which have been crossed and both parties are receiving their own telephone calls as well as those of the other.'

'Hmm!' mused the Doctor. 'Does it inconvenience you in any way?'

'Yes, Doctor, it does,' the middle-aged man replied. 'Sometimes I speak out loud and say the DARNDEST things!'

The Doctor sighed as he remarked, 'So I see from this report. Well, we shall have to commit you to an Observation Ward until we can get the matter straightened out, you seem to be living in two worlds at the same time.'

At the Doctor's signal the Attendant entered the room. 'Take him to Observation B3 please. I will see him later in the day.'

The Attendant motioned to the middle-aged man, and together they turned and went out of the Doctor's office. The Doctor sat motionless for a moment, then pushed his glasses up to his forehead and energetically scratched the back of his neck. Lighting a fresh cigarette, he leaned back in his swivel chair and put his feet on the desk.

'It seems we have a lot of people in nowadays,' he said to himself, 'who believe they are living twin existences. I suppose next we shall have people saying they are living in parallel worlds or something.' The 'burrr, burrr' of his telephone jerked him back to the present, and slipping his feet off the desk he reached out for the phone and got ready for the next patient.

    ·   ·   ·   ·

There are such things as parallel worlds because everything must have its counterpart in a reversed state, just the same as you cannot have a battery which is only positive or only negative; there must be positive and negative. But that is a matter to be discussed in our next chapter, now we have parallel worlds.

Unfortunately, 'scientists' who have been afraid of losing face or something, or sinking into matters beyond their depth, have confused the issue because they will not face up to the thought of having genuine research. Yet in India the Adepts of years gone by referred to their 'Linga Sharira', which means the part of the body which is in a different dimension—beyond the three dimensions of this world—and so cannot be perceived normally by a person existing in this three-dimensional world. We have to remember that upon this world we are confined to three dimensions, for this is wholly a three-dimensional world and to the average person who has not studied anything about metaphysics the fourth dimension is something to laugh about or to read about in some remarkable science fiction.

Not merely is there a fourth dimension, but beyond the world of the fourth there are the fifth, the sixth, the seventh, the eighth, and the ninth. In the ninth, for example, one attains realisation and is able to comprehend the nature of things, one is able to comprehend the origin of Life, the origin of the Soul, how things started and what part mankind plays in the evolution of the Cosmos. In the ninth dimension, also, Man—still a puppet of the Overself—is able to converse face to face with his Overself.

One of the greatest difficulties is the unfortunate fact that 'scientists' have set up all sorts of extraordinary and arbitrary rules and if one dares to contradict anything that these 'scientists' say, then one is really ostracised. An example of that may be found in the way in which the medical profession was completely crippled for hundreds of years because of the works of Aristotle, it was considered to be a great crime to do any investigation into the human body because Aristotle had taught all there was to know—ever. So, until the medical profession could escape from the dead hand of Aristotle, they could do no dissections and no post-mortems, and they could do no research.

Certain astronomers had much the same difficulty when

they taught that Earth was not the centre of creation because some early Wonderful Man had taught that the Sun revolved round the Earth, and that everything existed for the comfort of mankind!

But now we have to get on with our dimensions. Here on this Earth we deal with that which is commonly known as three dimensions. We see a thing and we feel a thing, and it appears solid and real to us. But suppose we had to deal with an extra dimension, the first thing would be—well, what is this extra dimension? Possibly we could not quite comprehend it. What could be a fourth dimension? Worse, what would be a fifth? And then go on up to the ninth, or even beyond the ninth.

The best thing is to consider first an ordinary tape-recorder because most people have access to a tape-recorder or have seen one. We have a tape-recorder running at a very slow, slow speed, less than an inch a second. At such a slow speed one could have a tape message last for an hour. But supposing we made that tape play back at, for example, a foot a second; then the speech would be quite unintelligible to us, the message upon the tape would not have altered in any way, the words would be the same, but in effect we would have moved our speech to another dimension and so we could not comprehend the speech. Before we could comprehend that which was upon the tape we should have to play the tape at the same speed as that employed in recording it.

Incidentally, marine biologists have used tape-recordings and have discovered that fish of all kinds talk. There is, in fact, a special phonograph record giving sounds of the sea in which there are the sounds of the fish talking to each other, and even lobsters and crabs communicating. If you find this hard to believe, remember that dolphins have had their speech recorded on tape; dolphins speak many, many times faster than humans, so the speech was recorded on tape and was quite unintelligible to humans, but the tape was slowed to a 'dimension' (speed) acceptable to human ears. Now the scientists are trying to decipher the tapes, and at the time of writing this it has been stated that these scientists are able to compile a vocabulary so that eventually they may be able to communicate *in extenso* with dolphins.

But—back to our parallel worlds. Many, many years ago, when I had escaped from the Russians and was making my

34

slow and painful way across Europe to eventually reach a free country, I chanced to stop in war-torn Berlin then being desecrated by the savage Russians. I was walking about wondering what to do next, wondering how to pass the time until nightfall when I should hope to be able to get a lift upon my way towards the French border.

I walked along looking at the still-smouldering ruins where allied bombing had reduced most of Berlin to shattered rubble. In a little cleared spot beneath twisted steel girders now turning red with rust, I saw a ramshackle stage set up surrounded by those bomb-racked buildings. There was scenery of a sort upon the stage, scenery made from bits of material salvaged from the wreckage. They had some poles, and from the poles were stretched pieces of sacking so as to obscure as much as possible a view of the stage from those who had not paid to enter.

I was interested and looking farther I saw there were two old men, one was standing before a curtain taking money. He was tattered and unkempt, but there was a certain air of—something—majesty, I suppose, about him. I forget now how much money I paid to enter, not much because none of us had much money in war-torn Berlin, but as I paid he put the money in his pocket and courteously motioned me through the tattered and bedraggled curtain.

As I went beyond the curtain I saw some planks bridging rubble, and on those planks people were sitting. I took my seat, too, then a hand came through the curtain and waved. An old, old man, thin, bent with the weight of years, shuffled to the centre of the stage and made a little address in German telling us what we were going to see. Then turning away he went behind the backdrop. For a moment we saw him with two sticks in his hand and from those two sticks depended a number of puppets, inanimate lumps of wood, roughly carved to represent a human shape, dressed up in gaudy rags, with painted features and lumps of hair stuck on top. They were crude, they really were crude, and I thought that I had wasted money which I could ill afford, but—I was tired of walking, tired of just ambling about attempting to evade Russian and German police patrols, so I kept to my hard seat and thought that as I had wasted the money I would waste some time as well.

The old man shuffled out of sight at the back of his little

ramshackle stage. Somehow he had rigged up lighting of some kind, these were now dimmed and on this very makeshift stage appeared figures. I stared. I stared hard and rubbed my eyes, for these weren't puppets, these were living creatures, gone completely was the crudity of hacked wood daubed over with colour, topped with horsehair and swaddled with bits of rag salvaged from bombed ruins. Here were living people, people each with a mind of his own, people intent on the task at hand, people who moved of their own volition.

There was no music, of course, and no sound, no sound that is except for the asthmatical wheezing of the old, old man now hidden in the back. But sound was not necessary, sound of any kind would have been superfluous, the puppets were Life, every movement, every gesture was expressive, speech was unnecessary, for these motions were in the universal language of picture, pantomime.

There seemed to be an aura around these puppets, these puppets who had now become people, they seemed to take on the identity and the personality itself of that which they were at the moment representing. No matter how much I peered I could not see the strings going from the heads, these were indeed artfully hidden against the background. Before me scenes of life were being enacted with absolute fidelity to the human counterparts. I lost myself in following the actions and the motives, we watched human drama and our pulses raced in sympathy with the under-dog. This was excitement, this was real, but at last the show came to an end and I roused myself as if from a trance. I knew that a real genius was controlling those puppets, a master of masters, and then the old man came out from behind his stage and bowed. He was shaking with fatigue, his face was white with the strain and covered with a thin sheen of perspiration. He was indeed an artist, he was indeed a master, and we saw not a tattered, battered old man, clad in rags, but the genius who manipulated those crude puppets and brought them to life.

As I turned away I thought of the things I had learned in Tibet, I thought of my beloved Guide the Lama Mingyar Dondup, and how he had shown me that Man is just a puppet of his Overself. I thought also how this puppet show had been a wonderful lesson on parallel worlds.

Man is nine-tenths subconscious and one-tenth conscious. You have probably read quite a lot about it because the whole

36

science of psychology is devoted to the various facets and idio-syncrasies of Man's subconscious. Remembering that Man is so little 'conscious' does it not occur to you what a shocking waste of time it is for a powerful, powerful Overself, gifted with all manner of abilities and talents, pulsing with the power of a more vibrant world and of a different way of life, who comes to this world laden with troubles and obstacles, and then to function at, at most, one-tenth of its ability? Supposing you had a motor-car, oh, let us say an eight-cylinder car because there do not seem to be any ten-cylinder cars to make the allusion more exact—let us say we have an eight-cylinder car, then, just for the purpose of this illustration.

We have this eight-cylinder car, but we find that it is work-ing on one cylinder alone, seven cylinders are not in any way contributing towards the function of the car, they are in fact holding it back even more because of the inertia. The perform-ance is deplorable. But think of it in terms of human exist-ence; mankind is like a ten-cylinder car only one cylinder of which works, the other nine are 'subconscious'. Wasteful, isn't it?

The Overself of a human—or any other creature either, for that matter—does not waste energy; the Overself of a human has a number of tasks which must be accomplished. Supposing we have an evolved Overself who is anxious to progress to other planes of existence, one who is anxious to go up and up and up to different dimensions. In that case the Overself might devote one-tenth of its ability to dealing with the body on Earth, and the rest of its abilities might go to dealing with bodies on other planets, or other planes of existence. Or it might even be without puppet bodies on other planes of exist-ence and be moving in what one might term, pure spirit, in-stead. But if the Overself is not that far evolved or has a different scheme of operations, it might do things in a different way.

Supposing our Overself is more or less of a beginner, then you can say that it is the same as a student in secondary school. The student has to attend a number of classes instead of hav-ing to learn just one subject, often this means that the student has to walk to different classes or to different centres, and that really does waste a lot of time and energy.

The Overself is in a far more satisfactory position. It is the puppet master. Upon this world which we call Earth there is a puppet which is the Earth body, and which functions with one tenth of the Overself's attention. Upon a parallel world in another dimension the Overself could have another puppet, or perhaps two, or three, or more puppets, and it would then be able to manipulate these between various tasks. To go back to our student, one might say that this is like a student who can remain aloof in his private room and send his deputies to the different classrooms so that he can gain all the experience required through these different sources and 'connect them up' later.

Let us assume that the Overself is having to rush things somewhat in order to catch up with the cycle of evolution. Supposing the Overself has been a bit slow or a bit lazy, and has had various setbacks, and this Overself does not want to be left in the same class or state after the others have passed on, so he has to take, in effect, a cramming course the same as a child or older student takes extra lessons in order that he may keep up with others who are more advanced, and so remain in close touch with them.

The Overself may have a person living one life in Australia, and may have yet another person doing something else in Africa. Perhaps there will be another one in South America, or Canada, or England; there may be more than three, there may be five or six or seven. These people might never meet on Earth and they would still be very much in affinity with each other, they may have telepathic rapport without in any way understanding why, but then occasionally they would meet in the astral just as travelling salesmen sometimes meet in the sales manager's office.

The poor wretched Overself with seven or eight or nine puppets would really have to get a move on to manipulate them all at once and avoid 'crossing the wires'. This is one explanation of some curious dreams because frequently when two compatible puppets are asleep their Silver Cords might touch, and would produce an effect similar to those crossed telephone lines wherein you hear pieces of others' conversations but, sadly, sadly, and to one's immense regret, we miss all the most interesting bits.

But what is the purpose of all this, you might ask. Well, that's easy to answer: By having a number of puppets the Overself can have vast experience and can live ten lives in just one lifetime. The Overself can experience riches and poverty

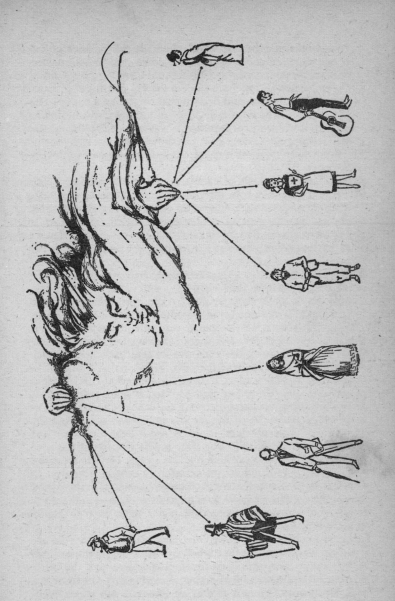

at the same time, and so weigh them in the balance of experience. One puppet in one country could be a beggar making a miserable living, hardly existing, in fact, while in some other country the next puppet could be a prince gaining experience of how to handle men and how to shape a nation's policy. The beggar would be gaining experience of misery and suffering so that when his lifetime of experience was blended to that of the prince-puppet the Overself would know of the seamier side of life, and would know that there are at least two sides to every question.

In the normal course of events people would perhaps come as a prince and then wait for another life to come as a beggar, or the other way about, but when they are rushed for time, when any given cycle of evolution is nearing its end as is the present case, then heroic methods have to be adopted in order that those who are slower may yet keep up with the rest.

We are now entering the Aquarian Age, an Age wherein much will happen to Man and Man's spirituality will increase —it is about time that it did, by the way. Man's psychic ability also will increase. Many people now living on the Earth will not be reborn to the Earth but will go on to different stages of evolution. Many of those who have not learned in this life or in this cycle of existence will be sent back like naughty schoolboys to start again in the next cycle.

If a boy is left behind by his class at school he is often dissatisfied and disgruntled that he is left behind, and he tends to be difficult with newcomers to that class, he tends to overplay his part and to show that he knows more, is better, bigger, and all that sort of thing, and the newcomers to the class almost always dislike the boy who is left over from the previous class. It is the same in the classroom of life, a person who has been rejected as not sufficiently evolved to go on to the next stage of existence has to come back and do that cycle all over again. His subconscious memory contained in the nine-tenths of the subconscious resents it, and he tends to get ahead in one particular way.

Many people after leaving this Earth will go on to a different form of existence, ever higher, for Man always must climb higher and higher, as indeed must all creatures, and the spirit of Man being gregarious by nature, delights to be in company with loved ones. Thus it is that an Overself will make really

40

determined efforts and will use many puppets in order that it may keep up with its fellows.

Let us accept, then, that a parallel world is a world in a different dimension, a world which is much like Earth, but yet is in a different dimension. If you find that difficult to comprehend, supposing you could go to the other side of the world instantly, in the twinkling of an eye. Now decide for yourself—are you living in the past? That is, have you gone back to yesterday, or have you travelled to the future? According to your calendar you will find that when you cross various date-lines you travel either backwards or forwards as much as a complete day. So it is theoretically possible to move a day into the future according to your basic time, or to a day in the past. Having agreed that that is so, you should be able to agree that there are various dimensions which cannot be easily explained, which nevertheless do exist, as do parallel worlds.

It is always amazing that people can readily believe that the heart can pump ten tons of blood in an hour, or that there are 60,000 miles of capillary tubing in the body, and yet a simple thing like parallel worlds causes them to raise their eyebrows in disbelief and thereby make an astonishing amount of muscles go to work.

Our subconscious is usually quite difficult to reach, difficult to plumb. If we could easily reach our subconscious we could at all times find out what other puppets of ours were doing in other worlds, or in other parts of this world, and that would lead to very considerable confusion, alarm, and despondency. For example, think—today you have done certain things, but if you could get into your subconscious and find yourself living the life of another puppet of yours who had done the same thing last week or who intended to do it next week, it would lead to quite amazing confusion. This is one of the many reasons why it is so very difficult to tap into the subconscious.

At times things happen whereby there is an involuntary breakthrough between the conscious and the subconscious. It is a serious matter indeed, so serious that it is usually dealt with in a mental home. It leads to all sorts of psychotic conditions because the poor wretched sufferer is unable to determine which is the body in which he is supposed to reside.

Have you heard of the book *The Three Faces of Eve*? A woman was possessed by three different entities. The whole thing has been written about by quite a number of reputable doctors and specialists who presumably know what they are writing about.

Have you read the story of Bridie Murphy? That is a similar case. Again a person was possessed by another entity, or in other words, there was a breakthrough in the subconscious from one puppet to another.

Then we have the matter of Joan of Arc; Joan believed that she was a great leader, that she had messages from higher sources. Joan of Arc, a very simple, uneducated country girl, turned into a warrior and a leader of warriors because the Silver Cords between two puppets became tangled and Joan received impulses designed for a man in a different body. For a time she acted as that man, as that leader of men, as that great warrior, and then when the lines were untangled her powers failed and she was once again the simple country girl who had to pay a penalty for temporary, and mistaken, fame; she was burned to death.

In the case of the victim of *The Three Faces of Eve* a multiple breakthrough, or breakdown, occurred and the poor woman was placed in unwilling contact with other puppets controlled by the same Overself. These other puppets were in a similar condition, they also suffered this breakthrough and as a result there was complete chaos. It is the same when you get two or three puppets and you are careless or inexperienced or let your attention wander, the cords become entangled, you pull a string which should control Puppet A, but because of the tangle you might cause Puppet B to kick and Puppet C to nod its head. In the same way, when you get a breakthrough between the conscious and the subconscious, an uncontrolled breakthrough, that is, then you get interference from and with others who are being controlled by the same Overself.

Bridie Murphy? Yes, that also is true, that was a breakthrough into the subconscious and again a tangling of cords and a transference of impressions.

Joan of Arc, as we have seen, was a simple country girl without education of any kind. She spent long periods alone in contemplation, and in one such period she quite accidentally broke through to the subconscious. Probably she did a special breathing exercise without even knowing it, because all this can be done deliberately and under full control. Anyway, she broke through to the subconscious, crossed strings with another puppet, and really got into a mess. She had all the impulses of

42

a warrior, and she became a warrior, she wore armour and rode a horse. But what happened to the poor fellow who was intended to become a leader, did he develop womanly traits? Well, if we speculate on that we can lead ourselves to all sorts of unfortunate conclusions. But—Joan of Arc became a leader of men, a warrior hearing voices from the sky. OF COURSE SHE DID! She was picking up impressions from the Silver Cord which, after all, is only our puppet string. Think of that, our puppet string. We have a Silver Cord that is also mentioned in the Bible where, as you may remember, in the twelfth chapter of Ecclesiastes it is said, 'Or ever the silver cord be loosed or the golden bowl be broken or the pitcher be broken at the fountain or the wheel broken at the cistern.'

People write about time and relativity, parallel worlds and all that, they use such big words that even they do not understand what they mean. But possibly you have got the general idea from this chapter. Remember, all this is true, all this is absolute fact, and one day in the not very distant future science will break down a few barriers and a few prejudices, and will realise the truth of—parallel worlds.

CHAPTER THREE

MANY MORE MANSIONS

'YOU ruined my radio!' yelled the hatchet-faced woman as she
tore into the little shop. 'You sold me batteries which RUINED
EVERYTHING!' she continued in a shriek as she rushed up to
the counter and thrust a small transistor radio into the startled
hands of the young man who was staring apprehensively from
the other side. The customer whose place had been so suddenly usurped by the belligerent woman sidled cautiously
away and, reaching the door unharmed, dashed into the street.

From the back room the Manager appeared, nervously
washing his hands with invisible soap and water. 'Can I help
you, Madam?' he enquired, gazing with some alarm at the
large, red-faced woman.

'HELP ME?' she shouted. 'You ruined my radio with your
bad batteries. IT WON'T WORK. I want a new radio,' she replied, her voice rising to a hoarse bellow as she thought of all
her 'troubles'. The young Assistant behind the counter feebly
fumbled with the set, at loss to know what to do. At last he
took a coin out of his pocket and gave a half-turn to two screws
at the back of the radio. Removing the cover of the battery
box, he slowly removed the four batteries.

'I will test them,' he said as he moved to the end of the
counter and reached for two leads. 'There!' he exclaimed, as
each cell indicated one and a half volts. 'They are GOOD!'
Gathering them up, he carefully placed them back into the
radio, turned the screws in the opposite direction, then turned
over the set. With a flick of his thumb he rotated the switch—
and the latest Beatle music blared forth.

The hatchet-faced woman stared at the Assistant, her mouth
dropping open with surprise. 'Well! It didn't work for ME,'
she asserted. 'You must have changed the batteries,' she added
truculently.

The Manager and the Assistant looked at each other and
shrugged their shoulders with exasperation. 'Madam!' softly
said the former. 'Are you SURE you put the batteries in correctly?'

44

'Correctly? CORRECTLY? What do you mean?' the woman asked, her face becoming purple with anger. 'ANYONE can put batteries in a radio. OF COURSE I put them in correctly.'

The Manager smiled as he said, 'There is one correct way and one incorrect way. If you put them in with the polarity reversed they will not work.'

Rubbish!' said the woman haughtily. 'They should work in any position—any position at all. I plug in my TV and I do not have to wonder which way the plug should go. You are making excuses, just like all you men do!' she sniffed expressively, and turned to pick up the radio which was still playing its raucous tune.

'Just a moment, Madam!' exclaimed the Manager. 'I will SHOW you, or we shall have the same trouble again.' Reaching past her, he took the radio and quickly removed the battery-box cover. Pulling out the batteries, he reinserted them in the wrong way and switched on the set, no sound, no whisper at all. Turning the batteries once again, he passed the now-playing set to the woman. 'Try it yourself,' he said with a smile.

'Well I never. Well I never did!' said the woman in a subdued tone of voice. Then—triumphantly pointing at the Assistant. 'Well, HE should have told me. How was I to know?'

The Manager reached for a battery on a shelf. 'Look, Madam,' he said. 'All batteries have polarity, one end is positive and the other end is negative. To make a battery work in a set at all it MUST be inserted with the correct polarity. Your TV is different, it takes alternating current which is changed inside the TV itself. EVERYTHING, batteries and magnets, and many other things, have polarity. Even men and women are of different polarity.'

'Yes!' sniggered the woman with a leer. 'We all know what happens when THEY get together!'

. . . . .

The telephone burred insistently; 'burrr, burrr, burrr' it went. At the other end of the garage the man in the grey overalls sighed in exasperation. Snatching up a piece of cotton waste he wiped his oily hands as he hurried to the still-burring telephone. 'Steve's Garage, Sales and Service,' he announced as he picked the instrument from its cradle.

'Oh!' exclaimed a feminine voice at the other end. 'I thought you would never answer.'

'Sorry, Madam,' said the garage man. 'I was busy with another customer.'

'Well,' replied the woman. 'This is Mrs. Ellis of The Ferns. My car won't start and I have to go to town very urgently.'

The garage man sighed anew, always WOMEN had trouble starting their cars, still, he thought, that was what brought in the rent money. 'Have you tried the starter?' he enquired.

'Of course I have,' the woman said indignantly. 'I pressed and pressed and nothing happened, the thing does not go round at all. Will you come over?' she asked anxiously.

The garage man thought for a moment, the woman's husband was a good customer and—yes—he would have to go. 'Yes, Mrs. Ellis,' he said. 'I will be over within thirty minutes.'

Just at that moment his assistant mechanic drove in from the town where he had gone for some spares. Steve hurried out to the truck. 'Put on the spare battery and the jumper cables, will you, Jim?' he said hurriedly. 'I have to go to see the Ellis car and I must wash up a bit first.' Hastily he went into the washroom and removed the dirt and grease, and peeled off his soiled overalls. Brushing back his hair, he strode out to the pick-up truck. 'Leaving you in charge, Jim,' he called to his assistant as he drove off down the road towards the suburbs.

The ten-minute drive to the Ellis house took him through a newly developed district, and he looked wistfully at all the new houses, thinking of all the potential business there was. But people just got into their big new cars and rushed away to the city to spend their money. Only the ones with old cars, or those whose cars would not start, shopped locally, he mused. Otherwise they all flocked to Flash Pete, or Honest Trader Joe, bedazzled by the gleam of chromium window frames and fluttering bunting.

As he drew up to the Ellis driveway, he saw the slim Mrs. Ellis hopping from foot to foot in her impatience. Seeing the pick-up truck, she hurried down the sloping driveway. 'Oh!' she exclaimed. 'I thought you were NEVER coming!'

'I've only been twenty minutes, Madam,' responded Steve mildly. 'Now, what is the trouble?'

'That's for you to find out!' said Mrs. Ellis tartly, as she turned and led the way to her two-car garage.

Steve glanced around, noting the spare tyres carefully fixed to the wall and the five-gallon drum of oil with the patent tap,

46

and the new, gleaming battery charger still plugged into the outlet and with its warning light still glowing. 'Hmmn!' he thought. 'THAT should rule out any battery trouble.'

Stepping over to the nearly new car, he opened the door and slid into the driver's seat. Looking about him, trying the clutch, and making sure the car was out of gear, he pressed the starter button. Nothing, no sign of life. No red light to indicate that the ignition was on, either. Getting out and lifting the bonnet, he saw that the engine was clean, with all ignition wires new. Testing the connections to the battery, he found them tight and clean. For a moment he stood puzzled and undecided. 'Oh! Do be quick, I'm late already, I MUST insist that you do SOMETHING, or I shall have to call someone else to start it.' Mrs. Ellis was really agitated. 'This is so stupid,' she said. 'My husband bought a battery charger yesterday so that our cars would start easily in the coldest weather, and now mine won't start at all!'

Steve hurried to his pick-up truck and returned with tools and a battery tester. Placing the leads across the battery terminals he discovered that the battery was completely DEAD.

'Oh, nonsense!' exclaimed Mrs. Ellis as he pointed it out. 'The battery was on charge all night, I put it on myself.'

Going over to the battery charger, Steve looked at it and found to his astonishment that the leads were unmarked, neither bore POSITIVE and neither bore NEGATIVE. 'How do you know which is which?' he asked.

Mrs. Ellis looked blank. 'Does it matter?' she asked.

Steve sighed, and explained. 'All batteries have a positive side and a negative side, and if you connect a charger wrongly you will DISCHARGE your battery instead of CHARGE it. So now your battery is flat and you cannot start.'

Mrs. Ellis let out a wail of annoyance. 'I TOLD my husband not to pull off those labels,' she exclaimed. 'Now what shall I do?'

Steve was removing the terminals and battery clamps as he spoke. 'Ten minutes and you will be ready to leave,' he said. 'I brought a spare battery to lend you while I charge yours properly.'

Mrs. Ellis, all smiles now, asked, 'Why does there have to be a positive thing as well as a negative?'

'There just has to be in order to have an energy flow,' answered Steve. 'EVERYTHING has its opposite counterpart

SOMEWHERE. Men have women as their opposite, light has darkness, in fact,' he continued with a laugh, 'I expect that SOMEWHERE there is a world with the opposite polarity to that of this Earth!' Getting into the car again, he pressed the starter and the engine roared into life.

'I must hurry,' shouted Mrs. Ellis, 'or my "opposite pole" will be angry if I am late meeting him for lunch.' Releasing the brake, she shot away, leaving Steve to put the dead battery on his pick-up truck.

Shaking his head in resignation, he muttered, 'WOMEN ...! But I wonder if there really COULD be another world of anti-matter, that was a queer tale I heard down at the Rose and Dragon the other night. I wonder ...!'

.   .   .   .   .

The river flowed on, swirling and gurgling around the stone piers of the Peace Bridge at Fort Erie, swinging around the bend to wash the banks of the Niagara Parkway. With un-dulating ripples it made the moored pleasure-boats toss and bob against their snubbing posts. Along the sandy beach at Grand Island it swept with a chuckling hiss as it rolled little stones with languid grace. Welcoming the Chippawa River to its bosom it flowed on, surging with increased force as every little river, stream, and spring added to the volume.

Farther on, the spray of the Niagara Falls sprang hundreds of feet into the air, to hang poised for a moment, then fall back to add to the torrent. Coloured beams of light played in ever-changing patterns upon the leaping waters and made multi-hued rainbows in the spray above. At the water-control station above the Falls the water divided at the whim of a man's hand, countless gallons going over the Falls for the delectation of tourists, and thousands of gallons swirling sharply left to enter a vast man-made tunnel and swoosh with ever-increasing force five miles downhill to the Sir Adam Beck Generating Station.

The mighty power of the harnessed waters closed in and swept with irresistible force against turbine blades, turning them with incredible speed, and rotating the coupled genera-tors so that stupendous amounts of electricity were generated.

Across Ontario power-lines hummed as the current flowed to meet the needs of civilisation. From Canada great grids of wires spread across the United States to New York City, bringing Canadian electricity to American homes and industries. Billions of lights spread their comfort and assurance. In busy hotels elevators whooshed along, taking guests to their rooms. In hospitals of two countries doctors and surgeons performed their tasks by the light of Canadian-generated electricity. Radios blared, and the flickering shadows called 'television' swayed and jumped behind their glass screens.

Droning across the well-lit land came aircraft from all over the inhabited globe. From England, Australia, Japan, South America, and from all the exotic names of the Travel Agency advertisements they came, converging in orderly layers to the great airports of New York State. Controllers in countless towers talked to the airmen, directing, guiding. Runway lights made the scene bright as day. Beacons threw great shafts of light into the sky, to be seen many many miles away by those still in the enshrouding darkness high above the ocean, still beyond sight of land.

Electric trains roared and thrummed below the ground, and clattered noisily across viaducts and bridges on the surface. In the docks great ships with commerce from the whole world rode at their moorings as swarms of ant-like humans engaged in frenzied activity to unload and load anew. Floodlights reversed the hours and turned the darkness of night into the brightness of day.

Away at the generating station the waters rushed endlessly by, turning, turning, that electricity should flow across two lands. Generating 'positive' and 'negative' so that the ceaseless struggle for one to reach the other would cause energy to flow, work to be done, and the comfort of Man assured. But somewhere—somewhere a little fault occurred. A short circuit took place. And what is a short circuit but a sudden coming together of positive and negative? They came together on a small scale at first, then, like surging football crowds, more and more positive electrons rushed to jump across to more and more negative electrons.

Relays became hot. The heat increased and points were welded together by the heat. Insulated cables grew hot, grew red hot, and threw off gouts of burning rubber. Motors roared and whined in an agony of excess power, then died and whirred into silence. Across two lands the lights went out. Elevators ceased to move, stranding passengers, and causing distress and fear. Beneath the ground the trains juddered to a screeching standstill as the current failed. Joy of joys—the shouting radios and the flickering television sets were silenced and extinguished. The presses came to rest in a tangle of torn paper and cursing men.

And all because 'positive' electricity wanted to meet 'negative' electricity suddenly, violently, without being tamed and controlled by first having to work. For when opposites meet, uncontrolled, ANYTHING can happen . . . and DOES!

·   ·   ·   ·

For centuries past the Adepts of the far, far East have known that there was an opposite world to this, the world which in the far, far East is referred to as 'the Black Twin'. For years Western scientists have scoffed at such things, believing in their ignorance that only things discovered by Western scientists could exist, but now, fairly recently, a man has been awarded the Nobel Prize for discovering various things connected with the world of anti-matter.

In 1927 a British physicist discovered that there was such a thing as a world of anti-matter, but he doubted his own work, apparently not having sufficient faith in his own ability. But then an American physicist by the name of Carl Anderson photographed cosmic rays passing through a special chamber. He found traces of an electron different from other electrons, he found, in fact, that there were anti-electrons, and for his discovery, which was anticipated by the British in 1927, Anderson received the Nobel Prize. Possibly if the British physicist had had sufficient confidence in his work he would have had the prize instead.

It is now clear even to scientists—it has been clear to people of the East centuries before—that a hydrogen atom and its anti-matter counterpart could make an explosion which by comparison would make the standard atom bomb as ineffectual as a damp squib. But let us look into this matter a little more.

All life, all existence is motion, flow, rise and fall, wax and wane. Even sight consists of motion, for the rods and cones of the eye merely respond to vibrations (motion) from the article which we say we have seen. So there is nothing whatever that is stationary. Take a mountain—it looks a solid structure, but by different sight the mountain is merely a mass of molecules dancing up and down, circling around each other like midges on a summer night. On a larger scale we could compare it to the cosmos, because in the cosmos there are planets, worlds, meteors, all circling around, all in constant motion, nothing is still, one is not even still in death!

In the same way that a battery must have a negative pole and a positive pole before any flow of energy can occur, so do humans, and anything else that exists, have negative and positive components. Nothing has ever existed which is all positive or all negative, because unless there is a difference there cannot be any flow of energy from one to the other, and thus life or existence would be impossible.

Most people are unaware of the world of anti-matter just as the negative or positive poles of a battery would not be aware of the existence of other poles. The positive terminal of a battery could have a direct pull towards the negative, or vice versa, but it is highly improbable that either pole could discuss the existence of the other.

There is the world of matter, but equal and opposite, there is a world of anti-matter, just as there is God and there is anti-God. Unless we have an anti-God there is no way of comparing the goodness of God, and unless we have a God there is no way of comparing the badness of anti-God. We who live upon this, which actually is the negative world or pole, are at present controlled by anti-God, the Devil, or Satan, or what we term 'the power of evil'. But soon the cycle of existence will change and we shall be controlled by God, more under His beneficent influence. We are of an alternating current system which changes from positive to negative, and negative to positive, just as our counterpart changes from negative to positive and positive to negative.

All life is flow, movement, vibration, oscillation, change. All existence is flow and change. If we examine the alternating current system we can see that each half wave consists of a negative cycle becoming half positive, and a half positive cycle becoming half negative. But then they go on and instead of becoming half negative the first becomes wholly negative, and the second wholly positive. In our ordinary household current, in England for example, the current changes its polarity fifty times a second, from negative to positive and positive to negative. In other parts of the world, such as Canada and the United States, the frequency of change is sixty times a second. We upon this form of existence known as the world, the solar system, and the universe, have a cycle system of our own. Here we travel along the stream of time just as electrons travel along the electric stream, we travel along our conception of time until we reach—or our Overself reaches—some much greater existence. If you will refer to *Wisdom of the Ancients* written by me, you will find that one different time cycle is 72,000 years.

But everyone and everything on Earth has a counterpart of the opposite polarity on another Earth, in another galaxy, in another system of time altogether. Obviously that system cannot be close to us or there would be such a tremendous explosion that the whole Earth, and many other worlds as well, would be destroyed.

It is now thought that the great earth-shaking explosion which occurred on June 30th, 1908, in the wastes of Siberia was caused by a piece of anti-matter much smaller than a football which had somehow got into our atmosphere. It travelled along at truly tremendous speed, and as it slammed into the Earth this piece of anti-matter, much smaller than a football, exploded with a noise which was heard more than 500 miles away. People 40 miles away were thrown off their feet with the blast and shock. So if a larger piece of anti-matter came there would be no longer an Earth; in just the same way as a spark can weld contacts together and so cause a short and complete failure of an electric system, so would a larger piece of anti-matter have caused complete failure to us.

We, then, in our present cycle and on our present world, are of the negative cycle. Thus we have frustration, bitterness, where the predominant force is evil. Take heart from the fact that this particular cycle is coming to a close, and in the years to come a fresh cycle will start in which conditions will become more and more positive, where we shall no longer be under the domination of anti-God, where no longer shall there be wars, but where all shall be good; for just as now we have wars against each other, in the cycle to come the only wars shall be against poverty and illness, and against evil itself. We will find that we have what can be termed 'Heaven on Earth', and Overselves everywhere will be sending their puppets to what then shall be the positive world as well as to the negative world.

Suppose you consider *Alice in Wonderland*: think of Alice going through the mirror into a world where everything was reversed. Supposing that you could suddenly pass through the veil separating the negative and positive, supposing that here on this world you were wondering how you could pay your bills, wondering how you were going to afford to keep going, and wondering why your neighbour disliked you so much. Then, unexpectedly you were pushed through the veil. You would find you had no bills, people were kind, you had time to help other people instead of thinking about yourself all the time. It is going to come, inevitably, it always comes, and each time there is a reversal of cycle we learn a little more.

It is an interesting thought that if we could catch a lump of anti-matter about the size of a pea, and we could shield it somehow from the Earth's influence, we could harness it to a vast spaceship, and then by exposing just a little to the Earth's influence that particle, no larger than a pea, would propel the spaceship upwards beyond this world, and out into deep, deep space. There would then be no need for rockets or other forms of propulsion, because that small piece of anti-matter, under proper control, would provide complete anti-gravity matter.

Again, there cannot be good without evil because no force would exist. You cannot have a magnet which is all positive or all negative because no force would exist. The magnet would not exist either! Let us imagine that the world is just a form of magnet with magnetic fields which radiate from the Arctic and the Antarctic, but connected to us by some bridge that we cannot see is another world of the opposite polarity. Then we would have the two poles of, for instance, a horseshoe magnet. Many scientists are wondering if anti-matter means that every single thing is duplicated on this other world. They wonder, for instance, if there are anti-people, anti-cats, and anti-dogs. Scientists do not know what these people are like because scientists are people of little or no imagination, they have to have a thing in their hands so that they can dissect it or weigh it. It takes an occultist to give information on this particular subject, because the competent occultist can leave the body and get out of the body, and out of the Earth as well, and once out of the Earth he can see what this other world is like—as I have done so very, very frequently.

Anti-people are merely people whose etheric direction is different from that of people on this, the world of Earth. They may, purely by way of illustration, have a yellowish and blue shell to the aura instead of a blue and yellow shell as here. If you find it difficult to visualise the world of anti-matter, consider in photography—we have a negative and we have a positive, and if we shine a light through the negative under sensitised paper and dip the stuff in various chemicals we get a dark patch where there was a light patch on the negative, and a light patch where there was a dark patch on the negative.

There are certain unknown flying objects—let us call them 'flying saucers'—which come to this Earth actually from the world of anti-matter. They cannot come too close or they would explode, but they are exploring just the same as we send a rocket to the Moon, or to Mars, or to Venus.

People complain that if there was anything in this flying saucer business the people aboard would land or would make contact with people upon this Earth. The whole truth of the matter is that they cannot, because if they touch down there is an explosion and no longer a flying saucer. If you will consider various reports you will remember that there have been incidents when some unknown flying object, which was very clearly seen on radar, suddenly exploded most violently as it came within 1,000 feet or so of the surface of this world, exploded so violently that no trace could be found. The same thing could happen if we could send a rocket to the world of anti-matter. We should annoy the inhabitants considerably by perhaps blowing a city right off their map!

There are other aspects of this world of anti-matter which are exceedingly interesting to those who have studied the matter thoroughly. For example, there are certain locations—fortunately but few—on this world of ours where people can 'slip through' into another dimension, or into the world of anti-matter. People move to such a location which oscillates slightly, and if they are unlucky they are transferred completely from our Earth. This is not imagination, but is a matter which has been proved time and time again.

Far away beyond the Shetland Islands in a very cold sea there is a mysterious island called Ultima Thule, the Last Land. Most mysterious happenings have occurred in the vicinity of that island and actually upon it. There is, for instance, a British Admiralty report of many years ago wherein it is stated that a party of British seamen landed on Ultima Thule, and there most peculiar things happened to them, and people appeared, people who were quite different from British sailors. Eventually the British sailors returned to their ship, a British battleship, by the way, considerably shaken by their unnerving experiences. At Ultima Thule whole ships' crews have disappeared never to be seen again.

There is off the American coast a place which has been known as the Triangle of Death. It is an area in the Atlantic Ocean where ships, and even fast flying aircraft, have disappeared. Would you like to check on some of this?

Here is a start: On February 2nd, 1963, a tanker called *Marine Sulphur Queen* left Beaumont in the State of Texas. This ship was bound for Norfolk in Virginia.

The ship left on February 2nd, and was in routine radio communication with land radio stations until February 4th, when she was stated to be near a certain area of land in the Gulf of Mexico. Then no more was heard of the ship.

On February 6th the ship was presumed lost. Planes took off to patrol the area, coastguard cutters steamed criss-cross patterns, and all ships in the area were asked to report any unusual wreckage. And so the search continued until February 14th, without any trace whatever of anything from the tanker.

Not only ships have been lost; in August 1963 two large four-engine tanker planes left an Air Force base South of Miami. The eleven men aboard the planes were to be engaged in ordinary refuelling operations—just an ordinary matter of training in refuelling.

During the flight the planes radioed their position as 800 miles North of Miami and 300 miles West of Bermuda, but that was the last heard from them, they reported their position and vanished to be seen no more.

These were new planes with highly trained crews. There was no fault in the planes at all, they had just radioed their position, and then they vanished.

Imagine the search which followed; aircraft went out and literally combed the area, some flying high so that they could see over the widest possible part of the sea, others flying low in the hope of spotting something of the two planes. Ships moved across and took up the search, but nothing whatever was ever found, no planes, no wreckage, no bodies—nothing.

Throughout years there have been reports of the mysterious disappearance of ships—ships lost without trace, lost without even a matchstick of wreckage to show that they existed. But never have there been the facilities for quick search by fast radar-equipped aircraft as at present, and no matter how one searches, no matter the means one employs, there is still no trace of what happened.

There is an area in the Atlantic on the Bermuda/Florida coastline where many ships have disappeared, and many aircraft, too, have disappeared. This is not a lonely area because the whole of the coastline is patrolled by coastguards, by the Navy, and by the Air Force. The list of disappearances goes back to the first part of recorded history.

Many years ago I became acquainted with a most mysterious area in the Pacific, South of Japan. Here there was a region known as the Devil's Sea where a ship, usually a junk, could sail along its peaceful way and then completely vanish before the startled eyes of people in other junks near by. On one occasion a line of fishing junks were sailing out over the Devil's Sea, the leading junk was perhaps a mile away from the next. It sailed on, and suddenly vanished without the slightest trace. The helmsman in the second junk was so paralysed with fright that he had no time or thought to alter course, and his junk sailed on over the course of the other and nothing happened to it. All the crews later reported a curious shimmer in the air above them, and a sensation which they said was oppressive and heavy like that often occurring before a very strong tornado.

Here is something that the sceptical among you could check; on December 5th, 1945, five torpedo-bombers took off from the naval station at Fort Lauderdale in the State of Florida. It was a peaceful, sunny day, without clouds, the water was placid, there were no storms, nothing at all to give one thought that a great mystery was about to occur.

These five bombers were going out on an absolutely routine flight during which time they should be within visual sight of the American coastline or some of the Caribbean Islands. At no time, considering the height at which they would fly, should they be out of sight of land. Every bomber had been carefully checked and every fuel tank was completely full. Every engine was at its best condition, as was certified by the pilots who had to sign examination sheets before taking off. Further, every plane had a self-inflating life-raft, and each man wore his own life-jacket, life-jackets which would keep a man afloat for days. The crew numbered fourteen, and every man had more than a year's experience of flying.

Presumably they all thought they were going for an ordinary pleasurable flight up into the blue sky, watching the jewels of islands which were the Caribbean Islands, and watching the

long, long coastline of Florida. Perhaps, too, some of them hoped to get another look down at the Everglades. But they took off carrying out their ordinary routine patrol, they were going to fly East for 160 miles and North for 40 miles, after which they would head back to the air station which they would reach two hours after take-off.

Sometime after take-off—about an hour and a half—a message was received at the Fort Lauderdale station, and it was a strange message indeed, it was a message of emergency. The leader of the flight was agitated, even frightened; he said they all seemed to be off course, and he said also that they could not see land. This was such a strange occurrence that he found it necessary to repeat it. 'Repeat, we cannot see land.'

As is usual in such a case the radio operator on duty at the air station sent a message to the flight of planes asking what was their position. The reply completely shattered the composure of the men in the airport control towers. The reply, 'We are not sure of our position, we do not know where we are.' Yet they were flying in ideal conditions, every man was completely experienced and their aircraft were excellent. But then a further message was received, a highly alarmed voice came through the speakers, 'We don't know which way is West,' said the voice. 'Everything is wrong, everything is strange, we cannot be sure of any direction, even the sea doesn't look as it should.'

Can you imagine an experienced man accompanied by thirteen other men being able to say the compass did not indicate correctly, they did not know where they were, they could not see land, and even the sea looked different? And yet, also, the sun which was shining on the air station was invisible to the fourteen men flying in a cloudless sky, they could not see the sun, and the sea looked different.

At about 4.30 p.m. of that same day another flight leader spoke by radio, and said that he did not know where they were. It continued, 'It looks as if we are——' And then the message ended, no further contact was ever made, no trace was ever found of these fourteen men, nor of the planes in which they flew, no wreckage, nothing.

Within minutes one of the American Navy's largest flying-boats, with complete equipment for survival and rescue, roared off the water carrying a crew of thirteen men. The flying-boat, nearly 80 feet long and with a wing span of 125 feet, was built to withstand the roughest landings at sea. One would have called such a flying-boat invincible and invulnerable.

During the flying-boat's journey out to the imagined position of the torpedo-bombers it sent out routine reports, but after twenty minutes all radio contact stopped and nothing whatever was ever heard again about the torpedo-bombers nor about the huge, specially equipped, specially manned flying-boat which had gone to their rescue.

The coastguard, the Navy, the Air Force—everyone—went out in a hurried search for wreckage, for men floating in life-jackets or in self-inflating life-boats, but nothing was ever found.

An aircraft carrier moved into the area and thirty planes took off at first light to search the whole area. The R.A.F. who happened to be nearby sent every one of their available planes into the air to search. But, again, never has there been the slightest piece of wreckage, and it is clear that all these planes just disappeared.

Disappeared? Yes, they went through a 'hole in time' into the world of anti-matter, just as throughout the ages ships and men and women, and animals too, have vanished without trace.

These incidents are not just isolated incidents that happened recently, they have happened throughout history, and if one digs deep enough one can find various highly interesting accounts of sudden disappearances. There is, for example, a well-documented case of a boy who went out of his father's farmhouse one evening. He was going to get water from the well, there was snow upon the ground, just a few inches of it, and the boy was anxious to get back to the fire, so he started out with a pail in each hand. His parents and some visiting friends sat by the side of the fire and waited for him because they wanted the water with which to make tea.

After a time the mother got restless and wondered whatever was keeping the boy. But knowing how boys dawdle she was not alarmed until almost an hour had passed. Then some strange feeling came over them and they took lanterns and went out in search of the boy, thinking that perhaps he had fallen into the well.

With their lanterns before them shedding light upon the snow they could follow his footsteps half-way across the field. Then, the father in the lead stopped with such horrified astonishment that those following bumped into him. He moved aside and pointed dumbly. The others looked in the snow, and there they found clear imprints of the boy's footsteps and then no imprints any more. The boy had vanished as if he had suddenly been drawn straight up into the air.

This is fact; the footsteps went in a straight line, and then they were no more. The boy has not been seen since.

There was another case of a man in full daylight. He went out into a field watched by his wife and the local sheriff (in the United States). He was going to get something for the sheriff from the field, and in view of these people he just vanished into thin air and was never seen again!

Do you have access to *Reynolds' News*? If you do you might like to consult the issue of August 14th, 1938. If you turn over those by now yellowed pages you will find the tale of an R.A.F. flying-boat that suddenly disappeared in an immense column of water and smoke while flying just a few feet above the surface of the sea off Felixstowe, England. There was no collision, no impact, but the plane just vanished and no trace of it has been found.

Here is another one: In the year 1952 in the month of March Wing-Commander Baldwin of the R.A.F. was flying with a patrol of planes along the Korean coast. He and his companions were all flying new jet planes. He flew into a cloud, his companions did not. They returned to base eventually but Commander Baldwin did not, there was no trace of him and no trace of his plane, and none of his companions could say what happened to him.

There are many, many such cases. For example, in 1947 an American Super-Fortress just disappeared without any trace and without any wreckage. It was flying in that triangle near Bermuda. This Super-Fortress, a very large plane, just vanished, and although a really intensive search was mounted no trace was found.

Do you remember the case of the British South American Airways plane, *Star Tiger*? The year was 1948, the month was January, well, almost February because it was January 30th. But this great plane, a four-engine affair, radioed the airport at Kindleyfield, Bermuda, that it was approximately 400 miles from the island. The radio operator stated that the weather was excellent and the plane was performing exactly as it should. The radio operator added that they expected to arrive on schedule. Well, they did not; the six members of the crew and two dozen passengers disappeared, and again, in spite of a most thorough search, nothing was ever found. About fifty planes of various types flew low over the area, but—nothing was found. In London there was an investigation based on all available evidence. These things are thoroughly investigated because of the insurance at Lloyds of London, but the only verdict the investigators could bring in was 'Lost, cause unknown'.

Do you want another? December 1948—a big airliner going from San Juan airport towards Florida. There were more than thirty passengers, and when the radio operator got in touch with his station he said that everything was going well and the passengers were all singing.

At 4.15 a.m. the radio operator contacted Miami control tower stating that they were 50 miles out and were in sight of the field. He asked for landing instructions.

The plane vanished, the passengers, everything vanished without trace, and no trace has ever been found. Again there was no wreckage. The investigators confirmed that the Captain and crew were highly experienced and yet—less than 50 miles from their destination a great plane vanished without the slightest trace.

Just one more—we have to mention this one because it is a sister of the *Star Tiger*, but this later one was called the *Ariel*. Again it got in touch with Bermuda and then passed on *en route* to Kingston, Jamaica. But at 8.25 there was a message which stated that the plane was 175 miles from Bermuda. The operator confirmed that everything was well and he was changing to the radio station at Kingston, but that was the last heard, the plane vanished without trace.

The United States Navy were in the vicinity of Bermuda, carrying out manoeuvres. The United States Navy and the Air Force, too, had had enough of these mysteries, so they bent every possible effort to solving the mystery. Two immense aircraft carriers put every one of their planes in the air, in addition there were light cruisers and destroyers, together with mine-sweepers and all manner of pinnaces. Yet although every square foot of water was covered, no trace was found, nothing at all.

The explanation is that there is a 'split in time' through which infrequently people go from one world to another. If

61

you imagine two large footballs rotating close together, and each football has a small split in it, you can see that if for some reason the two split-areas came into close proximity an unhappy little flea on one football could just jump straight into the split of the other football. Perhaps there is a similar state of affairs between this world and the opposite world.

If you find that difficult to understand, remember this; here we are in a three-dimensional world. We imagine that in our little box-like rooms we are quite safe and nothing can touch us, but supposing a four-dimensional person looked down at us, then possibly for him a ceiling or a wall would not exist and so he could reach down and pick us up.

It might be a good idea if we have a chapter devoted to dimensions, the fourth dimension, for example. What do you think? Shall we do it? The fourth dimension is a very useful thing if we understand it properly.

CHAPTER FOUR

MANY DIMENSIONS TOO!

IT seems rather appropriate to deal with the fourth dimension in the fourth chapter because when we leave this Earth we all go into the fourth dimension! Let us add an interesting point here; people who attend seances are often upset at the garbled messages they receive from those who have 'passed over'. They do not understand that the person who has left this Earth for another plane of existence is what we might term thousands of light years in the future. You will find an interesting parallel later in this chapter when we deal with the Hindu king and his daughter, but first what is a one-dimensional world? We cannot understand what four dimensions are unless we understand what one is. Suppose we have a piece of paper and a pencil; let us draw on the paper a straight line, and let us imagine that all the carbon from the pencil represents people so that in effect the straight line is a whole universe. There will be only two points for the people, one is straight ahead and the other is straight behind, they will be able to move backwards or forwards, and in no other way at all. Supposing that you could make a change in that line, then the one-dimensional people would think that a miracle had occurred, or if they saw the point of your pencil just lightly pressing on the paper they would think that a flying saucer had suddenly appeared.

You, as a three-dimensional creature, will have temporarily entered a one-dimensional world to rest the point of your pencil on the paper, and the one-dimensional being who saw that pencil point will be sure that a most unusual happening has occurred. Being one-dimensional he would not be able to see you but only that point of the pencil in contact with the paper.

Having some idea of what a one-dimensional world is, let us have a look at a two-dimensional world. This will be a flat plane and the people who live upon such a world will necessarily be flat geometrical figures. The world in which they exist will be to them much the same as our world except that if you draw pencil lines around them they will become aware of these as great walls preventing them from going beyond those encompassing lines, and they will probably decide that the lines they encounter must exist somewhere else, they will think of the third dimension in much the same way as we think of the fourth dimension; in much the same way as we sometimes have difficulty comprehending the fourth dimension, so will these two-dimensional people have the greatest difficulty in comprehending that third dimension which to us is so commonplace. In fact, if anything does stir their consciousness about a third dimension, and if they are foolish enough to talk to anyone else about it, they would be put away as lunatics and regarded as liars, phoneys, hoaxes, or similar.

A two-dimensional being senses lines, they cannot be perceived by this person because, being a two-dimensional person, he will not be able to look from above.

If only scientists were not so difficult! If only scientists would put aside all their preconceived notions and enter a research with an absolutely unbiased outlook. We have to face the fact that 'big names' have too much say in everyday affairs. For example, a man had some success as a General in a war so he is immediately made into President of the United States. Or we get an actor who pretends that he is a lady-killer on the screen. Actually, he is really quite hopeless in that department, but anyway he had some success on the screen so we immediately become inundated with photographic comments from the fellow, telling us how we should brush our teeth, how we should cut our hair, what sort of shavers we should use, and possibly helpful hints on a love life which this person could not possibly enjoy.

It follows, then, that one of the biggest difficulties—one of the biggest drawbacks—which we metaphysicians have to face is that people blindly follow the words of those who should know about such things, but probably do not.

Take people such as Einstein or Rutherford, or those of similar standing. These men are specialists in a particularly narrow field of science. They have the scientific outlook and they want to analyse everything according to mundane, outmoded concepts and physical laws which daily are being contradicted. People take the word of eminent scientists as gospel. They take the words of film stars as gospel also, and unfortunately the 'gospel' cannot be disputed and cannot be varied. Our problem is to delve into truths which some eminent people have strenuously attempted to conceal.

Fundamental laws should be regarded as 'fundamental'. That is, as being valid during the present state of knowledge, but such laws must be sufficiently flexible that they can be altered, amended, or even scrapped in the light of increasing knowledge. Let us remind you of the bumble-bee. According to the laws of flight—the laws of aerodynamics—the bumble-bee cannot possibly fly because the poor creature's structure completely defies all known laws of aerodynamics. Thus, if we believe the scientists with their fundamental laws, we must believe that the bumble-bee cannot fly.

They, reputable scientists, basing their statements on the laws of physics, have said that Man would never travel at more than 30 miles an hour because his blood system would break down under the strain, his heart would burst, his brain would collapse, etc., etc. Well, according to recent reports, Man CAN travel at more than 30 miles an hour! Having accomplished that, the scientists said Man would never fly; it was impossible. With THAT overcome they said that Man would never fly faster than sound. Never mind, undaunted they said that Man would never leave the Earth and go into space. According to rumours this has been done!

Going back a bit farther, to somewhere about 1910, all the wise men and pundits of science said that no man would send his voice across the Atlantic, but a gentleman by the name of Marconi proved that statement wrong and now we send not merely voices but pictures across the Atlantic. But possibly that is not much of an advantage, having due regard to the presentday state of television programmes.

Having got over to you—more or less—the idea that established scientists with their stereotyped, hidebound, immovable laws can be wrong, let us go a little farther. One of their fallacies is that statement that 'two solids cannot occupy the same space at the same time'. That is absurd, that is completely incorrect, for in the science of metaphysics two bodies CAN occupy the same space at the same time by a process known as interpenetration.

Scientists have shown that everything that exists is composed of atoms with great spaces between them, in much the same way as when we look up at the stars on a clear night we can see little dots which are worlds, and great black spaces which is Space. It follows, then, that if we have a creature small enough (you will have to stretch your imagination here) to look at what to us is a solid, that creature may be able to see not a solid as we do, but all the particles composing the 'solid'. Then to that creature, looking at our solid, the view will be similar to that which we see when we look at the heavens on a clear night. To remind you, that is much Space with just a few little pinpoints of light. But imagine this : supposing that there was a Being large enough so that in looking at our Universe He would see that Universe as a solid. At the other end of the scale, think of a virus : if you could catch a virus of a special type, you could drop that single virus into a porcelain cup and the poor creature would fall right through—would fall right through the bottom without touching anything on the way because it is such a small thing. This is not imagination but fact. You may be aware that one of the big difficulties in 'catching a virus' in a laboratory is that the things just go through the ceramic filters much the same as a dog can run wild on a moor.

To a creature small enough, the spaces between atoms in a 'solid' are as great in comparison as those between the stars in our Universe, and just as whole showers of meteorites or comets or spaceships can travel the empty spaces between the worlds, so can other objects occupy that which we term a 'solid object'.

It is quite possible to have two solids, or three or four solids so arranged that their 'worlds' do not touch each other, but one set of 'worlds' occupies the spaces between the other set of 'worlds'. You will appreciate that under this system there could be many apparently solid objects which occupy the same space simultaneously. Obviously we cannot perceive this in normal life, because we do not have a suitable nor an adequate range of perceptions. We need to increase our perceptions, and as here on this world we cannot easily enter the fourth dimension, we have to accept the printed words of explanation or taped voices of explanation.

To give you just a crude idea—suppose you have two forks, ordinary garden forks, if you like, or table forks. You can pass the tines of one through the space between the tines of the other. Thus, while one set of tines occupies the spaces between the other set of tines the two fork blades occupy what is essentially the same amount of space without impinging upon the 'living space' of the other.

Originally people thought that objects had length and breadth. But then matters improved somewhat and people came to the conclusion that there was length, breadth, and thickness, so that people lived in a three-dimensional world; i.e. length=one dimension, breadth=two dimensions, and thickness=three dimensions. But it is quite obvious that we live in a three-dimensional world. There are other dimensions, such as a fourth, a fifth, and so on. To give you something to think about—our three-dimensional object has length, breadth, and thickness, but here is another dimension; how long will it exist? So we have a further dimension of Time. Time becomes a fourth dimension in this case.

The average person, by way of illustration cannot see infrared rays without special equipment. This proves of course that there are things beyond the range of the average human perceptions, and it follows from this that objects emitting infrared rays and lying in a plane beyond length, breadth, and thickness would be quite invisible to the average person.

May we digress for a moment? May we remind you that there are sounds which are quite inaudible to humans, but which cats and dogs hear clearly? The soundless dog whistle, probably everyone knows about that! But if you look at the illustrations in Lesson Six of *You—Forever!* you will see what we term the symbolic keyboard. You will observe that after sound, we have sight, and there are certain cases in which sounds have been almost seen, 'apperceived' would be a better term, because under certain conditions if a person is very clairvoyant they can 'see' the shape of sound. You have probably heard someone say, 'Oh, it was such a ROUND sound,' or something similar, from which we may gather that quite a number of people have an idea of sound as a shape such as a round sound, a square sound, or a long-drawn-out sound.

But—let us get back to the point we were making before we digressed in the previous paragraph.

You will need to think of this; a three-dimensional object such as a house or a person or a tree casts a two-dimensional shadow, because the shadow has length and breadth but no thickness. Of course, in other planes of existence we should say that the shadow also has a further dimension, that of time, the time of its enduring. But let us forget that for a moment and go back and say that a three-dimensional object casts a two-dimensional shadow. We can assume that a four-dimensional object would show a shadow of three dimensions, so those of you who have seen a 'ghost' may actually have seen the shadow of a person in the fourth dimension. A ghost is a person who has apparent breadth, thickness, and height, but is of somewhat shadowy substance, as shadowy as a shadow in fact. So why should it not be that our four-dimensional visitor, who is invisible to us because of his four dimensions, nevertheless manifests to us in three dimensions, or as a ghost which has form without substantial substance.

Consider further, reports of objects which the Press rather foolishly call 'flying saucers'. These objects have appeared and disappeared at fantastic speeds and without any sound at all. They have changed direction at a speed far beyond that of a human body. Now, why should we not suppose that some flying saucers may be the shadow of a four-dimensional object? Consider their rate of change of direction, consider holding a mirror in your hand and focusing the Sun's rays on a wall. You can make that blob of light dance about and change direction at a rate far in excess of that which any human mechanism could manage.

Again, imagine a sheet of frosted glass facing a person or entity who had no conception of the appearance of a human being. Then supposing the human, who was concealed at the opposite side of the sheet of frosted glass, put four fingers and a thumb in contact with the glass. The person at the other side, knowing nothing of the shape of humans, would see five blobs —five dark smears—just as some people have seen blobs in the sky.

You may wonder what all this has to do with metaphysics. Well, it has a very great deal to do with metaphysics! You see, we live in a three-dimensional world, but the highest form of Truth can be perceived only when we go beyond a three-dimensional world. We have to go beyond Time and Space, for Time is relative. Time is merely a convention established by mankind to suit his own convenience.

You think that Time is not relative? All right, supposing that you have to go to the dentist, and you have to have a tooth or teeth extracted. When you are having your aches and pains time appears to stand still. It appears that you are in the dental chair FOR EVER.

Now, you have a very enjoyable experience with a person to whom you are deeply attached. You will find that time flies. So, Time is just a relative thing, it appears to drag or hasten abominably according to our mood.

Well, back into our dimensions. Let us suppose that there are some form of people who live only in a two-dimensional world, that is, they live on a world on which there is length and breadth but no depth. They are like shadows, they are thinner than the thinnest sheet of paper—but having no perception of depth they can have no perception of space, because space is that which is beyond the sky, and to bring in the sky would be to bring in a third dimension. Thus, to them space is inconceivable.

A railroad track is similar to a world of one dimension—length. A train conductor could indicate his position from just one point of reference, he could say where he was by referring to the known location of a station or from a signal, or from some other well-known mark.

Let us go farther and agree that a ship upon the sea is as a person occupying a two-dimensional world, for the ship is not confined to rails but it can go forward or sideways or even backwards, so it has the use of length and width.

An aeroplane is a creature of three dimensions. It can go forward, sideways, and up or down. That, you will perceive, gives us the three dimensions.

This theory (actually, to us it is knowledge) of dimensions will explain many things which otherwise must be considered as a mystery—teleportation, for example, in which an object is moved from one room to another without any visible person doing the moving. An object can be moved by teleportation from a locked room to another room. Actually it is quite simple because we merely have to think of our two-dimensional being. If we three-dimensionals had a series of boxes without any tops to them, the two-dimensional people who could be in those boxes would be completely confined, completely enclosed, because not having any conception of height they would not know that there was no roof above them. And so if we three-dimensional creatures reached in through the open roof and moved something from one box to another it would, to the two-dimensional people, be an absolute miracle in which an object in one secured room was moved to another secured room. Remember the two-dimensional person would have no conception of the roof above. In just the same way we three-dimensional people could have no conception of an opening which is quite clear in the fourth dimension, so that the person in the fourth dimension could reach down into a locked room (for the room would be locked in three dimensions only) and move that which he desired to move through what was an opening clear to four-dimensional people. The object would be moved from the three dimensional world and for a moment would be in the four-dimensional world, where it would penetrate through what we prefer to call solid walls. We have something of an illustration when we think of the way that radio or television waves can penetrate apparently solid walls and still activate a radio or television receiver.

Time, to which we have already referred, plays a very important part in the life of Man, but that which we call 'Time' differs from man to man and animal to animal. Again we suggest that you think about this under different conditions in your everyday life. When you are late for an appointment, see how the hand races around the clock face. When you are expecting someone and he or she (more usually she!) keeps you waiting, time appears to stand still.

Animals have their own conception of time, and their conception of time is quite different from that of humans. Animals live at a different rate. An insect which lives for twenty-four hours of human time can still have as full a life as a human living for seventy years, the insect can have a mate, can raise a family, and see its own family have their families in turn. If the allotted span of an animal is twenty years, those twenty years will appear as seventy years or so appears to a human, and within the space allotted to the animal he will be able to function just as a man could function in his longer lifespan. It is worth a thought that all creatures, insect, animal, or human, have approximately the same number of heart-beats in a lifetime.

All this about time was readily understood by the wise men of centuries ago. There is a very holy book, one of the great 'Bibles' of the Far East, which is called the Srimad Bhagavate, in which appears this:

Once a great king took his daughter to the home of the Creator, Brahma, who lived in a different dimension. The great king was most concerned that his daughter had arrived

70

at a marriageable age and still had not found an acceptable suitor. The great king was anxious to find a good husband for his daughter. After arriving at the home of Brahma, he had to wait for just a very few moments before he could be escorted into the Presence and thus make his request. To his intense amazement Brahma replied, 'Oh king, when you go back to Earth you will not see any of your friends or relatives, your cities or your palaces, for although it seems to you that you arrived here only a few moments ago from the Earth you knew, yet those few moments of our time are the equivalent of several thousand years of your time when you were on the Earth. When you go back to Earth you will find that there is a new age, and your daughter whom you have brought here will marry Lord Krishna's brother, Balarama. Thus, she who was born thousands of years ago, will be married to Balarama after several thousand more years, because in just the time it takes for you to leave my presence and journey again through Time to Earth several thousand years of Earth time will have passed.'

And so the bemused king and his daughter returned to the Earth which, according to their own estimate of time, they had left but a few minutes before. They found what appeared to be a new world, with what appeared to be a new civilisation—a different type of people, a different culture, and a different religion. So, as he had been told, several thousand years had passed in the time of the Earth although he and his daughter, travelling to a different dimension, had seen but a few minutes pass.

This is a Hindu belief which was written in the holy books of the Hindu faith thousands of years ago. One cannot help wondering if this is not possibly the foundation of some of the things that Dr. Einstein produced as the theory of relativity.

Probably you have not fully studied Einstein's theory of relativity, but very very briefly, he explained Time as a fourth dimension. He also taught that Time is not a steady, unvarying flow of 'something'. He realised that a second ticked on, after sixty such second ticks a minute had passed, and after sixty minute ticks an hour had passed. But that is convenient time, that is mechanical time. Einstein considered Time as a sense, as a form of perception. Just as no two people see precisely the same colours, so Einstein taught that no two people have precisely the same sense of time.

We call a year 365 days, but it is just a trip around the Sun—an orbit around the Sun. So we upon the Earth do an orbit of the Sun roughly every 365 days, but compare this with a person who lives on Mercury. Remember that Mercury completes its orbit around the Sun in eighty-eight days, and during that orbit it rotates just once upon its axis, whereas, as you know, we upon Earth rotate once in twenty-four hours.

Something else for you to ponder; do you know that if a clock be attached to a moving system it will slow down as that moving system's velocity increases?

Supposing that you have a rod made of some material—metal, wood, ceramic—anything you like, but it is a definite measuring rod of a definite length. If you attach that to any moving system it will apparently shrink in the direction of its motion according to the velocity of the system. All these things, such as changes in the clock, or the contraction of the rod, are not in any way to do with the construction of the things, nor are they of a mechanical phenomenon. They are instead to do with the Einstein theory of relativity. You may have your metre stick (let us say that our metal rod was 1 metre or 1 yard long), so now if it goes through space at 90 per cent of the velocity of light, it will shrink to half a metre and, in theory, if its speed is increased until it moves at the speed of light it would, according to the Einstein theory of relativity, shrink to nothing at all! And if somehow you could tie a clock of some kind to that metre stick, its rate of time-keeping would vary so that as the metre stick approached the speed of light the clock would go more and more slowly, or would appear to, until at the speed of light the clock would stop completely.

You must remember when you criticise this by saying, 'Oh well, I have driven the car, and I haven't seen the car contract,' that these changes can be detected only when the speed of the moving article approaches near to the speed of light. So, if you have a brand-new car and you race along the road, it doesn't mean to say that your car is going to get any shorter, because, no matter if you can do 100 or 120 miles an hour, that speed is still all too slow to make any measurable difference in the length of your car. But it does mean, according to Einstein, that if a spaceship should be sent into space and it

73

could approach the speed of light, then it would contract and disappear.

Do you know what that means, assuming that Einstein is right? We, being able to do astral travel, we know that Einstein is wrong, just as were those scientists who said that Man would never exceed the speed of sound. Einstein is wrong, just as wrong as the person who said Man would never exceed 30 miles an hour, but we have to learn by the mistakes of others. It might save us from having mistakes of our own. So let us see what would happen according to the theory of Einstein. Let us say that we have a spaceship, and the crew in the spaceship are all wise men who are able to make accurate observations. The ship is travelling at a very high speed indeed, almost approaching the speed of light. The ship is going to a distant planet, so distant that it would take ten years to reach from the Earth to that other planet. A light year is the time and distance it takes light to reach a certain point by travelling one full year, so ten light years is the time it takes light to reach that distant object.

This ship is going to travel at about the speed of light. (Let us forget all about Einstein for the moment, and let us say that this ship can travel at the speed of light.) So, supposing the ship is going ten light years to this distant planet, and then without stopping it is going to come back. After all, as we are 'supposing' anything is permissible! Thus, we have a journey which will last for twenty years—ten years out and ten years back. Well, naturally, the poor fellows aboard are going to be frightfully bored shut up for twenty years. Not only that, but they are certainly going to need a whole pile of food and drink with them. Anyhow, we are just 'supposing'.

If you are to believe Einstein, there won't be these difficulties, they won't need food for twenty years. If the ship is going to travel at even close to the speed of light everything aboard the ship will slow down. The men will be slow in all their functions, their heart-beats, their breathing, and their physical actions, and even their thoughts. Whereas with us a thought may take a tenth of a second, when travelling at the speed of light, according to Einstein, it might take ten seconds for a thought on Earth but ten weeks for the duration of the same thought when travelling near the speed of light. But travelling at the speed of light is going to have certain very important advantages according to Einstein. For example,

74

twenty years on Earth would pass, but to the people in the spaceship it would be just a matter of a very few hours. Do you want to have a better illustration than that?

All right: In 1970 we have made a spaceship which will travel at almost the speed of light. The ship is outfitted and ready to go on a journey far beyond our solar system, far beyond Mars, Venus, Jupiter, Pluto, Saturn, and all of them. It is going, instead, to a different universe. It is going to take, at the speed of light, twenty years. In 1970, then, the spaceship lifts off. It does ten years travelling to this far distant world. It circles, it takes some photographs, and then it returns —another journey of ten years—twenty years in all.

The crew are young men, one of them is just twenty years of age when he leaves on that eventful journey. He is married and his wife is the same age as he—twenty years. They have a child one year of age. When the poor fellow returns after just a few hours of travelling at near the speed of light, he will get the biggest shock of his life. He will find that his wife is twenty years older than himself. While he and other members of the crew have aged just a very few hours, the others left upon the Earth have aged by the temporal time, that is, twenty years. So this man of twenty and a few hours now has a wife of forty!

Here is an incident which the United States very much desires to keep quiet and keep out of the public knowledge. This particular matter which follows is absolutely authentic, absolutely genuine, and those who are sufficiently highly placed may be able to 'dig in' to some of the United States naval records.

In October 1943 an attempt was made to render a ship of the United States Navy invisible! This had disastrous results because some of the scientists were so hidebound that they could not use their imagination, but had to go 'by the book'. You will remember that in the Second World War the United States as well as other people advertised for ideas of how to make super-super weapons, etc. One idea was as a result of Professor Einstein's letter to President Roosevelt in which 'the unified field' theory was set out in some detail. There is no point in going into the technical aspects of the unified field, but we might say that it does embrace a certain amount of knowledge about the fourth dimension.

A certain Doctor of Science, a very clever man indeed, used

part of the theorems relating to the unified field, and working in conjunction with the United States Navy in October 1943 he was able to make a shield—a type of ray—which completely encompassed a destroyer. The field would extend about 300 feet from its centre of origin, and anything inside that field became completely invisible so that to the observer outside the ship and crew disappeared. Unfortunately when the ship again became visible many of the crew were insane. It seems that examining physicians afterwards used sodium pentathol to try to dig down into the subconsciousness of crew members to find out exactly what happened.

From our point of view, and in connection with the fourth dimension, it seems that on one occasion the invisible ship reappeared several hundred miles away in Chesapeake Bay. It is a pity that people in the area cannot go to the Public Libraries and consult the files of the local newspapers, or get hold of some of the records in such a book as *M. K. Jessup and the Allende Letters* compiled by Riley Crabb. A book was apparently published by Gray Barker in the United States called *The Strange Case of Dr. Jessup*.

This is a very serious discussion, this is not hoax or even hearsay evidence. The United States Government have gone to great trouble to try to silence anyone who has discussed such things as this, and there have been reports of people dying mysteriously after having been in possession of certain information.

The United States Government also seems to have had some success in silencing the Press; for that surely they deserve the Nobel Prize and a few Oscar's thrown in for good measure. But it does indicate that there is much in this invisible ship business.

There has been one report inadvertently released which says that the invisible ship materialised in a port, and some quite bemused sailors staggered ashore and fairly tumbled into a public house. They were seen by perhaps thirty or forty people, and in mid-sentence while they were ordering drinks they disappeared, disappeared, vanished, went into thin air. People who are sufficiently interested should read the books mentioned above and should also try to find some method of combing newspapers round about 1944 and 1956. There are hints, and in two instances actual reports.

It is clear that if one could suddenly switch a ship or a

special weapon into the fourth dimension and then bring it back to the third dimension at some designated spot the Chinese could be suppressed very thoroughly; it might even give the Russians a few frights! People laughed about the Laser Beam, but that little ruby light has proved to be all that was claimed for it and a few things besides. So—if research would only be continued with suitable safeguards it would be found that documents solidly locked in a bank vault could be removed by way of the fourth dimension because, remember, if a thing has four walls to you that is because you are in a three-dimensional world, and in a fourth dimension there may be an opening through which one could enter.

Returning to this matter of the invisible ship, it is thought that if the men had been conditioned to know what to expect they would not have gone insane, because the horrid shock of finding oneself in a different time continuum is enough to unhinge anyone's mind unless they are preconditioned.

Many many years ago, in the days of Plato, there was discussion about the fourth dimension, but even in those days scientists were not able to perceive that which was metaphorically perched on the end of their noses. Plato had a dialogue which seems to be rather applicable to this discussion about the fourth dimension and so as it is essential that in order that we may obey the Commandment, 'Man know thyself!' we must understand the relationship of the different dimensions, the first, the second, the third, and the fourth.

So let us have here to end this chapter the Dialogue of Plato the philosopher, and how he tried to make it clear to people that which was so obvious to him:

'Behold! Human beings living in a sort of underground den; they have been there from their childhood, and have their legs and necks chained—the chains are arranged in such a manner as to prevent them from turning their heads. At a distance above and behind them the light of a fire is blazing, and between the fire and the prisoners there is a raised way; and you will see, if you look, a low wall built along the way, like the screen which marionette players have before them, over which they show the puppets. Imagine men passing along the wall carrying vessels, which appear over the wall; also figures of men and animals, made of wood and stone and various materials; and some of the passengers, as you would expect, are talking, and some of them are silent!

'That is a strange image, he said, and they are strange prisoners.

'Like ourselves, I replied; and they see only their own shadows, or the shadows of one another, which the fire throws on the opposite wall of the cave?

'True, he said; how could they see anything but the shadows if they were never allowed to move their heads?

'And of the objects which are being carried in like manner they would only see the shadows?

'Yes, he said.

'And if they were able to talk with one another, would they not suppose that they were naming what was actually before them?

'Very true.

'And suppose further that the prison had an echo which came from the other side, would they not be sure to fancy that the voice which they heard was that of a passing shadow?

'No question, he replied.

'There can be no question, I said, that the truth would be to them just nothing but the shadows of the images.

'That is certain.

'And now look again and see how they are released and cured of their folly. At first, when any one of them is liberated and compelled suddenly to go up and turn his neck around and walk and look at the light, he will suffer sharp pains, the glare will distress him and he will be unable to see the realities of which in his former state he had seen the shadows; and then imagine someone saying to him, that what he saw before was an illusion, but that now he is approaching real being and has a truer sight and vision of more real things—what will be his reply? And you may further imagine that his instructor is pointing to the objects as they pass and requiring him to name them—will he not be in a difficulty? Will he not fancy that the shadows which he formerly saw are truer than the objects which are now shown to him?

'Far truer.

'And if he is compelled to look at the light, will he not have a pain in his eyes which will make him turn away to take refuge in the object of vision which he can see, and which he will conceive to be clearer than the things which are now being shown to him?

'True, he said.

78

'And suppose once more, that he is reluctantly dragged up a steep and rugged ascent, and held fast and forced into the presence of the Sun himself, do you not think that he will be pained and irritated, and when he approaches the light he will have his eyes dazzled, and will not be able to see any of the realities which are now affirmed to be the truth?

'Not all in a moment, he said.

'He will require to get accustomed to the sight of the upper world. And first he will see the shadows best, next the reflections of men and other objects in the water, and then the objects themselves; next he will gaze upon the light of the Moon and the stars; and he will see the sky and the stars by night, better than the Sun, or the light of the Sun, by day?

'Certainly.

'And at last he will be able to see the Sun, and not mere reflections of him in the water, but he will see him as he is in his own proper place, and not in another, and he will contemplate his nature.

'Certainly.

'And after this he will reason that the Sun is he who gives the seasons and the years, and is the guardian of all that is in the visible world, and in a certain way the cause of all things which he and his fellows have been accustomed to behold?

'Clearly, he said, he would come to the other first and to this afterwards.

'And when he remembered his old habitation, and the wisdom of the den and his fellow-prisoners, do you not suppose that he would felicitate himself on the change, and pity them?

'Certainly, he would.

'And if they were in the habit of conferring honours on those who were quickest to observe and remember and foretell which of the shadows went before, and which followed after, and which were together, do you think he would care for such honours and glories, or envy the possessors of them?

'Would he not say with Homer——

' "Better to be a poor man, and have a poor master," and endure anything, than to think and live after their manner?

'Yes, he said, I think that he would rather suffer anything than live after their manner.

'Imagine once more, I said, that such an one coming suddenly out of the Sun were to be replaced in his old situation, is he not certain to have his eyes full of darkness?

'Very true, he said.

'And if there were a contest, and he had to compete in measuring the shadows with the prisoners who have never moved out of the den, during the time that his sight is weak, and before his eyes are steady (and the time which would be needed to acquire this new habit of sight might be very considerable), would he not be ridiculous? Men would say of him that up he went and down he comes without his eyes; and that there was no use in even thinking of ascending: and if anyone tried to loose another and lead him up to the light, let them only catch the offender in the act, and they would put him to death.

'No question, he said.

'This allegory, I said, you may now append to the previous argument; the prison is the world of sight, the light of the fire is the Sun, the ascent and vision of the things above you may truly regard as the upward progress of the soul into the intellectual world.

'And you will understand that those who attain to this beatific vision are unwilling to descend to human affairs; but their souls are ever hastening into the upper world in which they desire to dwell. And is there anything surprising in one who passes from divine contemplations to human things, misbehaving himself in a ridiculous manner?

'There is nothing surprising in that, he replied.

'Anyone who has common sense will remember that the bewilderments of the eyes are of two kinds, and arise from two causes, either from coming out of the light or from going into the light, which is true of the mind's eye, quite as much as of the bodily eye; and he who remembers this when he sees the soul of anyone whose vision is perplexed and weak, will not be too ready to laugh; he will first ask whether that soul has come out of the brighter life, and is unable to see because unaccustomed to the dark, or having turned from darkness to the day is dazzled by excess of light. And then he will count one happy in his condition and state of being.'

CHAPTER FIVE

PAINTING WITH WORDS

THE ancient grey walls gleamed whitely under the harvest moon, throwing deep black shadows across the well-raked gravel of the drive. Old indeed, it was, and mellow with the love which is bestowed on well-loved things. From a wall facing moonwards an antique coat-of-arms proudly caught the moonbeams and tossed them back in age-faded colours. From the mullioned windows came the yellow gleam of electric light. The old Hall was gay tonight, gay with the joy that comes only to a betrothal so recently announced.

The moon sailed serenely across the luminous sky. The shadows marched slowly across the open spaces, turning the side trees to darkest ebony. A sudden burst of music and golden light as french windows opened and a young man and woman stepped on to the terraced balcony. Behind them the windows closed silently. Hand in hand the man and woman crossed to the stone balustrade and gazed out upon the peaceful scene before them. A vagrant breeze blew the gentle scent of mimosa to them. Tenderly placing his arm around the woman's waist, the man walked with her to the broad marble steps leading to the close-cropped lawn.

He was tall, and clad in some uniform with the buttons and badges flashing in the moonlight. She was dark-haired, and with the ivory skin which so often comes to such people. Her evening gown was long, and almost of the colour of the moon itself. Slowly they walked across the lawn, to join a tree-lined path. Infrequently, they stopped a moment and gazed at each other. Soon they came to a rustic wooden bridge crossing a placid stream. For a time they leaned on one of the rails of the bridge, murmuring softly to each other, gazing at their reflection on the unruffled waters below.

Resting her head on the man's shoulder, the woman pointed upwards to a hoot-owl staring intently down from a great oak tree. Unhappy at being watched, the bird spread great wings and soared off across the garden. The man and woman straightened, and strolled on, past well-tended bushes, past flowers now folded in sleep. Ever and anon small rustles and squeaks showed that the little people of the night went about their legitimate business.

The path curved and widened, and turned into a well-kept strand. The moonlight shed a broad white band across the softly heaving water. Tiny wavelets caught the light and turned it into a myriad of glittering jewels dancing on the water. A mile away a huge white liner clove her stately path through the sea, decks ablaze with lights. From her came faintly the strains of music as her band entertained the dancing couples upon her decks. The red of her portside light gleamed, and floodlights lit up the house-mark on her funnels. Phosphorescent foam came from the meeting of her bows with the water, and waves from her wake gurgled and tumbled upon the beach. The man and woman, arms about each other, stood and watched the majestic progress. Soon she was hull-down, and no more could the strains of her music be heard.

In the velvet-purple dimness cast by the shade of a tall pine tree, they stood together, telling each other only the things that lovers tell, planning the future, looking forward to Life itself. No shadow crossed the moon, the air was warm and balmy. Gently the little wavelets tickled the rounder pebbles and played with the smaller sand.

The night, beneath the harvest moon, was made for lovers. A night for poets too, for are not poems the essence of dreams, and life?

·   ·   ·   ·   ·

The sands of the desert were searing-hot beneath the blazing heat of the noonday sun. Even Mother Nile, flowing between hard-baked banks, seemed more sluggish than usual, with the heat-vapour pouring off her gleaming bosom and losing water which an arid land could so ill-afford. Unlucky fellaheen, condemned to work in the fields under the torrid sky, moved with heavy lethargy, too hot and weary to even curse the sweltering day. An Ibis-bird stood drooping by a clump of wilting reeds. The new Tombs of the Great Ones stood bright and tall, with the heat drying the freshly placed mortar between the immense blocks and capping stones.

In the relative coolness of the Embalming Room, deep beneath the burning sands, a wizened old man and his scarcely younger assistant worked as they stuffed aromatic herbs into a months-dead body.

'I reckon the Pharaoh is taking strong measures against the Priests,' said the more ancient of the two.

'Yes,' replied the other with gloomy satisfaction. 'I saw the Guards raiding some of the temples, arresting some, cautioning others, and carrying out bales of papyri. They looked very determined, too!'

'I don't know what the world is coming to,' said the Ancient. 'Never was like this in my young days. The world is going to POT, that's what it is, going to POT!' Sighing and mumbling, he picked up his packing rod and rammed more herbal mixture into an orifice of the unprotesting corpse.

'By Order of the Pharaoh!' shouted the Captain of the Guard as, surrounded by his men, he stalked majestically into the quarters of the High Priest. 'You are accused of harbouring malcontents who plot against Him, and try to cast evil spells that they may harm Him.' Turning to his men he gave the order, 'Search the place—and seize all papyri.'

The High Priest sighed and quietly remarked, 'It was ever thus, those who aspire to higher learnings are persecuted by ignorant men who fear to know Truth and who think that no one can know more than they. So, in destroying our papers of wisdom you extinguish the rush-lights of knowledge.'

The day was a hard one, with soldiers on the alert, Guards raising, and carrying off suspects—most often those who had been betrayed through a neighbour's spite. Slave-drawn carts rumbled through the streets laden with confiscated papyri. But the day ended, as days always have and always will, no matter how endless they seem to suffering victims of oppression.

A cool breeze sprang up and rustled the papyrus reeds with a dry grating sound. Small waves bounded across the dimming Nile to rebound from the sun-baked banks. Along the lower reaches of the river, ferrymen smiled with pleasure as their slatting sails filled with wind and sped them upon their homeward path. Free from the torrid heat of the day, small creatures emerged from holes in the banks and began their nightly prowl in search of prey. But humans were in search of prey, too!

The dark vault of the heavens was besprinkled with the shining jewels which were the stars. Tonight the moon would be late in rising. Faint glimmers of light came from mud huts, and scarce brighter gleams came from the homes of the wealthy. The air was filled with terror, foreboding. No roisterer loitered on the streets this night, no lovers clasped hands and made promises by the broad sweep of the Nile. Tonight the Pharaoh's men prowled the streets, heavy footed and coarse of mien, ready for 'sport'. The Purge was on, a purge against the scholars, the priests, and any who might threaten the Pharaoh by forecasting his early demise. It was DEATH to be abroad this night, DEATH on the pikes of the prowling guards.

But in the dark places of the city silent figures lurked and flitted from shadow to deeper shadow as the Pharaoh's men clumped noisily by. Gradually a pattern became apparent, silent, determined men, using every available cover in order to reach their destination unchallenged. As the guards patrolled noisily, and the eternal stars wheeled overhead, dark figure after dark figure slipped easily through an unmarked, un-lighted door. Slipped through to be seized by those behind the door, and held securely until identity was established. As the last man insinuated his silent way in, and was identified, wait-ing men placed great baulks of timber against the door to ensure that it was firm.

An ancient, cracked voice quavered, 'Follow me, let each man follow in line and place a hand on the shoulder of the man in front. Follow me and—NO NOISE! for Death stalks us to-night.'

With the merest suspicion of a shuffling sound, the line of men followed their leader downwards through a well-con-cealed trap-door. Down, down the slanting path, for a long long way, and at last they emerged in an old burial vault where the air lay dank and musty. 'We shall be safe here,' whispered the old leader. 'But let us not unduly raise our voices lest the minions of Set hear us and carry tidings of our meeting.' Silently they filed round and placed themselves among the funeral furniture. Squatting on their heels, they waited in ex-pectation for their Leader's words. The old man peered short-sightedly around the gathering, assessing, weighing. At last he said, 'We have today and for many days seen our most cher-ished possessions torn from us and burned. We have witnessed the evil sight of uncouth men, driven on by a power-mad tyrant, persecuting our learned ones and destroying the accumulated wisdom of bygone ages. Now we are gathered here together to discuss how our heritage of written learning may be saved.' He glanced shrewdly around as he continued, 'Much has been lost. Much has been saved. Some of us—at risk of savage torture, substituted worthless papyri and saved the good. That we have stored . . . SAFELY. Now, has anyone a suggestion that we may consider?'

For some time conversation ebbed and flowed in a muted undertone as man debated with man the feasibility of This or That. At last a young priest of the Temple of Upper Egypt stood up and in a different tone said, 'Reverend Sirs, I crave your indulgence for my temerity in addressing you thus.' Heads nodded in encouragement, so he continued, 'Last night on duty in the Temple I dreamed. I dreamed that the God Bubastes descended before me and gave me indisputable instructions. I was to state that the Ancient Knowledge could be concealed by Learned Scribes distilling the wisdom of the ages, and then concealing that wisdom in the lines of carefully composed poems. This, said the God Bubastes, would be beyond the comprehension of the illiterate, but clearly apparent to the Illuminatii. Thus posterity should not be deprived of our knowledge nor of the knowledge that went before.' Nervously he sat down. For moments there was silence as the Elders debated within themselves.

At last the Ancient One reached a decision. 'So be it,' he said. 'We will conceal our knowledge in verse. We will also prepare special pictures of the Book of the Tarot. And we will make much that the pictures can be a card game, and in the fullness of time the Light of Knowledge shall shine forth again, replenished and renewed.'

Thus it came to pass as was ordained, and in the years that followed men of high purpose and fearless of character strove to preserve all that which was worthy of preservation in verse and in pictures. And the Gods smiled and were well content.

.   .   .   .   .   .

Throughout the ages mankind, and sometimes womankind also, have used a special form of words that they might conceal and reveal at the same time. Verse can be used to enchant the reader or to mystify the intruder.

By a suitable rhythm of verse, metre, rhyme, and all that sort of thing, one can delve down into the subconscious messages which one needs or requires to become part of one's psychic entity.

When looking at a poem one should decide whether the poet is just lightly playing with words or if he has some special message which he is trying to get over. Many times a message which would be quite unacceptable in ordinary brutal prose can be so wrapped up that only the initiated can get the meaning. Many 'seers' wrote their messages and predictions in verse not because—as the sceptic says—they were afraid to put it in plain language but so that those initiated in such things could read the deeper meaning behind the poem. Frequently some illiterate author (and oh! what a lot there are!) will attempt to sneer at famous poems of predictions. Of course people who cannot write anything of their own can always get a market by pandering to the lower instincts of mankind, and so, as this is the Age of Kali, everyone is trying to reduce everyone to a common denominator. This is the age of cynical disregard for the elementary precept that all men are not equal; no matter that they be equal in the sight of God, all men are not equal upon the Earth, and there is a very prevalent form of inverted snobbery nowadays which makes a man say, 'Oh, I am as good as he is!' Now we see great leaders like Sir Winston Churchill, Roosevelt, and others, having their names and their reputations dragged in the mud, but only by the sorry little people who have no abilities of their own and thus obtain a fiendish pleasure by trying to harm those who have abilities.

Shall we look at a piece of poetry and then go deeper and look at the real meaning behind that poetry? Here, then, is a Tibetan poem, a very very famous poem, it is not just pleasant reading but it has special meaning attached to it. Here is the poem 'I Fear Not':

I Fear Not

In fear of death I built a house
And my house is a house of the void of truth.
Now I fear not death.
In fear of cold I bought a coat
And my coat is the coat of inner heat.
Now I fear not cold.
In fear of want I sought wealth
And my wealth is glorious, unending, sevenfold.
Now I fear not want.

86

In fear of hunger I sought food
And my food is the food of meditation upon truth.
Now I fear not hunger.
In fear of thirst I sought drink
And my drink is the nectar of right knowledge.
Now I fear not thirst.
In fear of weariness I sought a companion
And my companion is the everlasting void of bliss.
Now I fear not weariness.
In fear of error I sought a Path
And my Path is the Path of transcendent union.
Now I fear not error.
I am a Sage who possesses in plentitude
The manifold treasures of desire, and wherever I dwell I am
    happy.

Shortly we will delve down into the esoteric meaning of this
poem, but first let us have another poem. Again it is a Tibetan
one, again this is one with a very special meaning indeed. Here
is the second poem, 'Be Content':

BE CONTENT

My son, as monastery be content with the body
For the bodily substance is the palace of divinity.
As a teacher be content with the mind,
For knowledge of the truth is the beginning of holiness.
As a book be content with outward things
For their number is a symbol of the way of deliverance.
As food be content to feed on ecstasy
For stillness is the perfect likeness of divinity.
As clothing be content to put on the inner heat
For the sky-travelling Goddesses wear the warmth of bliss.
Companions, be content to forsake
For solitude is president of the divine assembly
Raging enemies be content to shun
For enmity is a traveller upon the wrong path.
With demons be content to meditate upon the void
For magic apparitions are creations of the mind.

Let us have yet one more poem, a Tibetan poem which was
composed by the Sixth Dalai Lama, a very erudite man indeed. He was a writer and an artist, a man misunderstood by
many, but one who definitely left his mark upon Eastern

culture. There are so few of his type in the world today. Here is a translation into English; I am afraid I do not know who made the translation, but no matter who it was, the translation cannot in any way do justice to the actual thing in Tibetan. One of the great sorrows of authors is that translations into another language rarely follow the same trend of thought as that which the author attempted to impart in the original language. But here is this translation by someone unknown of 'My Love':

MY LOVE

Dear love to whom my heart goes out
If we could but be wed
Then had I gained the choicest gem
From ocean's deepest bed.
I chanced to pass my sweetheart fair
Upon the road one day,
A turquoise found of clearest blue,
Found, to be thrown away.
High on the peach tree out of reach
The ripened fruit is there.
So, too, the maid of noble birth
So full of life and fair.
My heart's far off, the nights pass by
In sleeplessness and strife
Even day brings not my heart's desire
For lifeless is my life.
I dwell apart in Potala, a God on Earth am I,
But in the town the chief of rogues and boistrous
    revelry,
It is not far that I shall roam,
Lend me your wings white crane.
I go no farther than Li Thang and thence return again.

Let us now consider the poem 'I Fear Not' by that great man Milarepa. Milarepa wrote that the initiated may know certain things. Here is an inkling into the hidden meanings:

In fear of death I built a house
And my house is a house of the void of truth.
Now I fear not death.

The meaning of that has been variously translated and mistranslated. Actually, according to esoteric beliefs, it can be taken as meaning that even on other planes of existence one cannot stand still on a tight-rope, one must go forward or fall, one must progress upwards or one must slip backwards. It is necessary at all times to keep in mind that although here we are upon Earth, yet when we die we are reborn into another stage of existence. When we finish with what we might term the Earth Stage of existence we go on to another Round where there are different abilities, different standards. For example, upon this particular cycle of lives we are given so many senses. When we go to the next stage we will have more senses, more abilities, and so on. But we move up, never backwards unless it is by our own lack of energy.

So, in fear of death in the astral plane, I built a body, and my body had the emptiness of truth. With truth I fear not death. In other words, we know that when we die to one life we go on to the next. There is no such thing as permanent death, death is rebirth. I want to tell you this in absolute sincerity; because of very special training I have been able to visit other planes of existence normally inaccessible to one, a dweller on this plane. Special precautions have to be taken by those who guide one, of course, because one's vibrations—and we are only vibrations—cannot, unaided, speed up to make it possible for us to reach those higher planes. The experience was quite painful, it was like a blinding light, it was like passing through white-hot flames, yet I was shielded, protected.

I found that on a higher plane I was of about the same standard as would be a slug on this Earth compared to a high human intelligence. The greatest scientists of this Earth would find that they were no higher than that slug upon elevated planes. We have to progress all the time, and all the time, at the end of every life, we die, so called, so that we can progress upwards. Think of a caterpillar; a caterpillar is a creature which crawls about, then apparently it dies and becomes a butterfly which moves in a different element, which moves in air instead of crawling about on the ground.

Take the classic example of a dragonfly. From out of some stagnant pond painfully crawls some lowly worm, some grub. It crawls slowly up, perhaps, a rush or a projecting branch. It climbs up, and takes a fierce, tenacious hold. Then there is no more movement, the creature dies, it seems to decay. Eventually from the dead husk there comes a little plop and the dead

shell splits. From it emerges the dragonfly, limp, bedraggled. It spreads its wings, soon they become firm and iridescent. Then, with the sunlight upon it, the dragonfly rises up into the air and soars away.

Now, isn't that really like humanity? The human body, something like a worm you will agree, dies; from the dead husk emerges something which soars upwards into new life. That is what I like so much about dragonflies, they are a promise of eternal life, they are a promise that there is more than just this miserable flesh body. But I for one do not need promises, because I have experienced the actuality.

If we were to continue with 'I Fear Not' we might go to:

> In fear of hunger I sought food
> And my food is the food of meditation upon truth.
> Now I fear not hunger.

That, of course, means spiritual hunger, not physical but spiritual. If a person is in doubt he just doesn't know what to do, where to go to obtain knowledge. A person in doubt is a frustrated person, an unhappy person. 'In fear of spiritual hunger I sought knowledge, and I meditated upon truth, and now knowing the truth I fear not hunger.' I say to you that even in these humble little chapters you can learn much, you can have seeds of knowledge planted within you. A seed is a small thing, but from a small seed can grow a mighty tree. I am trying to plant a seed, I am trying to light a candle in the darkness.

Centuries ago all mankind had knowledge such as this, but certain elements of mankind abused the knowledge, and so there came the Dark Ages when the candles of learning throughout the world were extinguished, when Man burned books of knowledge, and sank for a time into abysmal ignorance, when Man was riddled with superstition. But now we are coming to a new era, to a new stage, wherein Man is going to have additional powers. I may become unpopular when I say almost in a whisper, atom bomb fall-out may not be altogether the harmful thing which it is so often supposed to be. Let us digress from poetry for a moment to get down to reality:

Mankind throughout the centuries has been deteriorating. If we want to get prize cattle, or prize animals, we do not let them mate indiscriminately and breed unfavourable strains. The animals are carefully picked and bred for quality, possibly

91

for some particular quality. If we have trees, fruit trees, we can carefully tend those trees and graft them so that we get bigger and better fruit, or fruit having a special flavour. But let us neglect these animals, let them run wild, let us desert our fruit groves and let them revert to nature, then all the good training they have had reverts back and we get inferior fruit, inferior animals. Think, for instance, of a most beautiful apple which can revert back to a crab apple. Humans are like crab apples, humans breed indiscriminately, and people with the least desirable traits usually have the most children, while people who have knowledge or characters which could actually increase the quality of the human race have no children at all. Often it is because of excessive taxation, or excessive import duties.

So possibly Old Mother Nature, who must know a thing or two after all these years, might see a different way of increasing the value of the human race. Give this a thought; possibly Old Mother Nature has made it so that a few strange radiations are let loose to produce mutations. Not all mutations are bad, you know. We get, for instance, a germ, a family of germs. They are treated by penicillin, many get killed off, but others change, they become immune to penicillin. Later they become not just immune, but they thrive on penicillin. How do we know that humans are not doing the same? Always we have to move upwards, always we have to progress, and it is my firm belief, which also is the belief of Eastern thought, that everyone has to know all these things before they can pass on to higher stages of evolution.

> *In fear of error I sought a Path*
> *And my Path is the Path of transcendent union.*
> *Now I fear not error.*

In other words—I did not know which way to move, I did not know where my Path lay, so I sought knowledge from Higher Worlds. I got that knowledge and now I do not fear that I am making a mistake of my life.

> *I am a sage who possesses in plentitude*
> *The manifold treasures of desire,*
> *And wherever I dwell I am happy.*

Again, I am wise that I have obtained from other sources knowledge of what is to be, knowing what one is required to

92

know. Thus, knowing that life upon Earth is, in the infinity of Man's spiritual lifetime, just a flickering of an eyelid, I can be contented wherever I dwell. Thus, I fear not.

Milarepa was a great sage, he was a man who retired into a mountain cave. People came to consult him and to study with him. Let me make it clear that those who came to study with him, attended to his body wants, cleaned his cave, looked after his clothing, prepared his food, ran messages. So many people of the West think, 'Oh, all knowledge should be free, you must not charge to teach people anything.' But, of course, that is just ignorance, asinine, crass ignorance. That is said by people with little knowledge and little knowledge is a dangerous thing indeed. Anything that is worth having is worth working for. Milarepa taught that one must be content, be content with knowledge. Milarepa taught that the body was as a monastery, and the monks within the monastery were the different powers and abilities of the body and of the mind.

For the bodily substance is the palace of divinity.

Again, the body substance, the flesh, or clay, or whatever you want to call your body, is the house wherein dwells the Overself or the soul who is here upon this Earth to gain experience of mundane things. In higher stages of existence one cannot meet those whom one heartily dislikes. The obvious answer is to come to Earth where you meet all of them all the time! You just think—if you really think with an open mind you will find that you dislike an amazing number of people, and you are sure that an even greater number of people dislike you. If you are honest you will agree that that is right. If you go to work you will be sure that somebody is trying to cut you out of your job, somebody is trying to deny you promotion, somebody has a spite against you. That's so, isn't it?

Well, the Overself has to come down to Earth to get those obnoxious experiences. Thus it is that the body is a fairly durable contraption, it houses the soul against undue shocks. One must be content with the mind, because within the mind one can store and sort out knowledge of the truth, and until you know the truth you cannot know holiness, holiness not in the sanctimonious sense, but in the true sense which recognises that the Overself is the controller of the body, and the body is merely a puppet.

Milarepa goes on:

Raging enemies be content to shun
For enmity is a traveller upon the wrong Path.

That means you must not have hatred or enmity for anyone because if you feel strong hatred for anyone it means that you are upon the wrong Path. You cannot stand still on a tight-rope, you either go forward or you go back because actually, you know, on our spiritual tight-rope you cannot fall off and be destroyed. Often in religions, in all religions, there is talk of eternal damnation, talk of eternal torment. Don't believe it, don't believe it! These things were said by the priests of old in the same way that the mother might tell her child, 'Now you be quiet or I'll tell your father. He'll take a stick to you!'

In the days of old people were very much like children. They perhaps lacked reasoning power which has developed throughout the ages, often they had to be threatened in order to help them. You might find that little Joe or Charlie won't eat his breakfast, you might say—if you are foolish—'Now you eat it up this moment or I'll call the policeman for you!' I have known that happen many times. Well, eventually little Joe or little Charlie thinks that all policemen are fiends, he thinks that a policeman is always ready to pounce upon him, take him off to jail, and do all kinds of unmentionable things to him for ever and ever and a bit longer. So in the days gone by the priest used to say, 'Ah! Devils will get at you, Devils will prod you in various unmentionable places, they will give you, in fact, the devil of a time.' Don't believe it! There is a God, it does not matter what you are going to call that God, there is a God, a God of good, and no person is ever called upon to suffer beyond his limits.

Some of us, though, have memories of other things. Some of us, as in my own case, have actual knowledge, not just memories, and some people without the memories and without the knowledge are called upon to suffer more than they need to suffer because they will not learn by lessons of the past. We live upon this Earth, we are, as you know, about nine-tenths subconscious, one-tenth of us only is conscious, or at least that is the popular figure. By the sight of some of the people on certain other continents one would doubt that people are even one-tenth conscious! But I want to say something here about other work which is done by the Overself.

The Overself, of course, is ten-tenths conscious. It has to be otherwise the human subconscious could not be nine-tenths awake. The Overself is not confined to dealing with one body alone, there are different systems of utilising the energies of the Overself, and let us just briefly look at them.

Some people come as a member of a group, for example, a young girl may be upon the Earth and she may be quite lost and inept without the company of her brothers, her sisters, and her parents. These people, they seem to function only when they are all together. Death makes a terrific gap, while when one gets married, then the married person is always running back to the family. These people may be as puppets all controlled by the same Overself.

Twins or quads often also are controlled by the same Overself. It seems as if the leaders of other Planes know that this particular round of existence is nearly at an end and another will start, and so they seem to be bringing people here to work in groups under the control of one Overself to each group, in much the same way as a Communistic dictatorship has cells of so many people under the control of one supervisor, and all the supervisors are under the control of a senior supervisor, and so on.

One has often seen groups of birds, perhaps fifty birds, wheeling and turning in unison as if under the command of one person. Well, that is as it should be because these birds are all controlled by one person, in just the same way as a colony of ants is controlled by one Overself, or a hive of bees is controlled by one Overself.

People who are more enlightened, more evolved, have a different system, and this is going to make you think. So, let us take it slowly and briefly because actually all we have to bother about is how we are managing on this Earth—let the other worlds take care of themselves until we can get round to them.

There are many different worlds like the Earth, not in the same—for want of a better word I can only call—'time'. But perhaps we should do better if we used a musical term— harmonics. We can have a musical note, a pure note, but then we can have harmonics to the note. The harmonics are all fundamentals of the original note. In much the same way there is this Earth, which perhaps we should call Earth D, then there are Earths C, B, A, and E, F, G, for instance. These are similar Earths, similar worlds, and they are called parallel universes or parallel worlds, whichever you prefer.

An Overself who has evolved and who realises that controlling just one puny little Earth-body is time consuming, and not sufficiently educational, can have a puppet on each of several worlds. So that in world A, for example, little Bennie can be a genius, but in world F little Freddie can be a moron. In that way the Overself can see two sides of the coin at once, and can gain experience on both ends of the scale.

A really experienced Overself might have nine different puppets, and that is the same as living nine different lives, which speeds up evolution quite a bit. But this subject has already been dealt with more fully in Chapter Two.

As was stated at the beginning of this chapter, poetry or verse or a definite rhythm-pattern is often used to drive a matter deeply into one's subconscious. Now we are going to have an example of the type of thing which the Egyptians used to do. Unfortunately it loses a lot of its power by being translated into English. In the original Egyptian the words swayed rhythmically and achieved the desired purpose, but just think for yourself, if you get a piece of poetry and you translate it from English or Spanish into, let us say, German, you get the sounds all wrong, you get the balance all wrong, and so it does not have the same effect. In fact, some poems cannot be translated at all into another language, so this 'Confession to Maat' is not as good as it would be in Egyptian.

This is a temple confession which was said in the Chamber of Maat in the Egyptian Temple of Initiation. It is as written in the Egyptian Book of the Dead, it was actually an invocation. Maat, you may remember, is the Egyptian word meaning 'Truth'. So the Chamber of Maat became the Chamber, or Temple, of Truth.

Here is the Confession to Maat which should be repeated every night before one goes to sleep. If one repeats this as did the Egyptians, then it leads one to a much purer life. Try it and see!

THE CONFESSION TO MAAT

Homage to Thee, Oh Great God, Thou Master of all Truth, I have come to Thee, Oh my God, and have brought myself hither that I may become conscious of Thy decrees. I know Thee and am attuned with Thee and Thy two and forty laws which exist with Thee in this Chamber of Maat.

In Truth I come into Thy Attunement, and I have brought Maat in my mind and Soul.

I have destroyed wickedness for Thee.
I have not done evil to mankind.
I have not oppressed the members of my family.
I have not wrought evil place of right and Truth.
I have had no intimacy with worthless men.
I have not demanded first consideration.
I have not decreed that excessive labour be performed for me.
I have not brought forward my name for exaltation to honours.
I have not defrauded the oppressed of Property.
I have made no man suffer hunger.
I have made no one to weep.
I have caused no pain to be inflicted upon man or animal.
I have not defrauded the Temple of their oblations.
I have not diminished from the bushel.
I have not filched away land.
I have not encroached upon the fields of others.
I have not added to the weights of the scales to cheat the seller and I have not misread the pointer of the scales to cheat the buyer.
I have not kept milk from the mouths of children.
I have not turned back the water at the time it should flow.
I have not extinguished the fire when it should burn.
I have not repulsed God in His Manifestation.

AFFIRMATION

I am Pure! I am Pure! I am Pure!
My purity is the purity of the Divinity of the Holy Temple.
THEREFORE EVIL SHALL NOT BEFALL ME IN THIS WORLD, BECAUSE I, EVEN I, KNOW THE LAWS OF GOD WHICH ARE GOD.

There are, as previously stated, occasions when prose in special form is used to drive into the subconsciousness a special message. Here is a Prayer which I composed, and which you should repeat three times each morning:

Let me this day, living my life day by day in the manner prescribed, control and direct my imagination.

Let me this day, living my life day by day in the manner prescribed, control my desires and my thoughts that I be purified thereby.

Let me this day, and all days, keep my imagination and my thoughts directed firmly upon the task which has to be accomplished, that success may come thereby.

I will at all times live my life day by day, controlling imagination and thought.

.   .   .   .   .

You should also have a Prayer to be said at night, three times each night before going to sleep. Here, then, is a specially composed Prayer (composed by me) which will instil discipline into your subconsciousness by night:

A Prayer

Keep me free from evil thoughts. Keep me free from the blackness of despair. At the time of my misery shine a light into the darkness that enshrouds me.

Let my every thought be good and clean. Let my every action be for the good of others. Let me be positive in my thoughts that my mind may be strengthened therefrom.

I am the Master of my Destiny. As I think today, so am I tomorrow. Let me therefore avoid all evil thoughts. Let me avoid all thoughts which cause distress to others. Let my Spirit arise within me that I may easily succeed in the task that lies ahead.

I am the Master of my Destiny. So be it.

CHAPTER SIX

A WORLD WE ALL MUST VISIT

THE gentle rain came pattering down, lightly washing the soot-laden slates of the old market town. Like the tears of new widows it fell from grey skies to tinkle across the garbage cans with musical fingers. To the soft sighing of the evening wind it danced and swayed across the roadways, tapping against windows and bathing the parched foliage of such scrawny trees as still stood with lower trunks immured in concrete sidewalks. The light of passing cars reflected from the glistening roadway, their tyres hissing through the thin sheet of water which collected from the poorly drained surface. 'Tap-tap-tap!' went the raindrops as they ran gleefully together from the old grey roof and flowed into the broken spout to fall on to the worn stone steps below.

Passers-by hurried along, muttering imprecations against the weather, turning up collars, and erecting umbrellas. Those caught unprotected hastily improvised shelter from unfolded newspapers. A cautious cat sidled along close-pressed to the houses, jumping puddles, and ever alert to find the driest places. Tiring of the wet, or possibly reaching home, the cat gave a long, cautious look around, then squeezed through a partly opened window.

From around the corner came a slight, hurrying figure clad in dark raincoat and sheltering beneath a small, black umbrella. Pausing a moment beneath a street lamp she consulted a slip of paper clutched between her fingers. Peering in the dim light she checked again the address and number before hurrying on. Here and there she halted her hurried flight to bend forward and read the numbers on the house doors. At last, with a small exclamation, she stopped by the corner house. Hesitantly she looked at it, a small house, a poor house, with paint sun-blistered on the door. The window frames were cracked for want of paint, and the stonework had seen much better days. Yet—she decided—it was a HAPPY house.

Hesitating no longer, she mounted the three small stone steps and knocked timidly at the door. Soon there came the sound of footsteps within the house and the slight creak as the door was opened.

'Mrs. Ryan?' asked the woman on the step.

'Yes, I'm Mrs. Ryan, can I help you?' responded the other, then, 'Won't you come in out of the rain?'

Gratefully the small woman folded her umbrella and stepped inside. As Mrs. Ryan took her wet coat the slight woman looked about her.

She saw an elderly, gaunt woman, with a kind face and work-worn hands. A woman who, like her house, had seen better days, but one who had well learned Life's hard lessons. The furniture was clean but well worn, and the linoleum was beginning to be shabby. The slight woman turned with a start and said, 'Oh, I'm SO sorry, my mind was wandering. I'm Mrs. Harvey. Mrs. Ellis told me about you. I DESPERATELY need help!'

Mrs. Ryan gazed at her gravely and said, 'Come into the sitting-room with me, Mrs. Harvey. Let us see what the trouble is.' She led the way into a small, neat room facing down the street. Motioning to a chair she said, 'Won't you sit down?'

Gratefully the slight woman sank into the comfortable chair. 'It's about Fred,' she cried, 'he died five weeks ago and I miss him so!' Memory overcame her and she wept with an agony of emotion. Fumbling in her handbag she withdrew her handkerchief and dabbed ineffectually at her streaming eyes.

Mrs. Ryan patted her on the shoulder and said, 'Now, now, just sit there and have your cry out; I will make a cup of tea and then you will feel better.' Hurrying from the room she entered the kitchen from whence soon came the clatter of tea-cups.

'I've had a TERRIBLE time!' said Mrs. Harvey later as they sat facing each other with the tea-tray between them. 'Fred—my husband—and I were very much in love and then five weeks ago he was killed instantly in an explosion at the Works. It was HORRIBLE! And every night I've had the strongest feeling that he was trying to get in touch with me, to tell me something.' She stopped, and twisted her handkerchief nervously, biting her lower lip and scuffing the worn carpet on the floor. Then—'Mrs. Ellis told me that you might be able to get in touch with Fred—I don't know what you charge—but I do so want to hear from him!'

'My dear,' said the elderly woman to the anxious young widow. 'We can only try and trust in God. Sometimes I can receive messages from those who have left this life, other times I cannot. Only the highest Adepts can always be telepathic and clairvoyant. If I can help you, then that is God's Will; if I cannot, then that is God's Will too. As for my charge'—she waved a hand round the room—'I do not look as if I over-charged and lived in luxury, do I?' She sighed and added, 'A machine could be constructed whereby this world and the Unseen could communicate just as we now telephone another country. But Industry is not interested . . . tell me about your husband, have you some personal article of his that I may attempt to contact him?'

Much, much later a smiling and greatly comforted Mrs. Harvey stood up to leave, and said, 'I know now that there are mediums and mediums; some are absolute swindlers as I have found to my cost. Some raise hopes falsely and without having any ability whatever. You—you are VERY different. Thank you, thank you so much, Mrs. Ryan!'

As she softly closed the door after the departing Mrs. Harvey, the gaunt old medium muttered, 'Lord! Lord! If only we could stop all the fakes and have real research, how easily we could then communicate.'

She turned back into the sitting-room and slowly gathered up the tea-things, thinking of a seance which she had once attended.

·   ·   ·   ·   ·

The shops had closed early, for it was the middle of the week, when all the pay packets were empty, and larders too were becoming bare in anticipation of the morrow's shopping spree. The shops had closed early, and from the great city had flowed clerks and accountants, typists and shop girls. Great rivers of humanity had stormed the barriers at the Tube stations and rushed like a roaring torrent down the escalators, sweeping along the subways to stand at last in a solid mass along the station platforms. From the deep tunnels came the reverberating vroom-vroom of the trains as they approached. At the first glimmer of train-light wavering in the darkness an uneasy surge swept the waiting masses. Strong ones pushed forward, weak ones were roughly shoved aside. As the train slowed into the station, to stop with a dying sigh of airbrakes, the crowd rolled forward and were engulfed by the carriages. A thud as the rubber-lined doors shut, and the dull throbbing of the air compressors pumping pressure to keep the brakes off, and the train rolled away, gathering speed, as the next wave of work-leaving humans poured down the subways to stand sheep-like on the so recently vacated platform.

At last the pushing crowds thinned and dwindled to a trickle. Soon the trains became less frequent, for this was the time of home-returning for the workers. Later the flow would be partly reversed as theatre-goers and window-shoppers returned for their evening pleasures. Soon Ladies of the Night would appear, to loiter in darkened doorways or flaunt themselves beneath the lamplights. Soon policemen would saunter through the shopping areas, leisurely trying premises for unlocked doors, peering into parked cars, and being unobtrusively alert for the unusual and illegal. But not yet, the workers had but recently left for home.

Far out in the suburbs people were getting up from their evening meal. Some were dressing for theatres, others were wondering how to spend an idle evening. Others were going to Meetings . . . !

Down the road, in twos and threes came a small group converging on a big old house that stood back somewhat from the road, like some old person trying to keep aloof from the common herd. The bushes hiding the façade were unkempt, untrimmed, reminding one of a man with long, uncut hair on his neck. Above the portico a single unshaded bulb glowed dimly through the mess left by singed flies and insects. Briefly a face appeared at an upstairs window and peered down the road, assessing the number of people approaching, and then vanishing in the twitching of a quickly drawn curtain.

Soon people were congregating at the portico, calling greetings to friends, eyeing new faces with unfriendly suspicion. Soon the door was opened, and a very large, very stout woman bedecked with strings of imitation pearls appeared. Washing her hands with invisible soap and water, she beamed toothily upon the group facing her. 'Well! Well!' she exclaimed archly. 'The Spirits told me that we should have a record number tonight. Now, if you will just come in . . .' She moved aside and people filed into the gloomy hallway. 'Leave your Love Offerings there,' said the stout woman as she pointed to a deep plate standing in an alcove. A banknote, weighted down with four half-crowns, already rested in the capacious bottom, giving silent hints as to the amount of 'Love Offering' expected.

Under the watchful eyes of the stout woman the congregation fumbled in pocket and purse and dropped their offerings into the rapidly filling plate. 'That's right!' said the woman. 'We must not let our Spirit Friends think their efforts are unappreciated, must we? The more we give the more we receive,' she added smugly.

The little group of people moved into a large room with what appeared to be a stage at one end. Hard wooden chairs were placed in irregular ranks and these were rapidly occupied by the crowd, with nervous newcomers being pushed to the back rows.

The stout woman moved ponderously to the stage and took her place in the centre, playing with her bracelets impatiently. A tall, thin woman appeared and sat down before a half-concealed harmonium and played the first bars of a hymn. 'Just a few hymns first to get the atmosphere right,' said the stout woman. 'Then we will get down to business.' For some minutes the organ played and the people sang, then the stout woman waved her hands imperatively and said, 'STOP! STOP! The Spirits are waiting!' The last notes died away from the organ in a wail of diminuendo as the bellows emptied of air. There was a rustle and creak of furniture as people sat and shuffled to become at ease. The lights dimmed, went out, and were replaced by red ones which shed an eerie glow over all.

Upon the platform the stout woman peered and pranced. 'Oh! Boys!' she exclaimed coquettishly. 'Wait—wait—you must speak in turn! There are many waiting to speak tonight,' she exclaimed to her audience in an aside, 'and they are very impatient. Many of you will have messages tonight,' she added.

For some time she writhed on the platform, giggling, and rubbing her head. 'Now!' she exclaimed at last. 'They have had their fun. So—to business.' Looking about her, she suddenly asked, 'Mary—the name is Mary. Has anyone here by the name of Mary lost a Dear One recently?'

Dubiously a hand rose. 'I lost my stepfather six months ago,' said a nervous young woman. 'He was a great sufferer, I'm sure it was a relief when he went.'

The stout woman nodded, and remarked, 'Well, he asks me to tell you that he is happy now and is sorry for all the work he caused you.' The nervous young woman nodded and whispered to her companion.

'Smith!' called the stout woman. 'I have a message for Smith. I am asked to say that you are not to worry, everything will be all right. You understand what I mean, don't you—— I can hardly talk about it in a meeting like this, but YOU understand!' Near the front a young man nodded his head in assent.

'The Boys are in great form tonight,' said the stout woman, 'they have SO MANY messages for you. I am just like a telephone, you know, giving the messages from our Dear Departed who are yet with us in the spirit! Wait—wait—what is that? OH! They say that I should ask for special contributions so that I may have this room decorated, they don't like to visit shabby rooms. Will you help? Will you contribute towards this worthy cause? Miss Jones, will you pass the plate round please? Thank you!'

     .   .   .   .   .

Let it be stated at the outset that it is quite possible under certain conditions to receive messages from those who have 'passed over'. At the same time it must be stated equally definitely that people who have left this world have a job to do, and they do not just sit around in groups waiting like a gang of youths on a street corner to get a word in somehow. Many of the messages are fake messages either from elementals or from ungenuine 'mediums'.

First we should deal with one or two of the very real dangers of occultism and metaphysics, and everything else that comes within that classification. Of course there is no danger whatever to the person practising occultism for a pure reason; I have quite a different thing in mind.

One of the biggest dangers which we face is that posed by cranks, crackpots, the mentally deluded, and those who think they are Cleopatra or some such similar reincarnation. The number of Cleopatras would probably populate the whole of New York and leave an overflow for the rest of the United States.

It is a most unfortunate thing that the emotionally unstable flock to occultism like flies to a jampot, and the bigger cranks they are the more danger they make for us who are trying to do a decent job.

Let me make this quite definitely clear; occultism is a natural thing, there is nothing mysterious about it, it is just the use of powers which almost everyone has, of which almost everyone has forgotten how to use. Put it this way: we have an ordinary, average person who shall be our guide-stick, or our yardstick. This ordinary, average person is our indicator. A person with less intellect is below average, so a denizen of a mental home can be very much below average. The sub-normals, those who are below average, do not engage our attention. But those who are in possession of abilities which our average indicator does not possess, then they are above normal, paranormal. People with occult abilities are para-normal, they have abilities which are not developed in the average person.

A savage has a very keen sense of smell, and often a very keen sense of sight also, he senses far above anything which the so-called civilised person does. A civilised person has the same potentialities for increased smell or sight, but conditions of alleged civilised life make the exercise of smell, power, and sight keenness a positive drawback. Think of going to some of those restaurants if one's smell was phenomenally acute, the stench would knock one over backwards.

The person with occult power, then, is not a magician, not anything like that, he is just a person who has developed certain senses possessed by everyone else. In the same way we all have muscles, but the weight-lifter has developed his muscles to a far greater extent than has the little old lady who sits in a chair all day long. And the man who engages in politics, he has developed his vocal chords far beyond that of the man who stays at home all the time; they both have muscles, they both have vocal chords, but the stages of development of those organs are different.

One of the most important of the occult laws is that one should not indulge in exhibitionism, one should not drag down occult power by what becomes a mere circus turn. How often does one hear a woman say, 'Oh, I met a wonderful man to-day, he came to my door, he's a Spanish onion seller in the mornings, in the afternoons he sells ladies wear, and in the evenings he gives occult demonstrations. He is so utterly wonderful, he can balance on one finger while drinking a cup of tea upside down.' Or how often do we hear of some poor little man, so lonely, so forgotten by the world, that he has to say, 'Ah, I have read a book about occultism. I will now set up as a great Teacher and a Master.' So he goes to work by day, perhaps canvassing from door to door, or perhaps being a meek little man under a domineering employer, and by night he sets off to his back room, puts on a mysterious look, flaps his eyebrows up and down, sights down the side of his nose, makes weird sighs and groans and perhaps also does a stage trick or two, says how wonderfully he can do astral travelling. Actually he has probably had too much supper or bad cheese, or something, and he has had a nightmare. Well, that little man is a real pest, he is a real danger to occultism and to himself. I am going to tell you that all these crackpots who put on stage shows and call it occultism are going to have to pay time after time until they learn better, they are going to have to come back to this Earth, and that should be a threat enough to put anyone off.

In India there is a sect of people called the Fakirs. They pose as holy men, they travel about India and no attractive woman is safe from them, but they put on stage shows, they put on tricks. Well I for one, if I want to see a conjuring show, I would rather pay and go to a good variety theatre. I don't want to see a dirty little man squatting on the ground trying to hypnotise a whole group of people, that doesn't prove anything spiritual to me. It proves, instead, that the person has not even the first conception of spiritualism. The Indian rope trick is just a simple matter of hypnotism. I am going to tell you, though, quite definitely that the real Masters who never prove anything to satisfy the idle curiosity seekers can actually do the so-called Indian rope trick by utilising natural powers, and that does not employ hypnotism. I will tell you quite truthfully that I and many others have seen levitation. Levitation is a very real thing indeed, and it is not at all mysterious. It is a matter of reversing magnetic currents. If you get hold of two magnets, two bar magnets for preference, if you hold them one in each hand and bring them together, they may jump together with a loud metallic clang, often pinching a bit of flesh in-between! But if you reverse the direction of just one, that is if you take the one in your right hand, and you put the South Pole where the North Pole was before and you try to bring these two magnets together, you will find that they make quite strenuous efforts to evade each other, they oppose each other, they have no magnetic attraction to each other, they have repulsion instead.

Another thing: One can have a form of induction coil connected to a battery or to the mains, and over a shaft which projects upwards one can drop an aluminium ring. If the current is switched on, the ring apparently defies gravity and floats in the air. If anyone doubts the truth of this, well, they should consult some scientific magazine or write to the United States for a demonstration kit. But let us get back to what we are discussing seriously.

Levitation is a method of altering our own magnetic attraction so that we do not weigh so much. In England about sixty or so years ago there was a young man called Home; he gave an actual demonstration of levitation in an English country house. Some of the world's foremost scientists witnessed the demonstration, but because the demonstration disproved the laws which those scientists had formulated they would not give an unbiased report. In Tibet and China—China before the Communists made a commotion there, that is—and Japan, before the United States soldiers made a commotion there as well, one saw a lot of levitation and similar things. But these things were never done as a circus turn, but only for the science of raising the Kundalini in sincere and genuine students.

Let us, then, be true occultists and let us very, very seriously suspect anyone who offers to give a demonstration of balancing on one finger or any of those really crackpotted asininities which the person with no confidence in himself and no occult powers at all tries to delude the unwary with. The true occultist never, never gives proof of his abilities unless there is a completely overriding good reason for it.

I should also include in this people like Dinah Dripdry, the back-street clairvoyant. This poor woman, perhaps for several hours a day, scrubs floors carrying around a bucket and a mop. Then at the end of her work she trudges off home (there is usually a bus strike, anyway!), she trudges off home and gets herself done up in some really outlandish fashion.

She sticks a colourful thing around herself, and then she wraps a sort of gaudy handkerchief around her head which she thinks looks like a turban. She has very dim lights in the room so the clients won't see how dirty it really is, then she is ready

107

to start business. Frequently she has got hold of some sort of crystal from somewhere, often it is kept as a showpiece exposed to the sunlight so that people will see this thing and think what a wonderful woman she is when she is not scrubbing floors. Well, there is nothing that ruins a crystal more thoroughly than being exposed to sunlight, it kills the odonetic power of the crystal.

Dinah Dripdry, then, has somehow lured a foolish client into her room. Usually she sits down opposite him, looks him up and down and gets him talking a bit. Most people are so fond of hearing their own voice that they tell all and a bit more. So Dinah Dripdry merely has to look in her crystal, seeing nothing but her own reflection, and repeat back in gloomy tones some of the things which her client has told her. Then she gets a reputation for being a great seeress. The client frequently doesn't remember having told her anything, and he parts with his money without a murmur! Dinah Dripdry cannot be a clairvoyant if she is doing it for money because that loses her the power even if she had it in the first case.

No average clairvoyant is clairvoyant all the time throughout the twenty-four hours. A person may be highly clairvoyant at a most inconvenient time, but then when there is need for clairvoyance the person is not clairvoyant, and if you are doing it for money you cannot say, 'Oh this is one of my off-days, I don't feel able to tell you the truth today.' So people like Dinah Dripdry have to make their money, and when they cannot see anything in the crystal—which is all the time with them—then they have to make things up.

You will have experiences of not being in top form all the time. You may say, 'I don't know what's wrong with me, I can't concentrate today.' Well, in the same way with clairvoyance; you don't concentrate in clairvoyance, you do just the reverse, so that if a person is tensed up or too excited then that person cannot relax, and for the time being the clairvoyant ability falls off. The second rule is, for the sake of your own pocket book, never, never pay anything whatever to have your fortune told by a crystal gazer or a person like that, they cannot do it for money and if they try to put it on a commercial basis, then they just have to 'make up' from time to time, and the more a person makes up things the more quickly they lose any clairvoyant ability which they might have possessed in the first case.

Another thing which should be made clear now is that no person can control the astral of another. You sometimes get an idiotic sort of woman who does a cackle of laughter, like a hen about to lay a particularly large egg, and says, 'Oh, I've got a hold on you, I met you in the astral last night and now I can control your astral.' If you ever meet a person like that the best thing is to call those white-coated attendants who carry the mentally afflicted off to a comfortably padded cell.

No person can suffer any injury when in the astral. No person can be controlled by another person while in the astral. The only thing to be afraid of is of being afraid. Fear is like a corrosive acid on the mechanism of a thing like a watch. Fear corrodes, fear corrupts. So long as you are not afraid, nothing at all bad can happen to you. So again, if any idiotic crackpot claims to be able to control you, then you'd better send them off to be examined by a psychiatrist or call the police, it's time the police did something anyhow!

It is not possible except under certain conditions and circumstances to hypnotise a person against that person's will. Of course those who have been trained in Tibet, and only in the Temple of the Inner Mysteries of Tibet, could do such a thing if they wanted to for a good reason, but every person who has been trained in the Inner Temple of Mysteries of Tibet has himself been hypnotically conditioned so that he cannot do anything of this type to harm anyone else but only to help someone else, and even then only in very unusual circumstances.

If someone starts gazing at you and trying to hypnotise you, then gaze straight back at the bridge of his nose between his eyes, gaze straight back, and if he doesn't know enough he will soon be hypnotised instead of you. You have nothing to fear whatever except of being afraid. Occultism is an ordinary thing just the same as breathing, or lifting a book, or taking a step. You can walk safely unless you are clumsy and careless, and then you can slip on a banana skin. Well that is your fault, not the fault of walking. Occultism is safer than walking because there are no banana skins in occultism. The only thing to be afraid of, I repeat, is of being afraid.

Of course it's quite difficult trying to reason with people, quite difficult trying to explain a thing to a person, because there is a definite law that in any battle between the emotion and reason, emotion always wins no matter how great one's

110

intellect, no matter how great one's reasoning power. If one gets really excited and enraged the emotion overrides the reason.

A person lives in a tall apartment building nine floors high, if you like. These buildings have a flimsy iron railing at the edge of their balconies, a good push would probably knock the thing over, but emotion tells us that it is quite safe because there is a railing there and we experience no fear at all. But supposing that railing was removed, then we should have great fear of falling even if we stood in precisely the same position as we should have stood if the railing had been there.

At all times, then, we should keep in mind that in any battle between emotion and reason, emotion always wins, and for that reason we should not let ourselves get unduly excited, instead we should try to get a step nearer to Nirvana which is the controlling of emotion so that no longer does it stop the workings of reason.

We must realise that some of these little back-street people who have read a book or perhaps have just heard of the title of a book, are not necessarily the best teachers. The only person who is qualified to teach anything to do with the occult is the person who obviously knows. A person who has been trained at a reputable place. I, for instance, can and have produced papers showing that I have been trained and hold medical degrees of the University of Chungking, and my papers describe me as a Lama of the Potala Monastery of Lhasa. Naturally, one does not produce such papers just for curiosity seekers or to settle bets as I have frequently been asked! Publishers have seen such papers and they testify to that in their Foreword to one or more of my books.

One would not go to a quack doctor, one who would give us a 'bonk' on the head with a mallet in order to make us unconscious and so oblivious to pain, one would only go to a qualified doctor. In the same way, one should not go to a quack who has no real knowledge of the occult except some imaginary sounds in the head; all too often, as you know, voices in the head may even be a symptom of mental derangement. You should choose your occultist as soundly as you choose your physical doctor.

When a person leaves this Earth they may be advanced people who have gone on to higher planes. In that case only a medium with very considerable power can make contact because in ordinary physical concepts those who have passed over have gone to a different time zone, and if you try to telephone Australia from England, then unless you know the time zone of your friend, you cannot get in touch, you may be trying to call in the middle of the night, for instance. But in our medium case we are trying to call someone who is already a few thousand light years into the future! Most times a medium who lacks experience will be deluded by those plausible Beings who are also known as elementals. Perhaps we should discuss elementals so that we may know something about the subject.

People have rather remarkable ideas about that order of Beings which we call elementals. Frequently they are confused with the souls of humans, but they are nothing at all like that. They mimic humans just the same as monkeys copy humans, and the average medium who cannot see into the astral will be led astray by elementals pretending to be humans.

Elementals are not evil spirits either, they are merely the thought forms which have been generated by constant repetition. For example, if a person constantly gets drunk, then that person will have confused thoughts and his excess energy, being no longer under control, will run wild and will perhaps conjure up thoughts of pink elephants or spotted lizards, or something like that. These things are elementals.

As we have said, each cycle of evolution is constituted by those leaving a cycle and those starting a cycle, so we get what is in effect a life-wave of living souls or Overselves, and each of these 'waves' has its own contribution to evolution, it leaves its own pattern just the same as an Oxford man leaves a different pattern on civilisation to the Yale man, and the Borstal man leaves yet a different pattern. So when this life-wave goes on their memory remains as a static force, and as there have been so many people concerned, the force is built up into what is in the astral plane a solid creature.

These creatures which have been built up and left behind by succeeding wave-forms or cycles of evolution are solid creatures, but they lack 'the divine spark', they lack intelligence, and instead they are only able to mimic or reproduce things which have entered into their consciousness at some time. You can, if you try hard enough, teach a parrot to repeat a few words, it does not necessarily understand the words but the parrot is repeating a sonic pattern. In the same way, elementals repeat a cybernetic pattern.

For those who are really interested in the subject, elementals are divided into many different types in much the same way as in humans there are black people, brown people, yellow people, white people, etc. In the elemental groups there are four main types attached to the Earth astral plane, and that is how we get some of the 'qualities' of astrology. The astrologer will know of the Spirits of Air, the Spirits of Fire, the Spirits of Water, and the Spirits of Earth, for they are the four main types of elementals.

The witchcraft people, or the alchemist, would refer to them as gnomes for one group, sylphs for the second group, salamanders for the third group, and for the last group undines.

If you want to take it a bit farther beyond the astrologer and beyond the witches you can go on to the stage of the chemists, because you can say that the Earth group represent a solid in which all molecules adhere. After the solid we have the liquid (water) in which molecules move freely. Next on our list is air, which also includes gases of various types, and in air the molecules repel each other. Finally, for our chemical correspondents, there is fire, and in fire molecules change or transmute into some other substance.

The term 'elemental' is almost always reserved for those Beings who occupy a place in one of the groups just mentioned, but there are other groups such as nature spirits. Nature spirits control the growth of trees and plants, and they help in the transmutation of organic compounds so that plants may be enriched and fertilised. These groups all have an Overself—Head, or if you prefer, an Oversoul; they are known as the Manu. The human tribe has a Manu, each country has a Manu, and nature spirits have a Manu, there is a Manu who controls and oversees the work of the tree spirits just as there is a Manu who controls the work of the rock spirits. In Egypt, many, many centuries ago, highly trained priests were able to get in contact with these Manus. For example, Bubastes, the cat God, the Manu of cats everywhere.

We must have negative or we cannot have positive, so just as there are good spirits so also are there evil spirits, demons if you like. They are evil to us here, but on another plane of existence they may be good. If you are at all electrically inclined this explanation might appeal to you; suppose you have a twelve-volt car battery; at the extreme is the positive and at the other extreme is the negative. But now supposing that you connect another battery, six or twelve volt, in series on to this first battery, then the negative of the original battery will be as the positive of the second battery, and the negative of the second battery will be more negative than the negative of the first battery! All this, stated simply, is that everything is relative and to be compared with each other. Thus we have evil here at present, but if we can find a worse world, then our evil would be as good on that world, and what is good on this world would be not very good at all on the higher world!

I said that Man was having different waves of evolution. Well, that really is so. For example, there was the Lemurian Race which mainly operated by instincts and passions, and then evolved higher emotions. After that there came the Atlantian Race which started off with higher emotions and then evolved a reasoning mind. The Aryan Race came next; this started off with the functioning mind and will eventually obtain an abstract mind. After the Aryan we come to the Sixth Race which starts with the abstract mind and eventually will obtain spiritual perception. With the Seventh Race, which will start with spiritual perception, it will go on to achieve cosmic consciousness.

For those of you who are interested in the theory of land drift, that is, that the whole world was covered with one continent at the start and that it broke up under centrifrugal rotation, there is now very considerable proof that this which was known as Pangea first separated into two super continents known as Laurasia which was in the North, and Gondwanalana in the South. These in time broke up into separate lands and continents, however that is taking us rather far from our original theme.

A medium is a person who through some difference in brain structure is able to receive messages from another plane of existence in just the same way as a radio can receive messages which the unaided human ear cannot.

A medium usually goes into a form of trance, either light or heavy depending upon the medium, and during that trance the consciousness of the medium is suppressed so that another entity can operate the 'controls' and give utterance to certain thoughts in the form of words.

Most mediums will have a spirit control from among those

114

who have been kept upon the lower astral for some specific purpose. The spirit control, or Guide as many call it, acts as a policeman and prevents—in some cases—mischievous elementals from doing harm to the medium.

The Overself of the medium has departed so as to give the Guide free rein, but the medium who is sitting in a chair or lying on a couch, will not be aware of anything at all. If you see that the medium is looking about taking too much interest in events, then you can be quite reasonably sure that you do not have a genuine medium. The whole point is that the medium should place his or her personality completely aside and function merely as a telephone. After all, if you are going to get a message from the other side of death you do not want the medium's interpretation, you want a clear unbiased statement, and the only way that one can obtain that clear unbiased statement is to let the spirit communicator communicate without interference from the medium.

Again you should remember that when one gets in contact with what we might term the spirits of the departed so that they may tell us of their experiences we merely listen to the accounts of their dreams in the other world, because the really evolved souls have gone on to a dimension which the average medium cannot possibly reach. It is only when one has a real Master that one can reach forward into time and call back a message from one of those very far-departed souls, and that is why it is so difficult to obtain really worthwhile statements from those who have passed over.

Supposing we try to look into the matter of the average medium. Let us say that the woman has some gifts in mediumistic work and she can obtain rapport with people who have passed over, but let us remember that these people who have just passed over are still in the lower astral, they are in what we might term purgatory, they are in the intermediate stage, they are in the waiting-room waiting for directions as to what to do and where to go.

Suppose you look upon these people as patients in a hospital, because it is a fact that many of these people do have to undergo certain spirit therapy to overcome the shocks of their Earth experience. So let us say that we are in contact with one of these people who is as a patient in a hospital; the patient is in bed and thus his only knowledge of his surroundings is that limited to the small area visible from his bed, he cannot see the whole work of the hospital, and if he can see other scenery, then possibly it is only that which he can see from the window.

Supposing you get a report from one of the Guides or some spirit whose special task is to assist those who are about to pass over or who have actually passed over. If they speak that is much the same as getting a report from some inexperienced little nurse or ward-maid at the hospital, and not even if you can go to a lecture of the hospital committee can you realise the full scope of what is going on, you can only make an evaluation by leaving the hospital and touring, as one might say, the town.

When one leaves this world which we call Earth one goes to the lower astral, which the Bible terms purgatory, and that may, as we have stated, be regarded as a hospital for sick souls where they are cured of many of the shocks which they endured or sustained upon this crude, crude Earth.

Unfortunately the lower astral would better be compared to a mental home, in which patients are received and their cases considered, just as a psychiatrist may sometimes discuss things with a patient so that he himself can state his faults and ailments, so in the lower astral can the newly arrived soul see what he did wrong on the Earth and see what he has to do about it to atone. Then for a short time the soul rests and recuperates, and perhaps walks in pleasant parkland, all the time receiving medication and treatment to assist him or her to carry on with the next phase of existence.

You will quite appreciate that people in the astral world are absolutely solid to each other. You upon this world can bump into a wall, but a 'ghost' would walk through that wall, yet in the astral and other planes the walls are quite solid to those occupants.

From all this you can see that if you make a commotion and go from medium to medium and seance to seance trying to get in touch with one who has passed over, then you are causing considerable harm to that person. Think of it in this way; a loved one has been taken ill and has been taken to a mental home or some other form of hospital, suppose you keep on calling and pestering that person, then you impede that person's progress. The doctors cannot get his full attention because you are meddling in his affairs, you are stopping treatment and causing considerable distress.

When you try to get in touch with an entity who has gone

116

beyond the lower astral, then you are interfering with a person who is trying to do a particular task. People who have left this world do not just sit about on clouds strumming harps and singing hymns, they have more work to do than they had upon this Earth! And if they are subject to continual distraction, then they cannot get on with their work.

Suppose you call a very busy executive, or a research scientist, or a surgeon who is doing a difficult operation, suppose you keep jerking at his coat-tails, then you distract him and he cannot give attention to what he is doing.

Mediums should never, never try to get in touch with the departed unless under very special conditions and with very special safeguards. Fortunately there is already a built-in safeguard; many worthy mediums, believing absolutely in their own sincerity, merely contact elementals who are having quite a bit of fun! That is all right if you know you are contacting elementals, but if you know that much why play with a gang of half-witted monkeys?

CHAPTER SEVEN

END OF A CHAPTER

THE dog whined disconsolately, ears drooping mournfully down towards the ground. Whined, and whined again, with his tail hanging listlessly between his legs. A sudden shiver of apprehension twitched his body and caused him gloomily to give utterance to a short, sharp bark. The leaves of the trees rustled as if in sympathy as the dog cowered at the door. For a moment he became alert, vibrant with suppressed energy as he listened to some distant sound, then slumped again in disappointed misery. On an impulse he leaped up and scrabbled at the door, tearing great gouges in the woodwork. Throwing his head back he gave voice to wolf-like shrieks and yells.

Soft, padding footsteps sounded round the corner of the house, and an old voice said, 'Bruno, BRUNO! Be quiet, will you? You cannot go in, the Master is very ill.' Then, as an after-thought, adding, 'Here—you come with me, I'll tie you up in the Potting Shed where you will be out of the way.' The old gardener fumbled in his pockets and produced a length of binder-twine. Passing one end through the dog's collar, he led him off to a distant clump of trees. Dispiritedly the dog followed, head down and whining.

'What's wrong, George?' asked a feminine voice from a kitchen window.

'Ah! The dog knows what's happening, that's what's wrong!' replied George, not pausing to say more. The woman turned to some unseen companion and muttered, 'Well, I never did, it just shows that dumb animals know what's going on, that's what I say?' Sniffing she turned her back to the window and went on with her task.

In the big old house all was quiet. No clatter of crockery, no sounds of housework. Silence. Almost the silence of the grave. Like an explosion, a hidden telephone burred and burred again before it was hastily seized. The tinny rattle of the distant caller's voice, and the reply in grave, masculine tones: 'No, sir, I am afraid not. There is no hope. The Doctor is with him now.' A pause while the tinny rattle sounded again, and the rejoiner, 'Yes, sir, I will give her your sympathy at the first available moment. Good-bye!'

From a distant door there came a gentle tinkle, short, and understanding. The 'shush-shush' of hurrying footsteps and the merest whisper of sound as a door was opened. 'Ah, yes, Father!' an elderly female voice said. 'They are expecting you, I will take you up.' Quietly the old housekeeper and the Priest made their way along the carpeted corridors and up the wide staircase. The gentlest of taps on a bedroom door, and a whispered word to the Priest. The door was opened silently, and a young woman appeared, came on the landing, and closed the door behind her.

'He is failing fast,' she said to the Priest, 'and he asked to speak to you alone. The Doctor will leave the room when you enter. Will you come with me?' She turned and led the way into the bedroom.

The room was large, very large, and was indeed a relic of a bygone era. Heavy curtains were drawn across high windows, shutting out both sound and light. Old paintings adorned the walls, portraits of almost forgotten ancestors. By the side of the vast old bed a green-shaded lamp threw an uncertain light around the gloomy room. A small, shrunken figure lay motionless on the wide double-bed. A man with skin like faded parchment, wizened and feeble. By his bedside sat a Doctor who rose to greet the Priest. 'He wanted very much to see you,' said the former. 'I will leave the room and wait outside. He is very weak, so call me if you need me.' Nodding, he walked round the bed and accompanied the young woman out of the room.

For a moment the Priest looked about him, then placed his small case on a bedside table so that he could take out certain ritual articles. 'Ah! I don't need THAT!' whispered a voice as dry as dust. 'Come and talk to me instead, Father!'

The Priest moved round the bed, bent, and clasped the hands of the old dying man. 'Is your Soul prepared, my son?' asked the Priest.

'That's what I want to ask you about,' wheezed the ancient voice. 'What will happen to me, what will I see on the Other Side? Is there a life after this?'

Quietly the Priest talked, telling only that which his religion permitted, or knew. The breath of the sufferer grew shallower and fainter. Quickly the Priest hurried to the door and beckoned to the Doctor. 'Shall I administer the Last Rites?' he muttered.

The Doctor moved to the bed and lifted a wasted arm. Feeling no pulse, he fitted his stethoscope to his ears and sounded the sick man's heart. Shaking his head sadly, he pulled the sheet over the dead man's face and muttered, 'I wonder, Father, I wonder, what IS the Other Side of Life? I wonder!'

For reasons of their own Western religions do not tell much about death, but, after all, death is a very serious matter for all of us just as is birth, and it seems that death should logically follow the chapter about mediums because if no one died, mediums could not try to get in touch with them. So we are going to discuss death because, no matter who we are, death is something that comes to all of us just as does birth. But, you know, death is actually birth! Let us see how that comes about.

A baby within its mother dies to that warm, comfortable life within, and reluctantly emerges into the cold, hard world without. Birth pangs are death pangs, death to the old, birth into a new state. A person dies upon Earth and the pains of death are the pains of birth into a different state of existence. Most times death—death itself—is a quite painless process. Actually, as death approaches, Nature, in the shape of various metabolic changes, introduces a form of anaesthesia into the body system, anaesthesia which culls the actual perceptions while allowing the body reflexes to make certain movements which people think of as death pains. People actually associate pain and death, or if you prefer, death and pain, because in the majority of cases people who are grievously ill die apparently in pain, but that pain, remember, is not the pain of death but the pain caused by the illness itself. Perhaps there is a cancer, something affecting body organs, grasping at nerve endings or eating them away. But let us remember that this pain is the pain of the illness, the pain of the complaint, not death itself.

Death, the actual state of transition from this world to the next, the actual state of leaving this physical body, is a painless process because of the anaesthetical properties which come to most bodies at the moment of death. Some of us know what it is to die and to remember everything, and to come

120

back still remembering. In the process of dying we have a body which is ailing, functions are failing. But remember this, the functions are failing, that means the ability to perceive or apperceive or to comprehend pain impulses is failing also. We know that people sometimes give an impression of pain at dying, but this again is an illusion.

The dying body is a body which has usually (except in the case of accident) reached the end of its endurance, it can go no more, the mechanism is failing, there is no longer the ability for metabolic processes to renew failing organisms. Eventually the heart stops, the breathing stops. Clinically a person is dead when no breath condenses on a mirror held before the lips; clinically and legally a person is dead when there is no longer a pulse or a heart-beat.

People do not die on the instant, however. After the heart has ceased to beat and after the lungs have ceased to pump, the brain is the next to die. The brain cannot live long without its precious supply of oxygen, but even the brain does not die instantly, it takes minutes. There have been absolutely authenticated cases where people have been beheaded, and the head, severed from the body, has been held up for public inspection. The lips have continued to move and a lip reader can distinguish the words being formed. Obviously only a lip reader can interpret what is being said because there can be no speech when the neck has been cut and the supply of air from the lungs terminated. It is the air supply going past the vocal chords which makes the sound.

After the brain has died, after the brain is no longer capable of functioning through this lack of oxygen, the rest of the body dies slowly. Various organs die throughout a day or so. At the end of three days the body is just a lump of decomposing protoplasm, but the body does not matter, it is the immortal soul that matters—the Overself. But let us go back to the instant of clinical death.

The body in this case is lying on a bed. The breathing has stopped. A clairvoyant who is present can see a cloud like a faint mist forming above the body. It streams from the body, usually from the navel, although various people have various outlets for the Silver Cord.

Gradually this cloud coalesces and becomes denser, its molecules are less dispersed. Gradually a shadowy shape forms above the body; as the process of death advances, the shape

121

becomes more and more that of the body. Eventually as more organs fail, the cloud gets thicker and larger, taking at last the exact shape of the body above which it floats.

The cord, which we call the Silver Cord, connects the physical body and the astral body, for the cloud is in fact the astral body. Gradually this cord thins until at the end it withers, fades away, and parts. Only then is the body really dead, only then has the real person flown off to another life, to another stage of evolution. Once that misty figure has gone, it does not matter at all what happens to the fleshy envelope, it can be cremated or buried, it does not matter which.

It is perhaps opportune to digress here for a moment to issue what may be construed as a warning because so many people make it difficult indeed for the newly 'dead' to continue to live! When a person has died that person should be left untouched for two or three days if possible. It is definitely harmful to take that dead body and prop it up in a casket in some Funeral Home and have a lot of well-meaning people go and mutter all sorts of wonderful tributes which most times they don't mean.

Until the Silver Cord be severed and the Golden Bowl be shattered, the astral form floating can pick up the thoughts of those who are making comments at its passing. Further, if a body be cremated in less than three days there is often intense pain caused to the astral figure, and the pain, curiously enough, is not the pain of hot fire but of intense cold. So if you value those who have gone on before, and if you will do as you would be done by, you will whenever possible ensure that a person who has died has three clear days in which to sever and disassociate completely from the physical body.

But we have got to the stage where the spirit or astral form has left the body, the spirit has gone on where it meets other spirits and, of course, to each other they are quite as solid as two people on the Earth. You can only see a so-called 'ghost' as a transparent or semi-transparent person because that ghost is at a higher vibration than a human in the flesh; but—and I am not making a joke of this—two ghosts are two solid people to each other just as are two ordinary humans in the flesh.

If one has a person of a different dimension, then they might possibly see humans in the flesh as ghosts, because think of this; a two-dimensional object casts a one-dimensional shadow, a three-dimensional object casts a two-dimensional shadow, but a four-dimensional object (the fourth dimension again!) casts a three-dimensional shadow, and how do you know that you, to a four-dimensional person, are not just a semi-transparent shadow?

The spirit, then, has left the body and gone on, and if it is an evolved spirit, that is if it is aware of life after death, then it can be assisted in going to what is known as the Hall of Memories where all the incidents of the past life are seen, where all mistakes are perceived and appreciated. This, of course, according to some religions is the Day of Judgement or the Judgement Hall, but according to OUR religion Man judges himself, and there is no sterner judge than Man judging himself.

Unfortunately it frequently happens that a person dies and he does not believe in an after-life. In that case he drifts about for some time as if in the dark, as if in some stupendous cloying black fog. He drifts about feeling more and more miserable until at last he realises that he is in some form of existence after all; then perhaps some early teaching will come to his aid, he may have gone to Sunday School, he may be a Christian, a Moslem, it does not matter what it is so long as he has some basic training, so long as he has some preconceived idea about things, he can be helped.

Suppose a person was brought up to some branch of the Christian faith, then he may have thought forms of Heaven and Angels and all that sort of thing, but of course if he was brought up in certain parts of the East he will think of a different type of Heaven where all the pleasures of the flesh which he couldn't satisfy while alive—or rather, couldn't satisfy while he was in a flesh body—are his for the asking.

So our man who just had a smattering of religion goes on for a time in an imaginary world peopled by thought forms which he himself has created, thought forms of angels or thought forms of beautiful maidens, depending on which part of the world he came from. It goes on for an indefinite time until at last he begins to perceive various fallacies, various errors in the surroundings. He might, for example, find that the angels' wings are moulting, or if an Easterner he may find that certain of the beautiful maidens are not so completely beautiful as he thought! The Christian may come to the conclusion that this is not much of a Heaven where people wear brass halos, because people couldn't be sitting on a cloud playing harps all the time dressed in their best nightshirts. So doubts creep in, doubt of the thought forms, doubt of the reality of that which is being seen. But let us take the other side.

The fellow wasn't a very good man, he thinks of Hell, he gets all sorts of pains and aches because he has an image of old Satan prodding him in various vital spots. He has thoughts of fire, brimstone, sulphur, and all those ingredients which would be of more use in a pharmaceutical laboratory. Again doubt creeps in, what is the purpose of all this pain, how can he be prodded so thoroughly when there is no blood, how can he have his bones broken every few minutes or so!

Gradually the doubts strengthen, gradually his spiritual mind becomes accessible to what we might term 'social workers' of the spirit world. At last when he is amenable to assistance they take him in hand, they clear away all the theatrical props which the man's imagination has built, they let him see the true reality, they let him see that the other side of death is a far, far better place than is this side (the Earth side).

Let us digress once more; this is becoming a habit, but—let us digress. Let us imagine a man in a radio studio facing a microphone. He does some particular sound—'Ah'. Well, that 'ah' leaves him, enters the microphone as a vibration, becomes translated into an electrical current, and travels along a very devious path. Eventually it goes through much apparatus and becomes a very much higher frequency version of 'ah'. In the same way, a body upon Earth is the low vibration of a voice. The Spirit, or Soul, or Overself or Atman, or whatever you want to call it, can be represented as being akin to the radio frequency of the 'ah'.

Do you follow what I am talking about? It is a rather difficult concept to put over without using Sanskrit terms or going into Buddhist philosophy, but we don't want to do anything like that yet. Let us deal with matter of fact things in matter of fact terms. Death is a very matter of fact affair, we all go through it time after time until at last we are free of the pains and tribulations of being born and dying to Earth. But remember, even when we advance to higher planes and to different forms of existence we still have 'birth' and 'dying' with which to contend, but the higher we go the more painless and the more pleasurable are these two stages in our existence.

Well, let us get back to this poor fellow who we left in the spirit world, he is probably tired of waiting for us, but the spirit world, remember, or rather the astral stage, is an intermediate stage. Some religions relate it to Paradise; there is the Earth plane, Paradise, and eventually Heaven—provided the victim doesn't get sent to Hell first.

Our man is in the spirit world to see what sort of a mess he has made of his life. Did he leave undone those things which he should have done, did he do those things which he should not have done? If he is a normal human the answer is 'yes' on both counts. So he goes into the Hall of Memories to see what he did in past lives, how did he fail to learn things which he should have learned? And then when he sees his faults and also sees his successes he discusses with special guides—who are not Red Indians, by the way, or Ancient Chinese with long beards, but very special guides of his own type of person, own basic beliefs, etc., people who know the problems with which he is confronted, they know what he has been through, they know how they acted in similar circumstances. They are a bit more evolved, a bit more trained, they can see what this man has to learn in much the same way as a Careers Guidance Counsellor can tell a person how to get a certain qualification so that he can later try for a specific appointment.

After this meeting, conditions and circumstances are picked so that the person can come back to Earth into the body of a small baby, perhaps as a male, perhaps as a female. It might disconcert some of you, but people come to this Earth as male and then as female, it all depends on which is most applicable to the type of lesson that has to be learned. It doesn't mean that because you are a very male male now, or an extremely feminine female, you will be the same in the next life or the life after, you might want a change of attitude, you might want to see what the other person has had to put up with.

After a person has been born time after time they come to a state when they have to be born no more to this Earth plane, but the person living the last life on Earth almost without exception has a very hard time, a time composed of misery, suffering, poverty, misunderstanding. Anyway, misery, misunderstanding, and all kinds of suffering are, as one might say, the leavening which eventually makes a person rise up to be a good spirit instead of an indifferent human.

A person living his last life upon the Earth is often regarded (on the Earth) as one of the unluckiest people ever, instead of

125

the luckiest in that they are living their last life here. All their hardships are because they are clearing up, getting ready to move out, paying debts, etc. They cannot learn through the flesh in the next life, so they have a good dose in this life. So they die, and most times, if they ever think about it, they are jolly glad.

Then back in the spirit world they get a good rest, for certainly they have earned it, they get a rest where they may be asleep for quite a few years, quite a few years by Earth time, that is. Then they get rehabilitated, built up, and all that, reconditioned one might say. After this they start all over again on the upward path, upward, ever upward. So the Great Prophet in one life who has learned all there is to know, or thinks he has, goes on to another stage of evolution where there are all sorts of different abilities, all sorts of varying talents which he has to master. It is like a boy who gets hold of a bicycle—the boy learns to ride the wretched thing, then when he can more or less stay on without falling off he tries a motor-cycle; this is a little more complicated because he has other controls to manipulate. From the motor-cycle to a car, from the car to an aeroplane, from an ordinary aeroplane to an even more difficult helicopter. All the time one is learning more and more difficult things.

When we go to sleep, all of us—well, let us be accurate and say about 90 per cent of us—do astral travelling, we go into the spirit world, into the astral world. As Christ said, 'In my Father's House there are many Mansions, I go to prepare a Way for you.' In the spirit world there are many planes of existence, many 'Mansions'. The one closest to the Earth plane is the astral plane, beyond that is what one might term the spirit world. People who have died to Earth go to the spirit world, but if they want to they can come down to the astral world to see those who are over at the end of the Earth day. This is something like visiting people in a prison, but it may be a comforting thought for you because when you are in the spirit world you may at times want to meet those with whom you were associated upon the Earth.

Going to a higher plane it will comfort you even more to realise that when you are in the spirit world (not the astral) you can only meet those who are compatible with you, you cannot meet those whom you hate nor those who hate you. You have people around you who are attracted to you, you can only

126

meet those for whom you feel compatibility, kindness, consideration, or love.

In the astral plane you often meet people whom you do not particularly like; you might dislike a person intensely while on Earth and then when you both leave your bodies at night you go to the astral plane and you might meet to discuss in the astral language, or in Spanish, English, German, or some other language, and you might decide that you will try to patch up the differences between you, you might feel that friction has gone on long enough. So you have a discussion, you and your adversary, both in the astral plane, you decide what you can do to patch up your differences.

Also in the astral you often discuss what you are going to do in the physical world of the Earth. In the astral you might meet Aunt Fanny who lives in Adelaide, or some other place like that, and she will say, 'Oh, Maria Matilda (or some other name), I wrote you a letter such-and-such a time ago, you should be receiving it tomorrow when you get back to your Earth body.' Then when you wake up in the morning you have a vague idea about Aunt Fanny, or whoever it is, and you half-heartedly keep an eye open for the mailman to come trudging to your letter-box, and then you are not too surprised that you have a letter from Aunt Fanny in Adelaide, or whoever it was that you were thinking about.

Again, when one is in the astral world one can often meet people from the spirit world who have access to some knowledge. The person will say, 'Now that you have done all you can down there on Earth, you are going to have an argument with a bus next week, or the week after, and the bus is going to win, so you'd better get your affairs in order, you have nearly finished your task for this life.' The man feels very happy while he is in the astral to think that his life on Earth is nearly finished, but when he gets back to Earth he feels a bit gloomy and apprehensive, and tells his wife, if he has one, that he has had such a dreadful nightmare in which he could see that she would soon be a widow. She, of course, conceals her pleasure at this and when he goes to the office or to the store, she hurries to look in the strongbox to see that that fat insurance policy is perfectly all right, with all the premiums paid up.

Another way that the better-evolved person can know about the future is this; he is able to travel beyond the astral plane and up into what, for want of a better term, we might call the

127

primary spirit world. There he can consult the Akashic Record and the Record of Probabilities because it is not at all difficult to see what the probabilities of a person or of a nation are. One cannot always say precisely what is going to happen to an individual to the actual minute or even to the hour, but one can most certainly say what is going to happen to a country or to the world.

Well, we certainly have dealt with death in this particular chapter, and so you should regard this as a very pleasant affair, just as do children when leaving day comes for them to finish with their school life. Let us consider for a moment how to prepare for death, because just as one prepares for a wedding, one can have a much better time if one knows what is to be expected.

In Tibet several books are devoted to such things; *The Tibetan Book of the Dead* is one of the greatest classics in the Eastern part of the world, it tells in minute detail everything that can happen to a soul leaving the body and going out on the journey to the next life. In Tibet a lama specially clairvoyant and specially trained will sit by the side of a dying person and by telepathy will keep in touch with him so that even after the astral has left the physical, a conversation can be carried on. Let me state here most emphatically that no matter what the sceptical Western people say, Eastern people KNOW that it is possible to get messages from the so-called 'dead'. Everything has been told in detail, precisely what happens, precisely what it feels like.

The Egyptians also had a Book of the Dead, but in those days the priests wanted to keep a lot of power for themselves, and so they made a lot of symbolic things about the Gods Horus and Osiris, and about weighing the soul against a feather. That is a very pretty story, but it does not correspond to actual facts except that the Egyptians who were taught such things went into death with minds stuffed full of preconceived ideas so actually saw the God Osiris, actually saw the Judgement Chamber, actually in the mind lived through all those curious things where the soul was seen to flutter like a bird and where the Cat God Bubastes and others were perceived. But remember, this is just a pretty picture which has to be shattered before anyone can go on to the Reality, it is like trying to live in a Walt Disney world instead of the true world.

Many people have preconceived ideas which perhaps have

128

been fostered by some particular belief or by the lack of any belief at all, they do not know what to expect when they are dying and so they are caught up in remarkable fantasies of their own creation, or even worse caught in some blackness, some blankness because of a lack of understanding.

I will ask you to consider this with an open mind, it does not matter if you believe or disbelieve, just keep an open mind and think of what I am going to say to you now, it will help you later.

Give an hour or two to meditation (see the chapter on Meditation later) upon the subject of death, be prepared to accept the idea that when your time comes to leave this Earth you are going to force yourself painlessly out of this awful clay body which is cooling and feeling uncomfortable, and then you are going to gather in a cloud above the recumbent body. Then in that cloud you will send out a mental call for help from loved ones who have preceded you into the next life. You may not know much about telepathy, but that does not matter, when you leave this life for the Greater Life you will have telepathic abilities automatically, but to help you now let me say this; try to remember when you are dying that you visualise the person whom you love most ON THE OTHER SIDE. Try to actually visualise that person, try to send out a thought that you want that person to come and meet you and help you. In much the same way, if you are going on a journey you sometimes send a telegram saying, 'Meet such-and-such a train.' Then let yourself rest in peace, you will find a sensation of lightness, a sensation that you have escaped from a tight compressing chamber.

Keep an open mind, do not scoff, do not believe blindly but reason it out, practise what you are going to do when you are dying, practise forcing yourself out of the dying body and into life. Think how similar it is to being born, think how you are going to call on the person whom you love most for help, then when the time comes you will find that your passing will be painless and anything that the flesh body is experiencing will not disturb you in the slightest.

You will find that as you float there above the body the Cord anchoring you to it will thin and thin, and dissipate like smoke in a breeze. You will drift off upwards into the arms of your loved ones who are there to meet you. They cannot do much for you until the Cord is broken, in much the same way that you cannot shake hands with your friends while the train is still moving into the station.

One of the things which puzzles many people about death is this: Why is the fear of death universal when beyond death lies only peace and greater evolution? The answer is very easy; if people on Earth knew how pleasant it was upon leaving this world, people would not stay here, there would be suicides and that would be a very bad thing indeed because suicide is wrong. So people come down to this Earth with a built-in fear of death. That is a provision of Nature to prevent people from committing suicide or trying to gratify their own 'death wish'.

As death actually approaches, however, all fear of that stage diminishes. So—if you are afraid to die while you are quite well that is a normal state of affairs because we have to be kept here just as children have to be kept in school, and children who evade going to school are not popular with the truant officer!

When your time of dying comes, then, keep an open mind, keep before your consciousness the thought that there are those very willing to help you, remember there is no such thing as Hell, there is no such thing as eternal damnation, there is no such thing as a vengeful God who desires only your destruction. We do not believe that one should 'fear God', we believe instead that if God is good, God should be loved, not feared. And—death also is good, it should be loved and welcomed with open arms when that time comes, but until that time comes live according to the rule, 'Do as you would be done by.'

If you are willing to devote a bit of time and patience and a whole lot of faith, then most certainly you should be able to investigate the matter of death as a seriously interested on-looker, but you will find that such investigation will entail some sacrifices. For example, you cannot go to parties, you cannot go to the pictures, you cannot call in and get a 'quick one'. Instead, you have to be as a hermit.

I am a hermit, and I prefer to be a hermit because I have all those powers about which I write, and many of which can be yours if you try hard enough and with enough faith. I can do astral travelling, I can see the Akashic Record, and later in this particular chapter I am going to deal with prophecy.

A great amount can be done by meditation, and by concentration. For this, obviously, one has to be a hermit. Hermits, monks, lamas, call them what you will, are solitary people withdrawn from the ordinary circle of social life, withdrawn at their own choice so that they may concentrate, meditate, and go forth in astral travel. This astral travel business is very, very real, it is a fact, but it is as simple as breathing. The trouble is that you cannot take any luggage with you, it is useless to travel across the ocean to another country and think that you will stay for the week-end with friends. The difficulty is that your friends, unless they are of the same stage, may not be able to see you, the trouble is that you can neither take anything with you nor can you bring anything back that is material or solid.

One very interesting thing is in the astral one can see the Akashic Record provided one is of the fortunate few who have what I might call special permission. Let me say here and now that many of those people who pretend to go into the astral world and consult your Akashic Record are fakes and, in fact, swindlers. They take your money, usually round about fifty dollars, but they are quite unable to do what they claim to do. So if anyone tells you that he is going to go into the astral world and bring back your Akashic Record for fifty dollars— hang on to your fifty dollars!

It is a fortunate provision that not everyone can see the Akashic Record because think what a terrible weapon it would be in the hands of blackmailers or criminals. Indiscriminate use of the Akashic Record would cause untold harm. Thus, it is that only those who are of pure intention can gain access to the Akashic Record.

What is this Akashic Record? It is like a cinematograph film. For example, you have some great epic of the silver screen and if you know how, you can get to any particular part of the film, and you can see any particular part at will. In much the same way, everything that has happened in the past is on record. Look at it in this way—let us assume something that is only possible in the astral, assume that in the physical we could travel instantaneously to a far, far distant planet thousands of light years away. Then supposing we had an instrument which would enable you to see what was happening on Earth—you would not, of course, see Earth as it is now but you would see Earth as it was years ago, because light has a speed, everything you see is after the thing happened. The speed of light is very, very fast, relatively speaking.

But let us consider sound instead. You see that man down there half a mile away? He has an axe in his hand, he is chopping wood with great energy. You see the axe hit the wood and then, an appreciable time after, you hear the sound. Again, a supersonic jet plane screams across the sky, you look up to where the sound appears to be coming from but by that time the plane is about five miles or so ahead of the sound that you are hearing. The speed of sound is slow compared to the speed of light, and light, remember, is near enough sight.

Supposing you have the ability to go instantly out into space and stop at any particular instant and see clearly the light picture which is arriving from Earth, go out a few years, a few light years that is, you know, then you will see—what shall we say?—we might see Napoleon marching away to Moscow, or we might see General Eisenhower practising his golf. But go a bit farther and you would see much of the country of the United States covered with bushes, with wigwams and with Indians, and perhaps here and there a few of the famed covered wagons.

Go farther back, go back 1,000 years or so, 2,000 years, go back into the pages of history. You would find that history is very different from that which is written in the history books. History is written to fit the politics of the time, to fit the mood of the country and the beliefs of the country. A journey into the Akashic would show you the truth. As an illustration let us quote Francis Drake, the great hero of England. What is it to be? Sir Francis Drake the great hero of England, or, as the Spanish people view him, Francis Drake the pirate, the buccaneer, the man who tried to ruin the Spanish trade?

Look at the Spanish Inquisition. What was the truth of it? Were the inquisitors saints or was it similar to Belsen and other concentration camps in Germany? The Akashic Record will tell you.

But the Akashic Record, you know, is not just what happened in the past, you can see also the great probabilities for the future. Here in this particular time we are like a man alone on a winding road, a road with many obstacles beyond which he cannot see, but put that man up in a helicopter and he can see farther, he can see past the obstacles, he can see the road ahead. So it is with the Akashic Record, you can see the probabilities which lie ahead.

132

Now this does not mean that all the future is predestined. The main events are, yes. As an example let me say you know that there will be a tomorrow and a day after tomorrow and a week after that, you can safely forecast that, but you cannot safely forecast the minor minute details. You can say that a bus will go from here to some distant point, the timetable tells you that it will leave at such-and-such a time and that it will arrive at intermediate stations at such-and-such a time, and eventually arrive at the destination at the prearranged time. You have no fear that the bus or train will fail to arrive, in other words you are forecasting what will happen. You are forecasting the future of that bus.

There is a very complicated theory which is actually a very true theory about parallel universes, and to the effect that everything has already happened and that we are living in a different time continuum. However, we do not propose to go into that here, instead let it be stated that the Seers of old could see into the future, the Seers of the present can do so also. Now I am going to give you an illustration of this. This is something which happened to me, which happened under full control. I went into a trance and this is what I saw:

I saw first a probability that a war would be starting. Now, looking back, I can say that—yes, that was so, that was the war which started in Vietnam after the French withdrew, after the Foreign Legion was disbanded. But that was proved to be correct.

Other things are: In the future Italy will be conquered by Communism. For the time being the Christian religion will be lost and the Vatican will be closed, cardinals and bishops will be killed, Communism will seep throughout Europe. It will not be the Communism which we know at the present time, it will be modified somewhat. The original Communism of Russia was a much rougher, tougher affair than it is now, more like the Chinese Communism. England and the United States will eventually amalgamate for protection, and England will come under the direction of the United States and will, in fact, have an American as its Governor, which is quite an amusing thought when one thinks that people went from England to found America, and now the Americans are going to go back and rediscover England.

Eventually the surface of the Earth will crack. If you have read the reports of the International Geophysical Year you will know that there are great areas of stress beneath the ocean, areas where alterations are taking place. Already the sea-beds are rising. Lost continents which are now the sea-bed will rise and form new lands, present lands will sink and the world will for a time be in panic and turmoil. New York will be levelled to the ground and eventually shall sink beneath the waters of the Atlantic. Los Angeles and San Francisco, Seattle and Vancouver on the Pacific coast, will be levelled to the ground and then shall sink beneath the rising Pacific. Most of the coast-line will be inundated, the whole land will change. From over Alaska will come rockets with bombs from Communist Russia, great devastation will be caused in the United States and Canada. Of course, through retaliatory methods of these countries, great devastation will also be caused in Russia, but on the North American continent a few survivors will cluster on top of the Rocky Mountains, enough to repopulate the continent later.

In Canada the Great Lakes which are now fresh-water lakes shall reverse the direction of their flow through the tipping of the Earth's axis, so that the sea shall flow from Quebec to Montreal, from Montreal to Buffalo, Buffalo to Detroit, and the water shall pile up at Chicago and flood the city and flood the land, and cut for itself a salt waterway into the Mississippi. The rushing waters, made into a raging torrent by the tipping of the world's axis, will soon erode away a lot of the land so that there a new island is formed. All that which is divided by the water and facing the sea shall be a new land.

In Europe the bed of the Mediterranean shall rise and become high land and there shall be opened great tombs, part of sunken Egpyt and part of the land sunk years before.

The whole of the South American continent shall be disturbed by earthquakes. The Falkland Islands shall be islands no longer, but shall unite as high land with the lower third of Argentina. At about the lower third of Argentina a great rift shall appear so that there is access from the Pacific to the Atlantic through a gap which shall be no wider than the gap between the Mediterranean and Gibraltar. Under the change of weight distribution the Earth shall tilt even more and the seasons will change, the Poles will melt and much land will become available in these areas, together with wondrous ores and many new resources.

134

Japan and Korea and part of the Chinese coast will sink beneath the waters, but other lands shall emerge from the seas. The Russians will have moved great satellites into space. Soon the Chinese will get into space also, for they will have seized scientists from the United States who fled from the floods and destruction. The year 2000 will see great events in space, not always for peace, for there shall be great rivalry between the branches of Communism, the Russians and the Chinese. In the year 2004 there will be a tremendous war between China and Russia in space. On Earth, people will huddle in deep shelters and many shall be saved. More lands shall sink and more shall rise.

One part of this prophecy gave me so much cause for thought I wondered if I should be discreetly silent and not mention it, but what does it matter, let us tell the truth, let us, as we have gone so far, go a little farther.

In the year 2008 or so the Russians and the Chinese will settle their differences under the stimulus of a much greater thing. From far out in space, from beyond this whole system, will come people, humans, who will come here and want to settle on this Earth. The humans already here will be frightfully cross about it all, and they will look upon their unwanted guests with a jaundiced eye. For a time there will be a considerable commotion, however, eventually common sense and reason will prevail.

The people from outer space will demonstrate peaceful intentions, and that is a thing sadly lacking on this Earth. In time the people from outer space shall settle down with the people who are native to this Earth, they will intermarry, all races will intermarry so that at last there shall be only one race and it shall be known as the Race of Tan because the mixture of all colours, white, black, yellow, and brown, will result in a very pleasant tan shade.

At this stage in the evolution of the Earth it shall be the Golden Age, the age of peace, the age of tranquillity and of high occult knowledge. It shall be an age when Man, whether terrestrial Man or extra-terrestrial Man, shall get along harmoniously.

The future beyond that? Yes, that is clear also, but let us be content with this first episode because it is, in fact, a true episode.

Do you laugh, are you cynical, sceptical? Well you are en-

titled to your opinion as I am entitled to my knowledge. If you had my knowledge you would not be listening to me now, and you would not be laughing.

A very short time ago it was stated that Man would never send a message across the Atlantic by radio. Then it was said that Man would never fly the Atlantic in an aeroplane. It was stated that no one could possibly go faster than the speed of sound because people would die, it was also reported that Man would not be able to get into space because the heat generated by the speed would burn him up. Man has gone into space, and Woman also. Things which are utterly impossible today are commonplace tomorrow. Now we bounce television programmes off an artificial satellite, now we bounce radio messages off the Moon, Mars, Venus. How can you say that my prophecy is not true?

It is a sad thing that people condemn that which they do not understand. It is a sad thing that if people cannot do this or that or something else, then they are inclined to say, 'Oh, but that is impossible, quite impossible, such things are beyond human knowledge.' This, of course, is nonsense, because when one can see the Akashic Record of everything that has happened one can also see the Record of Probabilities.

And if you wonder what the Record of Probabilities is let me give you a simple illustration. Probabilities are those things which you expect to happen, you expect that tomorrow, the day after, and for years after, ships will steam upon the seas, planes will fly across the sky, and cars will go spewing noxious fumes throughout the countryside. You really expect that will happen because it is so probable. The future of a race or country can be forecast with the highest degree of accuracy, and the Record of Probabilities indicates what all that will be. Here you have had an insight into what will happen, but there are other things, little incidents which point the way. Do you want some more?

All right—in years to come England will be a state of the United States in much the same way as Hawaii and Alaska are states of the United States. Eventually England will be controlled by and from the United States, and eventually England will subscribe to the Federal Laws of the United States.

Canada will be one of the leading countries of the world in centuries to come, Canada and Brazil. Brazil at present is in a decline, but Brazil shall rise and shall be perhaps the second greatest country of the world, it shall in fact become 'High' Brazil once again.

France and Russia will unite in years to come to really squash Germany. France and Russia both feel menaced by Germany, and they will unite forces to end that threat, and the German race will be scattered among other nations in the same manner as Jews are now scattered among other nations.

The United States and Russia will combine to defeat China, the new China which poses a threat to civilisation everywhere, and so the Bear and the Eagle shall unite to defeat the Dragon, and not until the Dragon is defeated shall there be any enduring peace.

Those of you who are astrologically inclined will remember that on February 5th, 1962, 16 degrees covered the Sun, the Moon, Mercury, Venus, Mars, Jupiter, and Saturn during an eclipse at that time. The next time that will happen will be on May 5th of the year 2000, and shortly before that time Halley's comet will return in April 1986. All these configurations will lead to momentous occurrences throughout the world. It will be the opening of a New Age, the time when hope flourishes again like the gentle spring flowers which revive and bloom anew when the winter snows give way to sunshine, and as the spring flowers are renewed by the seasons, and the renaissance which comes about every year, so shall Man, Man's hopes and spiritual aspirations become renewed after the year 2000.

It might be as well here to say something about the changing climate of this world, because almost everyone in the world must have noticed great changes. The climate also is a worthy subject of prediction.

In the years to come there will be many earthquakes, land will rise and land will fall, and much land will become water. Out in the Pacific there is a great fault extending thousands of miles. It is a crack in the Earth's surface, and if many more nations start letting off many more atom bombs or worse, the crack will open a little and shift a lot, and then there will be a whole series of earthquakes and floods.

For hundreds of years it has been possible to more or less predict the weather. One could consult charts kept at meteorological offices and these charts would indicate that the temperature of, say, Canada normally would fall between such-and-such limits at such-and-such a time, while, for example, in Buenos Aires there were different limits of rise and fall. It was possible to predict the weather in Moscow, or Timbuctoo, or anywhere, by consulting records which indicated what the average temperature should be at other equivalent times for many, many years past. We have known what would happen during each season, we have known if the summer was going to be hotter than winter and what the limits of cold were going to be, and what the limits of heat were going to be, but all that is changing, and changing rapidly, through a whole conglomeration of causes, most of them man-made.

Have you noticed that quite recently there have been increasing reports of freak weather? In the United States there have been absolutely abnormally cold winters. In Georgia the weather has been quite a lot below zero. Arizona, that too, has had a great deal of cold, at times 40 degrees below.

I have had letters from friends in Canada and the United States and I get reports of freak weather, stunning cold. Then a week later, almost a heatwave. I had a report the other day from Niagara Falls, Canada; the weather was extremely hot, sweltering hot, and then it became frightfully cold. In Detroit, U.S.A., the weather has been stunningly cold, then suddenly it turned hot.

In the North and East United States there has been dryness, in fact April of this year was the driest ever recorded on the United States weather stations. There was no water for the plants, no irrigation system worked. Plants withered in the parched ground.

I don't know how many of you have been to the United States, but in Montana, not so far from the Canadian border, there is a big National Park, and in that Park there is a glacier, in fact there are several, but some have completely melted and others are greatly diminished.

Certain areas of the United States and Canada depend quite a lot on ski programmes, programmes calling for snow and ice. Well, there has been no snow or ice and so these people depending on such climatic conditions have been ruined.

In the mid-West there have been tornados, tremendous tornados. The number and speed and ferocity of tornados has been increasing. Quite recently there have been more than 800 tornados a year in mid-United States.

But let us leave the United States. There are other parts of the world. I get mail from all over the world, and it does not need mail but newspapers, to bring in information about the weather. In England there has been absolutely freak weather, the coldest on record, and in England they have had the worst blizzard ever, traffic was at a standstill, people were short of food and were freezing, cattle died through exposure and through starvation.

In the Mediterranean weather has been completely freak, abnormally cold for instance, and about a metre in depth of snow in Sicily which advertises as Sunny Sicily. Well, they might have had sunshine but they have certainly had searing cold as well. It is all freak weather, the climate of the world is changing. In Rome there was ice, on the River Tiber there was ice, ice for the first time in 500 years. One associates Rome, Italy, with warmth, with a kind benevolent climate, not with ice on the River Tiber on which people could skate.

And another part of the world—Japan. They have had the roughest winter in living history. Storms, crop failures, they have had everything bad.

In Russia, on the other hand, the climate seems to have been getting milder. Siberia is less frigid, and of course with all these changes in climatic conditions more changes are caused, for if we heat an area of land the air above it rises and forms cumulus clouds. It may be that so many atom bombs have obscured the direct radiation of the Sun to the Earth and back into space, that that has altered zones of temperature throughout the world. Thus it is, as has been predicted, that in the not too distant future things are going to change on this Earth.

Have you ever thought of this? If the ice at the North Pole and South Pole melted the water level all around the world would rise by at least 600 feet? Think, even if some of the ice on the coast of Russia were to melt, the resulting flood could inundate New York or Montevideo; in fact, it would not take many feet of water to completely flood Uruguay. But in case Uruguayans want to rush out and get water-wings and bathing suits, let me say this; according to predictions that part of the world will rise so that instead of being flooded it will be quite a long way above water level. New York will sink beneath the waves, so it is predicted, and down near the end of Argentina a rift will be caused dividing the tail of Argentina from the body, so there will be in effect an island there, and a quicker passage through to the Pacific Ocean. That in itself will cause a bit of commotion, because the Pacific is saltier than is the

Atlantic, and so we have more or less of a paradox; the Pacific water will be warmer but heavier, and so it will sink in the colder waters of the Atlantic because the Atlantic is not so salty, and is, therefore, lighter.

The Russians are busy altering the weather to their own advantage by tampering with the Gulf Stream, which causes warm water which normally should go to Europe to flow along the sides of Siberia, so that Siberia is becoming thawed out and will become the far land of Russia. But in the swing of the balance England could have another Ice Age, and ice could sweep across quite a lot of Europe.

Normally the Earth is surrounded by layers of air, some of them travelling as air currents in the same way as there are water currents. Normally the amount of cosmic rays entering and striking the Earth is fairly constant, but now because of the meddling with the upper atmosphere by rockets traversing and bombs going off, the outer atmosphere's jet streams have been disturbed and diverted. Thus there are temperature inversions so that hot air perhaps cannot rise and whole lands become parched through lack of rain and through excess of heat. Temperature zones throughout the world are changing, mainly for the worse, and unless mankind rises up to control those who desire war, then mankind is going to have a pretty sorry time before they have a better time. However, we are now in the Age of Kali, the Age of pain, suffering, and despair. Soon will come the dawn when Man can again hope and know that he is progressing towards greater things, greater happiness, greater spirituality, and greater faith in his fellow men.

CHAPTER EIGHT

MEDITATION

THE great tree towered heavenwards with branches groping blindly towards the Giver of Light. Upon the ground its shadow stretched black and long, becoming longer and yet longer as the Sun sailed across the latening sky on its eternal journey. The tree basked and thrived beneath the life-giving rays. In its branches, concealed by a multitude of leaves, birds fluttered and called and occasionally flew swiftly to other trees in pursuit of their business of living. From some hidden recess within the tree's foliage came a sudden sharp squawk of an outraged bird in protest against an invading monkey. The squawks continued and rose in a crescendo as a whole troupe of monkeys swung from branch to branch. Suddenly, as though at the turning of a switch, expectant silence fell upon the people of the tree. HUMANS were approaching!

Along a faint path through the bushes a bent old man stumbled and made his way. Clutching a sturdy stave in a gnarled hand, he plodded grimly forward. Behind him two young men carried small bundles. The old man stopped and pointed to the tree. 'We shall stop THERE!' he said. 'We shall rest awhile and I shall meditate through the night.' Together they moved forward into the little clearing where the great tree's bulging roots made deep furrows and mounds. Together they walked around the mighty trunk, seeking the best position. Soon they found a spot where a large flat-topped boulder protruded from the ground on the sunward side of the bole. A monkey was sprawled upon its top, leisurely scratching. At sight of the approaching men it screeched in fright and leaped straight up to disappear amid the concealing branches.

The younger of the two Assistants carefully gathered some withy branches from a nearby bush. Binding them tightly with a length of pliant vine, he soon had a serviceable brush with which he attacked the top of the rock, sweeping it clean of debris. With loving care the other Assistant took a sharp-edged stone and went with it to a lawn-like stretch of brilliant green moss. Kneeling, he pressed deep with the sharp stone

142

and moved along until he had cut a rough outline of the
boulder's top in the moss. Gently he peeled the layer of moss
and rolled it back like a carpet. With the aid of the younger
man he carried it forward and spread it out upon the rock,
forming a thick cushion that aged bones might be protected
from the harsh stone. Tightening his tattered robe, the old
man clambered with surprising agility to the verdant surface.

The brilliant rays of the fast-setting Sun sent multitudinous
colours across the wooded countryside, here gilding a tree top,
there shining blood-red through the lower branches. Quickly
the elder of the two Assistants prepared their simple meal, a
little parched barley, a sprinkling of rice, a small ripe mango
fruit, and sparkling water from a nearby stream. Soon the
meagre repast was finished and the utensils cleaned and put
away in the small bundles.

'I will meditate,' said the old man, settling himself cross-
legged and drawing his robe about him. 'Do not disturb me, I
will say when I am ready.'

The two Assistants nodded in respectful acknowledgement.
Turning away, they retired some many feet from the rock,
rolled themselves more tightly in their robes and composed
themselves for sleep. Suddenly the Sun plunged below the rim
of the Earth and the soft, scented purple iridescence of an
Indian night reigned as the Lord of the Night awakened all the
small nocturnal creatures to set about their business. Somewhere a sleepy bird muttered a last 'churp-churp' to his mate
before settling down to dream, maybe, of fat worms and juicy
fruits.

Slowly the purple of the night turned to lustrous silver as
the Goddess of Lovers climbed into the sky and showered her
Light upon the sleeping world. The gentle breezes of the night
came to sweep away the odours of the day, to fondly ruffle the
small forest flowers now folded in sleep, and carry fresh scents
to those who dwelt by night. The hours crept slowly on. The
Moon lowered her light below the distant horizon, and light
fleecy clouds sailed serenely above the Earth. The old man sat
erect, unmoving, withdrawn, meditating. Little creatures came
forth from burrows and warrens to peer with round, unwinking
eyes, and seeing no danger to them, went on with their lawful
business.

The old man sat erect, unmoving, meditating, as the first
streaks of light flitted across the sky. Sat unmoving as the

streaks widened and turned into the grey gloom of early dawn. Somewhere a sleeping monkey was jostled and shrieked and gibbered in drowsy fury. Swiftly the light grew brighter and a tinge of warmth swept across the night-chilled land. From the trees came the calls and fluttering of newly awakened birds. With a scream of terror a small monkey—inexperienced yet— lost his grip and fell a dozen feet before fear-paralysed limbs could reach out, grasp a branch, and swing to safety. The old man sat on, unmoving, as his Assistants climbed to their feet, rubbing the sleep from their eyes.

Much later in the day, as the hot Sun poured down its waves of heat, the old Monk ended his long meditation and partook of a frugal breakfast. Turning to the elder of the Assistants, he said, 'It is time YOU learned the art of meditation, my son, for I have observed you well and your time of instruction has come.'

'But is it so difficult to meditate, Master? Cannot ANYONE do it?' asked the younger.

'No, my son,' replied the old man. 'Some people never meditate because they are not worthy, and some, who are worthy, do not meditate because they do not know how. Meditation is an art which must be imparted, it is an art which can lift one's ego to sublime heights.' He paused in thought for a moment, then said to the younger, 'Today you travel alone to seek out food. I must instruct your senior. In time, if you are worthy, your opportunity will come.'

. . . . .

So many people say that they are 'going to meditate', but of course most of these people have not the faintest idea of what real meditation means. They think that it is some mystical thing whereas, as in the case of most metaphysical matters, meditation is simple and is just a means to an end, a method whereby one can obtain certain results.

One of the great difficulties confronting the average student of metaphysical matters is that most of the original training and most of the original research was done in Tibet, and in India, where civilisations flourished centuries before there were any civilisations at all in the Western world.

Of course, there was also the great civilisation of Ancient China, but although China has been lauded as being of great religious stature, actually China was more interested in the arts of war. The civilisations of China gave us such dubious assets as explosives, high-flying kites which discharge showers of poisoned arrows, and, surprisingly enough, the Chinese of centuries ago were the first to employ rocket warfare. Their 'atom bombs' were great masses of flaming material carried on rocket-heads; these flaming masses were fired into the enemy positions where they set fire to men and material indiscriminately.

China also gave us arts and crafts, which of course is to be commended, but China mainly took the religions of India and altered them to suit Chinese ideas.

Japan can be disregarded because until a few years ago Japan was a secluded island country impervious to the influences of other countries, and as the real history of Japan tells us, they merely copied their religions and their culture from the Chinese. Where the Japanese found their cruelty as shown in the Second World War can only be a matter of conjecture, but assuredly they lead the world in crude and cruel practices, and it is somewhat of a surprise that these little people are now tolerated among other nations. No doubt this is called commerce instead of friendship.

One of the great difficulties—to get back to our original theme—is that in translating Sanskrit and other Eastern languages it is not always possible to convey the exact meaning in a Western language such as English. The Western languages deal more with concrete matters, whereas the languages of the Far, Far East deal with abstract concepts, and thus it is that so many things which depend upon the precise use of an idiom, and which are not paralleled in another language, lead translators astray, and cause grave misunderstandings. An illustration is in the case of Nirvana, a term which we really should understand in the Eastern meaning and which will, therefore, shortly be referred to before going on to meditation, what it is, and how to do it.

India had a great civilisation, a civilisation which was highly spiritual in nature. India, in fact, was the cradle of true religion in this particular cycle of evolution, and many nations copied and altered Indian religions.

In some stages of the culture of Ancient China, when spirituality and veneration of one's ancestors was of greater importance than Chairman Mao or war, religions flourished, but some of the Chinese and some of the Indians, too, took their religious beliefs too literally because religion should be a signpost, a guide, a manual of behaviour. The Indians and the Chinese forgot that, and it was often the case that a Chinese or an Indian would spend his life sitting beneath a tree in idle contemplation thinking, 'Oh, I will just take it easy during this lifetime, I can make up for it when I come to this Earth again.' That is not a figure of speech, that is not an exaggeration, it is a fact, and until a very short time ago it was perfectly possible for a Chinaman to incur a debt in this life on the understanding that he would pay it back with interest in the next life. Can you imagine a Western moneylender—I see now they call themselves high-class finance companies—advancing a sum of money today on the understanding that it would be paid back to him when he came in his next incarnation? Certainly it would lead to some amusing book-keeping!

To repeat—Eastern languages deal mainly with abstract and spiritual concepts, whereas Western languages deal with terms dealing with aviation, money (or the lack of it!), and other mundane subjects. You may be interested to know that a few years ago the Japanese had no ideographs, no written form of expression which would deal with technical terms in radio or engineering, and so to my own personal knowledge Japanese technicians could only discuss radio, engineering, and other scientific concepts by learning the appropriate terms in English. There is nothing particularly remarkable about that because we have somewhat the same state of affairs in Western countries where two doctors of different nationalities and not understanding a word of each other's language, could still discuss medical terms and treatments by using the common language of Latin.

Radio operators, including amateurs, can converse quite well by using abbreviations and highly stylised codes so that they can understand each other even though the language of each is unknown to the other. Possibly you have heard of 'Q.R.M.' meaning noise or static, or 'Q.R.T.' which asks a person to be silent.

Nirvana is a word or concept which is usually quite beyond Western comprehension. Probably Nirvana is the most misunderstood of Eastern terms. People in the West think that the good Easterner just wants to sit and smell the flowers—in this case the lotus—and make himself into nothingness. It is often thought that Nirvana is total extinction of life leading to a

146

state where nothing exists, where nothing is, where there is no memory, no action, nothing. Nirvana is too frequently regarded by the Westerners as an example of the perfect vacuum, and they shun Eastern religions which they think, in their ignorance, lead to a state of complete and utter nothingness.

This is absolutely incorrect, Nirvana does not mean a Heaven or the opposite, it does not mean a place where there is nothing whatever—not even a place! It is not possible to exist in a state of nothingness, and yet again, the average Westerner thinks that the Adept, or Master, or Guru, or Enlightened One, strives to attain to a state where he forgets everything which he has striven to learn and in which he no longer knows anything, no longer feels anything, no longer exists. This is ridiculous! This is fantastically absurd, and one would have thought that ordinary commonsense would have indicated that there is no possibility of existing where nothing can exist.

The Adepts, the Guru, the Master or Enlightened One, or whatever you like to call him, seeks Nirvana. Nirvana is not the negation of everything as is usually supposed, it is instead the elimination of those desires which are wrong, it is the elimination of scandal, the elimination of perjury, greed, lust, and other faults. The Enlightened Ones strive so that they are empty of evil emotion, and thus their soul can rise within them and leave the body at will.

Before people can do conscious astral travelling they have to purge their thoughts, they have to be sure that they do not want to travel just for idle curiosity or so that they can peer in on the private affairs of another person. It is absolutely essential that before a person can astral travel consciously and under full control, they must get rid of gross lusts and desires.

In the Far East many people can astral travel consciously, many people who are on the spiritual Path, that is. But in the East the facts of life are treated differently, and we may have cause to deal with that later. In the Western world it is rare indeed for a person to consciously astral travel while the sins of the flesh keep the souls enchained. One of the more usual methods of keeping the soul in bonds is the wrong sort of sex life. There should be no sex life whatever unless the man and woman are in love; if these people are in love, then a normal sex life increases the strength of the auric current of each,

147

bringing lustre and clarity to the colour of the aura as any clairvoyant can tell.

If a man and woman engage in a sexual life just for mere animal pleasure, then they darken the colours of the aura and they weaken the fluctuations of the current. Many of the Eastern schools of occult thought, warn and warn again that the wrong sort of sex should not be indulged in if one is trying to progress. Unfortunately Western translations, or mistranslations, state that the Easterner has no sex life at all in spiritual planes. This again is wrong. Sex is all right if the two people need it and if they are truly in love.

In the Indian temples and in the Tibetan temples, too, there are pictures which Western people in their blindness have thought to be erotic, obscene, or pornographic. It is not so, and it does not in any way upset the Easterner to gaze upon these pictures. They see the pictures for what they are, they see that this is a reminder of what can be. The sexual act is the generation of life, it is the generation of stronger auric currents, and the pictures which truly adorn the walls of temples in India and Tibet show the true sexual life, and also the wrong sexual life, so that the initiate may compare the two because, after all, how can you know what is wrong unless someone shows you, and how can you do a thing correctly unless someone tells you that also? The wrong form of sexual life leads to unpleasant manifestations, frigidity, nervous troubles, and causes a suppression of the better instincts of Man and of Woman, while the correct form of sexual life, for those who need it, leads to an increase in the spiritual abilities of both.

After a time as the initiate progresses and becomes the Enlightened One he can do without the fellowship of those around him, he can do without a sex life, and contrary to what certain people believe he does not lose anything thereby. Sex life on Earth is a very physical thing, but as one progresses higher and higher the experiences are even stronger, even better, and, you may be surprised to know, when one leaves this Earth for the next life it is utterly necessary, a 'must' in fact, that one has a knowledge of the opposite sex in order that one can obtain balance!

This is a good point to say that we should not be deluded by all those peculiar people who claim that they are great experts, great Masters, great know-all's in fact, because they have read a few books; books do not give experience, one can read a book

148

and be without knowledge after. It is fantastic for a man or a woman to proclaim from the housetops that he or she is a great Enlightened Adept because he or she has read a book by such-and-such a person, and that so often occurs. Quite recently I had a letter from an illiterate fellow in Australia who claimed to be a great Teacher and a great Master. He assured me he was an Avatar, he knew he was this because his wife had told him so and because he had read a book or two and talked a lot!

The real yardstick is, what experience has a person had? Would you, for example, trust your life to an airline pilot who had only read a book about flying? Would you sail from here to another continent on a ship commanded by a Captain and officers who had merely taken a correspondence course on ship management and navigation? Obviously not. Using the same reasoning you should not entrust your training to any person who has just read a few books or who has a correspondence course which they want to sell you for high payments for the rest of your life. Before you study anything you should be acquainted with the experience of the person whom you are going to trust to teach you.

Well, it is time we got back to meditation. So many people do not know what meditation is. What is it? Meditation is a special form of concentration or directed thinking which disciplines the mind, and which forms a special attitude of mind. Meditation is that form of directed thought which enables us to perceive through the subconscious and other systems that which would not be possible for us to perceive in any other way.

Meditation is of extreme importance as it awakens the mind to higher consciousness, and permits the mind to 'tap in' more freely to the subconscious, just as a person can have a large library and go to his books for special information. Unless that person knows where to look he can have his large library, but they will be just so much waste paper.

The discipline of meditation is essential if one is to make any real progress in spiritual attainment. Just as an army would be useless without discipline and without drill, so the human psyche becomes as a member of a rabble without the discipline and training of meditation correctly applied.

It is useless to try to practise meditation by reading a book which has been written by a person who cannot himself meditate. So many occult books are just indigestible conglomerations of misunderstood Eastern parables; books which are written by people who really do not know the first thing about meditation, for it is clear that unless one can meditate oneself one cannot tell other people how to meditate!

It should be remembered that in many countries of the world—non-Christian countries, that is—attendants at a temple would meditate before entering the temple, they would meditate so that their mind was clear and opened ready to receive, what one might term in Western parlance, Divine Revelation and Instruction. It is quite useless to pray, for example, if one is just giving a babble of instruction to one's God. It is useless to pray that one shall win the beauty contest, or that one shall win the Irish Sweepstake. The process of praying should always be commenced by a period of meditation which clears the mind of the garbage of thought, and makes one ready to receive information from higher planes. To repeat—too many people flap down on their knees and start ordering their God to 'deliver the goods', then they say that prayer never works. Well, let them try meditation first. Meditation actually has four different parts:

1. The first part is that meditational practice which assists in the development of the true personality of the meditator, and if one can meditate and develop one's personality then one obtains a happier and more successful life. One becomes happier in the personal aspects of life and one becomes more successful in association with one's fellows, that is, in work. Successful meditation here also increases the mental capacity.

2. The second stage of meditation is that which almost automatically follows from successful completion of the first stage. The second stage of meditation is that which brings the physical body in rapport with the Overself and brings the Overself in rapport with the Manu of the nation. Before one can meditate to this, and higher standards, it is essential that one has a pure and lust-free life.

3. The next stage of meditation is that which gives one all the benefits of stage 1 and stage 2, but which enables one in addition to have full occult understanding. That is, when one reaches the third stage of meditation one is able to comprehend and apperceive.

150

Apperceive, of course, is different from perceive. Apperceive is the mind's perception of itself (all that which enables the Overself to improve its own spiritual condition).

4. Lastly, there is the mystical meditation, so called because it is so far removed from earthly concepts that it is rather beyond the understanding of those who have not succeeded in reaching that stage. The fourth stage of meditation takes us by way of the Silver Cord up to our Overself, and then by way of the Golden Cord of our Overself into the presence of that Great Entity which, for want of a better term down here, we call 'God'. But the first two stages of meditation are the essential steps and you should concentrate on them first.

Before taking up meditation it is essential that there shall be a Discipline because if one is playing with meditation, one is playing with fire. You would not allow a child to play with a barrel of gunpowder and a box of matches, at least you would allow him to do it only once! In the same way, you must exercise great restraint in practising the higher stages of metaphysics.

If you get a little weed of a man who suddenly decides that he wants to gain the muscles of Mr. Atlas, he has to undergo certain exercises, the poor fellow cannot suddenly grab a barbell, etc., and put in twenty-four hours a day at exercises, he would have a breakdown. In the same way it is quite necessary that meditation be regarded as the exercises of the soul, and if you rush into the practice of meditation like an American tourist rushing through the Vatican just to say that he has been there, then you will find that your enthusiasm will wane. You must practise according to a prearranged plan with discipline and much prior preparation because our weedy little man—if he practises too much and lifts too much and exercises too much, he will find that he is so stiff in his muscles that he can hardly move. But you, remember, with meditation, you can become stiff in the mind and that is a horrible state of affairs.

So in spite of all this, you want to meditate? You want to really go in for this thing? Well, let's see how you like the next bit; to meditate you must have an absolutely quiet time in your day, and you should make that time in the early morning. This is one of the reasons why priests, etc., meditate before they eat. You should have no food before meditating, and you should not meditate in bed, if you try that you will fall asleep. So—make arrangements to awaken an hour earlier than usual, and when your alarm goes off and wakens you, get out of bed, wash and dress, because the process of washing and dressing will awaken you so much that you will not be tempted to crawl back into bed and sleep.

If you really want to do this thing seriously you will have one corner of a room as your own Inner Sanctuary. You will have a little shrine which will enable you to fix your attention on that which you are trying to do. So, for those who are truly serious, here is how to proceed:

Have a room, even a box-room will do, as a Sanctuary, and keep the door of that room locked when you are not in it. Have a little table in a corner covered with a white cloth. Upon the white cloth have an image of, for example, a Ho Tai the symbol of Good Living (no, you are not worshipping graven images! Ho Tai is merely a symbol). Have an incense burner and a stick of thick incense which you should light and then blow it out so that it just smoulders in pleasant smoke. It will help if you have previously timed the burning of the incense such as, for instance, to the half hour, so that when your incense goes out you cease your meditation.

The serious meditator will wear a special meditation robe because the whole idea of the meditation robe is that you are shielding yourself from outside influences. The meditation robe must be very full, with long, loose sleeves, and with a cowl to pull over the head. You can get these of thin black silk, or if you find that too expensive, thin black cotton. When the meditation robe is not in use it should be put into a black silk case where it cannot be touched by other clothing. You may think all this is rather theatrical, but it is not you know, it is the best way of getting the desired results, and if you want the desired results you have to work according to the rules. So— wear your meditation robe when you are going to meditate.

Now that you have your room, your meditation robe, your Ho Tai, and your incense, go to that room and sit down quietly. It does not matter how you sit, you do not have to sit cross-legged. Sit in any way which is comfortable to you and which prevents you from getting cramps or twinges because in the early stages you cannot meditate if you are in discomfort. When you have sat for a few moments in quiet CONTEM-PLATION, you should repeat the prayer:

Let me this day, living my life day by day in the manner prescribed, control and direct my imagination.

Let me this day, living my life day by day in the manner prescribed, control my desires and my thoughts that I be purified thereby.

Let me this day and all days, keep my imagination and my thoughts directed firmly upon the task which has to be accomplished that success may come thereby.

I will at all times live my life day by day, controlling imagination and thought.

You will have seen that the room is not light, of course, but very well shaded, fairly dark in fact so that everything appears grey rather than black. You will soon find the amount of darkness which suits you best.

If you take a glass of cold water and hold that glass between your two hands so that your palms and fingers are around the glass but not overlapping on to the top, you will find that you will be in a suitable position for another exercise. Now slide the fingers of one hand so that they fit in between the spaces of the fingers of the other hand, so that you have as much of your hands and fingers on the glass as you can manage.

Sit quietly and take a deep breath. Try those exercises which are mentioned in *Wisdom of the Ancients*, but take a deep breath and allow the air to be exhaled with a long, long, drawn-out sound. The sound is 'Rrrrrrr Aaaaaaa'. You must do it aloud, you do not have to shout it, you can do it softly although very clearly, and you must treat it seriously because it is a serious practice. Repeat this three times, then sit and watch for several minutes as the odonetic, or magnetised, water focuses the etheric of the body into a cloud around the glass of water. It will condense (the etheric) so that you should easily see the quite heavy haze which will remind you of blue cigarette smoke condensed into a cloud, or if you prefer, remind you of incense smoke condensed into a cloud.

When you have done this for a week or two, or perhaps a month or two, depending upon your seriousness, you will be able to see some of your life-force in the water, and when the life-force gets into the water it charges the water just the same as soda water sparkles, but the sparks and sparkles that you will see from your own life-force will be flashes of light, lines, and swirlings of various colours. Do not rush things because

154

you have plenty of time; after all, you do not grow an oak tree overnight, and the more serious you are the more success you will have and the success eventually will turn that glass of water into a miniature universe with sparkles of multi-hued fire darting and swirling within the confines of the glass.

You should arrange your meditation into a definite pattern, or timetable. It is a very good idea to have a rosary so that you can keep check on your stages of meditation. You can obtain a Buddhist rosary, or you can make your own rosary of different sizes of beads, but no matter what method you use you should keep to a very rigid timetable. You must meditate in the same room and at the same time and wearing the same meditation robe. Start by selecting one thought or one idea, and sitting quietly before your little altar. Try to eliminate all outside thoughts, centre your attention within yourself, and there meditate upon that idea which you have decided upon. As you concentrate you will find that a faint shaking starts within you; that is normal, that faint vibration shows that the meditation system is working. Suggestions:

1. Have as a first meditation the meditation of love. In this you think kind thoughts towards all creatures who live. If enough people think kind thoughts, then eventually some of it will rub off on other people, and if we could get enough people to think kind thoughts instead of vicious thoughts the world would be a very different place.

2. After the first meditation of love, you can concentrate on the second meditation which causes you to think of those in distress. As you think of those in distress you really 'live' their sorrows and their miseries, and out of your compassion you send thoughts—rays—of understanding and sympathy.

3. In the third meditation you think of the happiness of others, you rejoice that at last they have attained the prosperity and all that for which they long. You think of these things, and you project to the outside world thoughts of joy.

4. The fourth meditation is the meditation of evil. In this you allow your mind to meditate upon sin and illness. You think how narrow is the margin between sanity and insanity, health, and sickness. You think how brief is the pleasure of the moment, and how all-encompassing the evil of giving in to the pleasure of the moment. Then you think of the sorrow which can be caused by pandering to evil.

5. The fifth meditation is that in which we attain serenity and tranquillity. In the meditation of serenity you rise above the mundane plane, you rise above feelings of hate, you soar above even feelings of earthly love because earthly love is a very poor substitute for the real thing. In the meditation of serenity you are no longer bothered by oppression nor do you fear, nor do you want wealth for its own sake but only for the good which you can bring to others with it. In the meditation of serenity you can regard your own future with tranquillity knowing that you at all times are going to do your best and live your life according to your own stage of evolution. Those who have attained to such a state are well on the way of evolution, and those who are can place reliance upon their knowledge and upon their inner knowledge to free them from the wheel of birth and death.

You may wonder what comes after meditation. Well, trance comes after. We have to use the word 'trance' for want of a better term. Actually trance is a state of meditation in which the real 'you' goes out and leaves the body as one would part from and leave a car.

Now, as we all know frequently to our cost, if one has a parked car one sometimes gets that car stolen by car thieves. In the same way, if people meditate deeply enough to enter what we must term the trance state without clearing their mind of lusts, etc., then they invite 'stealing' by other entities. The trance state is a highly dangerous state unless one first practises under capable supervision.

There are various forms of elementals and discarnate entities who are always prowling about to see how much mischief they can do, and if they can do a lot of mischief by taking over a person's body, then they are very happy to have some fun just as teenagers will sometimes steal a car to go racing round the roads; no doubt the teenagers fully intend to return the car unharmed, but frequently the car is harmed. And so when a body is taken over frequently it is harmed.

Let me repeat that if your thoughts are pure, if your intentions are pure, and if you are without fear, then you cannot be invaded, obsessed, or taken over, there is nothing to fear except fear itself. Let me repeat that; if you be not afraid you radiate an aura which protects your body much the same as a burglar alarm can protect a house, and if your thoughts are pure and you have no lusts, then when the lust of taking over a body tingles your consciousness you immediately look down the Silver Cord and see what it is, just the same as a farmer keeps a watch on his orchard to protect his apples! You cannot be obsessed or taken over or invaded unless you are afraid. But if you are afraid of such things—well, for your own peace of mind and for your own peace of body do not play with the deep trance stage of meditation.

I am greatly opposed to hypnotism except with the very greatest of safeguards, for if you are put into a hypnotic trance by an inexperienced person he can have an awful lot of fears wondering if you will be all right, wondering if he can get you out of the trance, etc. The hypnotic trance is a passive trance, it is a trance which is caused by a series of powerful suggestions strengthened by a person's belief that he or she can be hypnotised. Actually, when a person is hypnotised conditions are much the same as when a person goes cross-eyed because the etheric double is thrown slightly out of synchronisation which means that the physical and the etheric bodies are no longer in complete coincidence with each other.

If you get a bad hypnotist he can do a tremendous amount of damage, he can harm you for years. After all, you would not go to a surgeon who had just learned his surgical technique by taking a correspondence course, you want a person who can operate surely and competently. So—for the sake of your health and your sanity, do not allow amateurs to meddle about with you. If you want for some reason, or you have for some reason, to be hypnotised, then get in touch with some medical association in your own area and they will be able to tell you of some ethical medical hypnotist who has been trained under carefully supervised conditions. You may think that I am over-stressing the dangers, but—oh! You should see some of the letters that I receive about harm which has been caused by inept, criminally careless dabblers in hypnotism. Remember that when you are hypnotised your soul is pushed out of coincidence with the centres of your consciousness.

In the case of mediums, they are often people who get into a dreamy state of trance, a dreamy state of hypnosis, for consciously or unconsciously they lightly hypnotise themselves so that they are hyper-suggestible, and in such a case they can be used as a telephone by people on the other side of life. But remember what we have said, what we have learned together

157

about discarnate entities. The really good people who have passed over are too busy to fool around giving messages at seances.

Under certain conditions, of course, one can have a very skilled and conscientious person who can go into this trance in the physical and still remain alert in the astral, and so can in effect supervise the type of person who is giving messages to the group of sitters below. This is a very useful tool when one is doing detailed research, but it is utterly essential to make sure that the seance be not interrupted by noise or by the unexpected entry of other people.

There is a very special form of occult trance, the Adept calls it 'temple sleep', and this is an absolutely different type of trance from any of those previously mentioned because the Initiate who has studied all this under temple conditions knows what he is doing, and he can throw himself deliberately into the trance state just the same as a person can 'throw himself' into a car and drive off, he is under his own control and cannot be obsessed by others. But, of course, this depends upon having years of practice, and until a person has had the necessary experience he should always be under the most careful supervision of a person who has had such experience.

The average person playing about with trance states has a very useful protective system; you try playing about with a trance, and if you are a normal decent person you will find that you fall asleep! That prevents you from being invaded by discarnate entities. But even here there are two grave danger spots, for example: You are awake, even though in a trance state, but then you fall asleep. Now at the instant when you are between awake/asleep you are vulnerable to obsession just the same as you are vulnerable to obsession when (under these conditions) you have gone to sleep and now awaken. Please note that this only refers to when people are playing about with hypnotism or trances, and there is no danger whatever in the awake/asleep and asleep/awake of ordinary day and night living.

It follows from all this that you would not be very wise to meddle with trance states unless you are carefully supervised, doesn't it?

In certain temples the person being trained is supervised by two senior lamas who are able to keep contact with whatever the acolyte is thinking, and by their gentle but firm guidance the acolyte is prevented from doing any harm to himself or having caused any harm to anyone else. When the acolyte can pass certain tests, then he is permitted to go into deep trances by himself and usually one of the first things he will do is to go into a very deep trance, what we term the 'trance of vision'. This is a deep trance indeed, and the Initiate will be completely immobile, he might appear to be utterly rigid, even with hard flesh. In this particular state he is still within his body, but is very much like a man on top of a high tower who has a high-powered telescope which enables him to see very clearly and greatly magnified. The man with the telescope can turn in any direction, and can see what is going on with startling clarity.

One does not get out of the body in the trance of vision, instead you have to wait and practise the trance of projection before you can get out, and in this case the body is limp and flaccid, and is in a cataleptic condition with all consciousness being withdrawn and the body remaining, as it were, under the supervision of the caretaker. Breathing goes on at a very much reduced rate, and the heart-beat is reduced and life just flows very leisurely indeed.

First of all, when you get in these trances you will wonder if what you are seeing is imagination, but with practice you will know that which is real and will easily detect that which is merely a thought projection from some other entity, whether incarnate or discarnate.

To give you an illustration; you are somewhere, anywhere you like, sitting at peace and doing deep trance meditation. If you let your consciousness wander willy-nilly without having much control of it you might find yourself near a person who has had too much to drink, and you may be horrified to see all manner of queer animals wriggling around him. Yes, those striped elephants really do exist in thought form! Worse than that, though, supposing you allow yourself to just wander and you find yourself near a very, very bad-tempered man with murder in his heart; if he is thinking of murder, then you, you poor sufferer, will see the actual scenes as if they were reality instead of just thought, and you may come back to your body with such a jerk that you will get a headache for the next twenty-four hours thinking that you have witnessed a murder or worse!

The initiated metaphysician can easily recognise that which

159

is real and that which is imaginary, but it is again advised that unless you have some real reason for deep trance, you leave it alone.

If you will not heed that advice, well heed this; if in a deep trance or in the astral you find horrible entities making faces at you or worse, then you merely have to think strong thoughts at them that you are not afraid, and if you do that you will find that these people disappear. They can only feed on fear, and if you are not afraid they are actually repelled.

In sincere friendship I advise you not to allow yourself to be hypnotised except by a competent medical person, and I advise you not to undergo trance except under qualified supervision. The ordinary meditation is perfectly safe, no harm at all can come to you because you are in full possession of all your faculties. So—meditate and enjoy it immensely. Avoid hypnotism and deep trance because they will not further your development one iota

CHAPTER NINE

IS ASTRAL TRAVEL FOR *YOU*?

THE dark mists of night gradually turned grey and slowly retreated from the rising sun. For some time dank tendrils of fog rose up from the long grass. Soon one could discern the old-world village of Much Nattering nestling deep in the valley formed by the Cotswold Hills. A forest spread down the slopes as if threatening to engulf the little village, through the centre of the main street a small brooklet twinkled and tinkled along, carrying with it all the refuse of an older civilisation.

Much Nattering was a typical English village with small stone houses thatched with yellow rushes from the nearby marshes. At the far end of the village was the Village Green, in the centre of it the ducking pool where the scolds were dipped in the chair at the end of a long beam projecting far out over the stagnant, slime-covered water. Farther along, nearer the village side of the pond, was a small stone platform, probably the remains of an old basalt eruption from the mountain-side. Here it was the custom to take witches and throw them in the water to see if they sank or swam. If they sank and drowned they were innocent; if they swam, then it was adjudged that the Devil was supporting them and so the poor wretch would be thrown back again until eventually 'the Devil's arm got tired' and she drowned.

The maypole was still decked with its ribbons, for yesterday had been a Holy Day and the youth of the village had been dancing the maypole and plighting their troth.

As the light increased and the day advanced, small trickles of smoke seeped up from holes in mud roofs, or from small chimneys in thatched roofs, signs that the yeomen of England had bestirred themselves to get their breakfasts before setting out for their work. Breakfast—ale to drink and dry rough bread to eat, for in those days there was no such thing as tea or coffee, no cocoa, and rarely—perhaps once a year—did they eat meat of any kind, only the richer families knew the taste of any meat, the rest—that which they could produce in their own locality.

There came the sounds of much bustle, the sounds of much movement. Soon men were pouring out of doors going to shippens or barns or going out into the fields to catch and harness horses. The womenfolk were busy inside their houses, clearing up, dusting, making, and mending, and wondering how to make do with the small amount of money available, for so much was done by barter, and now everyone in the village knew what everyone else had, and it was time for some of the Travelling Men to come and bring new items.

The morning wore on, shining bright shafts of sunlight along the village street reflecting brightly from the greenish bull's-eye glass in some of the windows. Soon there came a great commotion; Mistress Helen Highwater pounced out of a house at the end of a street and pounded down the cobbled way, her old elastic-sided boots peeping shyly from beneath her voluminous skirts as they swirled slightly with the speed of her passing. Beneath the beribboned poke-bonnet which she wore her face shone bright red and was covered with a thin film of perspiration. On she swept like a full-rigged schooner racing before a winter gale, 'clack clack, clack clack, clack clack', tapped her heels on the tops of the smooth cobbles. Every so often she turned her head without stopping her headlong flight, turned to peer over her shoulder as if she thought she might be pursued by the Devil. Just a glance, then on she went with renewed vigour, her breath coming in short puffs and pants. Soon, by the time she reached the end of the street, her breath was coming in a series of staccato grunts.

At the end of the cobbled street she turned right to where the apothecary's shop stood in solitary splendour just apart from the rest of the houses. For a moment she paused in her headlong flight and looked about her once again, then she looked up at the leaded windows above her. Peering around the side of the house she saw that the apothecary's horse was not tethered, so returning to the front again she dashed up the three worn stone steps and pushed open the solid oaken door. 'Clang clang, clang clang' went a little bell as she pushed her way into a dark and gloomy room.

Odours assailed her from every quarter, musk and cinnamon, lemon, sandalwood, and pine, and other strange scents which her nostrils could not identify. She stood there panting and puffing and trying to get back her breath, when from a

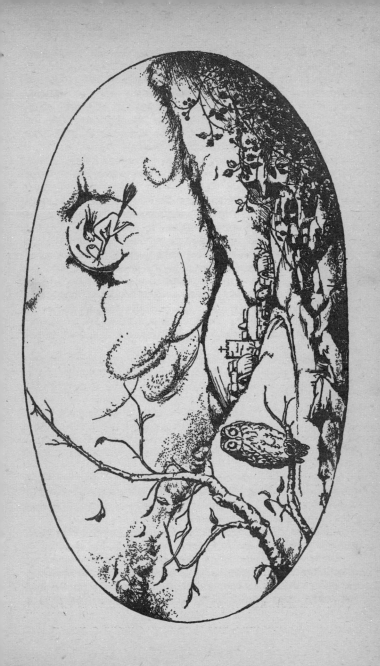

room behind the shop appeared another woman, the apothecary's wife.

'Oh, Ida Shakes!' said Helen Highwater. 'I saw it agin last night, there she was up in the sky with the moon as her background, she was nekkid, nekkid as a jaybird and riding on a big birch broom.' She shuddered and looked as if she was about to faint, so Ida Shakes hurried forward and guided her to a chair by the side of the little counter.

'There, there,' she cried, 'just you get yourself set down and tell me all about it. I will pour up a measure of ale and then you will feel better.'

Helen Highwater sighed dramatically and allowed her eyes to roll heavenwards. 'There I was,' she said, 'standing in my shift before the bedroom window looking out upon God's glory of the moon and the night sky.' She paused and sighed again. 'Suddenly,' she continued, 'I looked towards the right and a big old owl flew across the window, and as he flew across I saw that he was fleeing from something. I craned my neck to the right, and there SHE was soaring across the sky, with not a bit of a shift upon her, and I thought, "Oh dear me, all those men who were out benights and the gypsies down by the covert, whatever would they think to see a Satan's Daughter sailing overhead so!"'

Ida Shakes poured out more ale and they drank together in silence for a while. Then the apothecary's wife said, 'Let us go together and tell this tale to our priest, the Reverend Mr. Doguid, he will know what to do with it. Now you just get your breath back while I get my bonnet on and we will be out together, I will have the apprentice look after the shop.' With that she turned on her heel and hurried into the back room where Helen Highwater heard her giving orders in a short, sharp tone of voice.

Soon the two ladies, chattering away like magpies, were hurrying down the side road towards the parsonage, and towards a conference with the worthy pastor and keeper of their souls, the Reverend Mr. Doguid.

Miles away in a small village far from London, the fierce Cardinal Wolsey turned restlessly on his bed. He was making his plans to hunt witches, making his plans to make and unmake kings and bring austerity to princes as well as to paupers. He had retired to his country mansion at the Village of Hampton, some miles from London Town. Even then he was planning to rebuild the mansion and make it into a veritable Court to rival that of the King in London. But now the Cardinal, who little knew that in future years his name would be a trademark for underwear, tossed restlessly, while throughout the length and breadth of England his Special Investigators prowled, watchful, hoping to be led to witches that they could be tortured and burned at the stake to the glory of God and to save their souls.

The worthy Cardinal pondered upon all these things, and he leaned back upon his soft cushions and thought with smug complacency how he would reorganise Heaven when he eventually got there, although he had no plans to leave the Earth at the moment as he was enjoying much power.

Back in the Village of Much Nattering, the two ladies stood up to take leave of the Reverend Mr. Doguid. 'Well, then ladies,' he said sombrely, 'we will keep watch on that widow of whom you spoke, and we will see what we shall see, and having seen we shall act to the glory of God.' He nodded gravely and ushered Ida Shakes and Helen Highwater out of the parsonage door.

For the rest of the day little groups of women could be seen furtively whispering to each other, and peering up towards the forest which loomed at the perimeter of the village. There was much nodding of heads and shaking of heads, much folding of hands beneath aprons. The men, ignorant of what was going on, looked mystified at the strange doings of their womenfolk, as men always do anyhow, and just put it down to a form of moon-madness which came upon women every so often.

Down by the maypole a small group of boys and girls twirled and twisted and pranced around as they practised the steps for a new maypole dance which they were shortly going to perform before visitors from another village.

Soon the shadows of night gathered, and back from the darkening fields came the men who had laboured long throughout the day, drooping with weariness they trudged along the cobbled streets and lurched into their homes. In the shadow of the parsonage four men waited silently, leaning up against the wall, talking in the lowest of low whispers. Then as the darkness became more profound a figure appeared from the side door of the parsonage: it was the Reverend Mr. Doguid himself. The four men respectfully touched a forelock to the parson, he said, 'Follow me to the widow's cottage, I

165

have sent a messenger to fetch the interrogators.' So saying, he turned and strode off circumnavigating the main part of the village and heading towards the forest. For some twenty minutes they walked, and then they entered the dark shadows cast by the pine trees. Here progress was quite difficult, here there was only the purple loom from the night sky which filtered down through bare branches, but through familiarity they could feel and detect their way, so they pressed on, trying to be as silent as they could. At last they approached a clearing and passed by a pile of hazel twigs and some remnants of charcoal. Passing that they turned to the left and saw the dark outline of a rough hut ahead of them. Now their caution was extreme, they moved carefully with complete circumspection, softly they tiptoed across the clearing to the hut.

In single file they approached the window which was roughly curtained, but the merest chink of light shone out. The priest moved forward and put an eye to the chink, and looked inside. Inside he saw a sparse room, roughly furnished with home-made furniture cut from the trees themselves. The light he saw was the light from a burning pine knot on which the resin still dripped down. As it flared and sputtered, he could see that in the centre of the room was an old woman sitting on the floor. By carefully listening he could detect that she was mumbling something, but some moments he stood there watching and listening. Then out of the darkness swooped a bat, it dived down and clutched the hair of one of the men; with a shriek of terror, he leapt to his feet and then fell flat on his face, petrified with fright.

As the priest and the three other men looked in stupefied astonishment the door of the hut creaked open, and in it stood the old woman. The priest was galvanised into life, dramatically pointing a forefinger at her he shouted, 'Daughter of Satan, we have come for you!' The old woman, struck with terror, and well knowing the fate in store for her, fell to her knees wailing. At a sign from the priest, the three other men, now slowly followed by the fourth who sheepishly climbed to his feet, went to the old woman, two held her arms roughly behind her and two entered the hut. They rummaged around, and not finding any spells or signs of magical instruments, they overturned the pine knot into a pile of pine needles so that the hut flared, and as the men retreated, burned to the ground.

In the basement of the church the old woman knelt before

the priest. 'I have sent for the Interrogators,' he thundered. 'You are a Daughter of Satan, you have sailed across the sky naked in company with Satan!'

The poor old woman shrieked with terror, knowing that as her house had been burned, judgement had been passed upon her without any trial. 'You are going to be kept in a cell for the night to await the pleasure of His Majesty's Investigators,' said the priest, and turning to the four men he instructed them to take the old woman to the local prison and keep her locked up until the next morning.

Late the next morning there was the thunder of hooves along the hard-packed earth road, ending in a clatter as the horsemen joined the cobbled main street and reined-in at the parsonage. From the leading horse descended His Majesty's Interrogator of Witches, a surly, bloated-faced man with narrow pig-like eyes. He was followed by his Assistant and two Torturers who lovingly removed the bags containing their instruments of trade from the horses' backs. Together they went into the parsonage where the priest was expecting them. For some time there was animated discussion, and then the men left the parsonage and made their way to the room which was used as the local jail. Entering they seized the old woman, who was now gibbering with terror, and stripped her of her clothing. Examining her minutely, inch by inch from head to foot, they jabbed sharp pins into her to see if there was any spot which was immune to pain, one of the standard tests for witches.

Soon also they put thumb-screws upon her and tightened them until she screamed and the screws ran red.

Still having no confession from her, for in truth she had nothing to confess, they seized her by her hair and dragged her out at a run all the way down the cobbled village street to the ducking pond, where by now a crowd of avid, eager spectators had collected in the hope and knowledge of seeing a witch drowned.

The old woman was held upright naked on the stone platform while men went to each side of the pond. Then the priest stood in front of her and said, 'In the name of the Father, the Son, and the Holy Ghost, I urge you now to make your true confession that according to God's mercy you may die knowing that your soul be saved. Confess ere it be too late.' With that he made the sign of the cross in the air and stood aside.

The old woman was speechless with terror.

Four men grabbed her by her arms and legs, and swung her high into the air. Up she went, and turned a somersault in the air before falling head first into the scummy, stagnant pond. For moments there were just ripples on the surface, and then her streaming hair and head appeared. She threshed wildly at the water and seemed to make some headway at swimming. Then some spectator threw a heavy rock which caught her on the side of the head. Other rocks followed. The poor old woman gave a horrid, soul-wrenching scream, and an eyeball was seen dangling down her cheek. Further rocks dislodged it and the body sank beneath the water which was stained red. For a minute, perhaps more, there seemed to be turmoil beneath the water and a whole fountain of red, blood-stained water spurted up in a little mound.

One of the Investigators turned to another and said, 'So! Satan did not save her; perhaps, as she claimed, she was innocent after all.'

The man to whom he spoke shrugged and turned aside as he said, 'Oh well, what's it matter? We've all got to die sometime, we put her out of her misery!'

Unnoticed, isolated, and alone, an aged hunchback lurked in the shade of a little clump of trees. From his eyes tears slowly oozed and coursed down his seamed and wizened cheeks. From time to time he attempted to wipe them away with the back of a gnarled hand. Intently he peered forth from beneath white, shaggy eyebrows. Spasmodically his left hand gripped and re-gripped the twisted old stick which he used to assist him in his painful movements of walking.

As the poor old woman sank beneath the water surface for the last time, to become in her death agony entangled in the clinging weeds below, he muttered, 'Sad, sad.'

A woman hurrying along the path to try to see something before it was all over, spied the twisted old man and stopped beside him. 'What 'appened to her, grandfer?' she asked in a shrill voice.

'Murdered!' replied the hunchback in surly tones. 'Murdered on the altar of ignorance and superstition. She was no witch, I went to school with her. She was a pure soul who had no evil in her.'

The young woman glowered and said menacingly, 'You'd better be careful what you're saying, grandfer, or you'll find

168

yourself in that pond with her, there's been some ugly rumours about you, you know—if I wasn't a good granddaughter I'd tell on you myself.' So saying she hurried off to peer with avid fascination at the surface of the now still pond, a surface ruffled only occasionally by a bursting bubble plopping to the surface.

The hunchback stared towards her with brooding eyes, and then muttered to himself, 'Superstition, superstition, always the enemy of progress. We who do astral travel are the prey of the wicked, the ignorant, and the jealous, those who cannot do it themselves and who give the wrong thoughts to we who can. I must be careful, I must be careful!' Sadly he looked again towards the pond, for now Investigators had brought the old woman's clothing, which they dumped upon the stone where she had stood. Solemnly, with many a religious incantation, they applied flint and tinder to the torn old wrecks. Fanning the first sparks into flame they had the clothing blazing, and small particles of blackened burnt material swept upwards on vagrant wind.

The old hunchback turned away sadly, shrugged his shoulders, and stumbled blindly into the sheltering woods.

Yes, throughout the centuries those who could do astral travel have been persecuted and penalised by the jealous ones who cannot do astral travel, and who resent the thought that others can do what they cannot. Yet almost anyone can astral travel if their motives are right, if their thoughts are pure, and if they practise. Let us see what it takes to do astral travel.

In the first place, one must have absolutely pure thoughts because when one can travel in the astral it is a simple matter indeed to go to a person's house and see them, no matter where they are in that house, no matter what they are doing. It is possible to look over the shoulder of a person who is writing a letter, and read the letter; it is possible—but wrong, criminally wrong. The genuine person doing astral travel would never think of so intruding upon the privacy of another, and if one did intrude by accident, then one would never, never talk of what one had seen. So, unless you are sure, completely sure beyond the slightest shadow of a doubt that you do not want to intrude upon the privacy of another, then you will find that it is very difficult indeed to get into the astral consciously. Almost everyone gets into the astral subconsciously, that is, when one is asleep, but consciously—that is a different matter.

I get a vast number of letters asking me to visit such-and-such a person by astral travel to say what is wrong with him or her, but even if I was prepared to do this there are still only twenty-four hours in the day and it would be an utter impossibility to go to all the places because of the time consumed. In any case, it is morally wrong to rush along to someone's house and peer at them in the bedroom or elsewhere. Too often people want an astral visit because they are too lazy to take the necessary steps to cure themselves, or just for idle curiosity!

Another bar to astral travel in the awake state is imposed on people who want to astral travel so that they can talk about it and show how clever they are. If you do conscious astral travel you never talk about it because it is a very great privilege to be able to do it, and one only talks about it when one is trying to help others. So if you think that astral travel will take the place of a guided tour or provide more entertainment than your television—that would be easy!—think no more about astral travel, for if you think thus it is not for you.

A third bar is imposed upon those who want to astral travel so that they may control the affairs of others. There are many people who are 'do-gooder's', they want to rush around the world in the astral putting things right without knowing why things are presumably wrong! It is very wrong indeed to force a person to have help. After all, the person concerned knows his own affairs best, so if someone bumbles along in the astral and tries to peer and pry and then tells the victim that this, that, or something else should be done, that is taking an unwarranted liberty.

You may wonder what can be done by astral travel if there are so many limitations. Well, all right, this is what can be done—you can visit any of the great libraries throughout the world, you can visit any part of the world, you can learn from ancient manuscripts, you can (yes, this is quite true!) visit other worlds when you advance sufficiently. But if you want to travel and you succeed in astral travelling, and then you give way to temptation and you just peer at someone in the privacy of their own home, then you are doing wrong and possibly you may not astral travel again.

One of my interests is to watch people going off at night. I like to sit by a window, preferably from a high vantage point, and watch over a sleeping city. Shall I tell you what it is like? Shall I tell you how I see things?

Night has fallen and above us the ageless stars twinkle with silvery, or blue, or red light. The air is clear and calm, the street lights shed some slight radiance into the sky and make it appear that there are dancing motes bubbling above the streets.

From the rooftops of the city comes the bluish white haze as if an impalpable mist is rising. The mist rises perhaps 30 feet, perhaps 100 feet, becoming bluer and bluer. Then the surface of the mist bubbles like the bubbles on a pot of boiling tar. The bubbles burst and gleaming streamers of pale blue-white light emerge and streak up into the night sky, the threads of light become thinner and thinner but they are always there, they radiate in all directions, to the North, to the South, to the West, and to the East. Some go straight up, straight up into the infinity above, and yet curiously enough some go straight down as if searching for another form of life in the core of this earth of ours. The bodies of the people of this city are asleep, but their astral bodies are travelling, as proof whereof their Silver Cords are agleam in the darkness of the night. They stretch up and up, and ever and anon a little thrill or ripple comes racing along the Silver Cord, and there is a jerk and a twitch and the Cord contracts, and soon the astral body comes down, disappears into the blue mists and afterwards goes into the body again. These are people who have been disturbed by perhaps the opening of a door or the tossing of a partner, these are the people who awaken in the morning with a headache and memories of a horrid nightmare. Just about everyone does astral travel, but unfortunately because of the teachings of the West most forget what they have learned and what they have done when they return to the body, and if an astral is 'reeled in' suddenly it gives rise to nightmares and a complete shattering of all memories of the actual experience.

Most people have had the experience of a violent jerk as they were falling asleep, most people have had an experience of a rising and falling, and a sensation that they were falling out of a tree or off a cliff. That was verging upon remembering astral travel, but again, remember that astral travel is a thing which almost anyone can do consciously if one remembers the provisos previously mentioned in this chapter.

Some distance away within my line of sight there was a great building, a prison. Around the walls the lights burned throughout the night and occasionally a bright spotlight would flicker along the walls, but at this time of the night most of the cells were dark—yet not dark because the lights of the Silver Cord go up, the imprisoned men escape by night into the astral, for truly it is said that iron bars do not a prison make; iron bars restrain the flesh, but they are no bar to the astral. Thus it is that those adjudged guilty, and the innocent alike, mingle and go up about their separate travels in the night.

All too frequently from the pent-houses atop the high buildings one gets terrible sordid thoughts, and even the Silver Cords which protrude from such places are often duller and tainted. For those who pander to the lusts of the flesh do not travel to the highest planes, instead they are confined to the lower astral where they meet depraved and unevolved personalities to match their own.

Supposing you have gone through all this, and you have decided that you have no lusts, no desire to peer at others in the privacy of their own homes, suppose you decide that you are one who can travel consciously, well, this is how you should go about it:

Make a definite experiment, make an arrangement with some very close friend that you will, with his or her permission, visit the house that night. Have your friend agree to put something, perhaps some written message on a table so that you can read the message put there for you and repeat it back the next day to test your progress.

When you go to bed make sure that it is at a reasonable hour, that is, fairly early. You should not have a heavy meal before going to bed, and of course you should not drink too much before retiring otherwise your rest will inevitably be disturbed, and getting up in the night may cause you to forget your astral travelling experiences.

When you rest upon your bed make sure that you are completely comfortable, not too hot and not too cold, and it is better if you sleep alone with your door locked because if you are sleeping with your partner and there is restlessness during the night you will be brought back from your astral journey with quite a shock, which will cause you to forget anything you have experienced.

Decide where you are going to go. You may be going to your friend's house, in which case you will know the way, or you may be going to a different country. But supposing you are going to one special house or one special person, then visualise the house, visualise how you would visit that house if you were going by car or walking. Solemnly affirm before you allow your body to sleep that your astral will go to the house and that when you awaken in the morning you will have a complete memory of all that happened, you should affirm that this will occur and you will remember. Repeat your affirmation three times, and then let yourself drift off to sleep thinking of all this as you do so. If you succeed this is what will happen; you will feel your body getting heavy, you will feel your eyes becoming tired, and you will fall asleep in a perfectly ordinary, normal manner. But then as you fall asleep you will have an experience similar to going out of a dark room into a brilliantly lighted 'outdoors'. At the time of the passing, your physical body will jerk slightly, and if the jerk does not awaken you in the physical body, your consciousness will expand and become clearer, you will experience a truly wonderful, a truly joyous feeling of exhilaration and freedom from bounds.

You will feel as if you are sparkling and bubbling all over with vitality. It will occur to you after a time to wonder what it is all about, and then you will look about and you will see that you are attached to your physical body by a glowing, pulsating, blue-white cord, like a child being attached to its mother by the umbilical cord.

With some horror and distaste you will look at the lump of clay which is your physical body resting there, perhaps in a contorted bunch of twisted limbs. You will feel horror that eventually you have to get back into that confining body. But the time is not yet. You gaze about you, looking at things from an unfamiliar viewpoint. You can rise up and look closely at the ceiling or the walls, but then as you wander about the room you find that it is boring to be confined to such a small space, and you think of how to get out of the room—well, it's no sooner thought of than done. You find that you are out projecting beyond the roof with no memory of how you got through perhaps other bedrooms in your way, now you are out, floating above the rooftop at the end of your blue-white cord.

For moments you float there gently lifting as if on unseen currents. Perhaps you look down and identify your house and friends' houses, perhaps you watch some late car speeding along the highway. You are seeing your town or your district as if from a balloon, but the impression grows upon you that this is just a waste of time, you are doing this for another

173

purpose, there is nothing to be gained by just lying looking down at a sleeping city.

You think of the plans you have made, you think of the places you would like to visit—where shall it be, Bulgaria, Buenos Aires, London, Berlin? Anywhere! Perhaps you will be content to go just to a friend's house to read a carefully prepared message so that you can repeat it back to him for his confirmation on the morrow. Immediately you think where you are going, and you think how to get there. Perhaps from Dublin in Ireland you decide you would like to visit New York. As you think of this your astral cord extends and extends, and you rise up and up far higher than the astronauts, or cosmonauts either, have reached. As you rise up you see the Earth turning slowly beneath you, you see the ocean which from this height looks like a placid village pond, and then as you peer down you see your destination, New York. Here the time is four hours earlier so people are not going to sleep yet, they have their city lights on and it provides an excellent beacon for you. You 'set your sights' on New York City, and you fall down towards New York City almost with the speed of thought. As you get closer and closer, and the city becomes larger and larger, you can pick your actual desired destination. Perhaps it may be Manhattan, perhaps you want to look in on the crowds swarming out of Broadway theatres, perhaps you want to have a look round Radio City or float over the docks and see the great liners lying at their moorings. As you think about it, so you achieve it.

In many great blocks of buildings you will see lights shining out, many of them are office buildings. Well, you can look around, see the cleaners at work and perhaps some 'high pressure executive' at work too. But many of the lights will be apartment buildings. A caution here—do not intrude, do not force your way into the privacy of those apartments because you would not like people spying on you and perhaps chuckling a little maliciously at you, would you? Well, respect the privacy of these people, and you will be able to continue your astral travels without hindrance.

Throughout the period of your travel keep in your consciousness the thought that you will remember, you will remember, you will remember. Never lose sight of that thought, keep it tucked away somewhere so that all the time you are getting a jog that you must and will remember. With practice

174

you will have no difficulty at all in remembering. First when you are back in the body you will think that you had a dream, but if you allow yourself to visit the same place the night after you will realise that it is not a dream but actuality. So with confirmation you will find that it becomes easier and easier.

But you are in the astral looking at New York City from the air. The night grows darker, down below policemen in their prowl cars wander in and out of back alleys, the city grows quieter, although New York is never quiet. Soon you find that there is a strange impression of unease, an impression that you are wanted. Soon you find there is a tingling coming to you along the Silver Cord. If you are wise and experienced you will immediately head home, in this case you left from Dublin, remember. If you are not experienced you will be reeled in unceremoniously like a fish reeled in by an eager angler.

As you, being one of the wiser ones, allow yourself to return, you head straight up into the sky again so that, looking down you can see the darkness darker and darker over the United States and over Europe the light is beginning to come brighter. You find that over Dublin you have the first faint streaks of light coming over the edge of the world, so you allow yourself to go down and down, you see the roof of your house approaching and the first time or two you instinctively brace yourself for a hard landing, but—nothing happens, you go down straight through the roof without even being aware of it, and then you find yourself in your bedroom again floating a few feet above your slumbering physical body. You look down at it and you shudder once more at the thought of losing the freedom of moving with the speed of thought. However, nature will not be denied and you find that you are settling, settling, settling. Soon you are almost in contact with the body which seems to be shimmering and vibrating slowly, and then you become aware that you are vibrating much faster. You have the task of synchronising your vibrations to those of the physical body, but this is largely an automatic matter, and then you find you are sinking back into the physical body, you will feel as though you are tightly encased in a cold, damp, rigid garment. It is a thoroughly unpleasant feeling first because there is an impression of being stifled and constricted, and it will make you shudder and wonder why on earth people have to have bodies. Then the answer will occur to you—well, of course, you have to to be on Earth!

You will still be keeping before you the thought that you have to remember everything, you have to remember everything, and you lower your astral farther down so that it fits exactly into that cold, clammy body of yours. As it fits exactly there will be a sudden 'snap' and a jerk, and an impression that you are sinking down through dark, woolly dust. You may sleep for a few moments, in which case the next thing you will know is that daylight is upon you and you are opening and rubbing your eyes, and perhaps yawning as well.

Very clear in your mind is the knowledge of all that you did in the night. Now is the time to write down everything you did—write it down immediately, using paper and pencil put at your bedside for that purpose. Do not be 'clever' and feel that you can remember all because you will not—not for the first few times anyway. Instead, you will forget everything unless you take the elementary precaution of writing it all down before the returning day causes you to forget. So write it down and read it, and do that for your first half dozen astral trips around the world.

All this so far has dealt with astral travel on the mundane plane, that is bumbling around the world, seeing the great libraries, the great art galleries, and the great cities of the world. Well, perhaps you want to visit the astral world beyond this, what the old scribes called 'Purgatory' and 'Paradise'.

In that case remember that it is quite easy, remember that in the ancient Hindu Scriptures are very vivid descriptions of men travelling to the Moon, to the Sun, and to the stars, for when you are in the astral, difference in temperature and lack of a breathable atmosphere makes no difference to you, it does not inconvenience you at all. Unfortunately people nowadays are just playing with rockets and a few silly things like that, forgetting that 10,000 years ago the Hindus were able to travel in space by astral projection. This is not fiction, this is fact, and if you can get anyone to translate Hindu scriptures for you, you will soon see that for yourself.

If you want to visit friends in the astral you will have to be specially trained, that is if your friends are highly evolved, because in the astral, that is in the higher planes of consciousness, an hour or two of Earth time will be several thousand years of astral world time because it all depends on the speed of thought, etc. It takes, as a crude illustration, a tenth of a second for thought to travel from a man's brain to wiggle his big toe or turn a wrist. Well, in the astral planes it might take ten-thousandths of a second. There is a different time system altogether. But you—when you do astral travel daily or nightly, will find that you are able to operate your mind more and more in the higher planes, and thus you will not be limited by physical boundaries.

To give you some idea of the difference in time-cycles, let me say that we on this Earth are now living in the Age of Kali; the Age of Kali in celestial years is equal to 1,200, but in human years it is 432,000 years.

But beyond our Earth system, beyond our whole system of time and dimensions, there is the 'Creator of the Universe' system which is quite a long time, one, in fact, in which $4,320,000 \times 1,000$ human years constitute just one day of 'super' time, so before you can actually locate an evolved entity you have to be sure of his place in a certain time sequence. All of which makes it clear that the back-street medium really doesn't have a chance!

But you want to get out of this world and into the astral world—well, tell yourself what you are going to do and when you go to bed determine that you really are going to leave this world and go up and up into the astral, picture yourself rising up beyond the Earth and into space, and into another dimension altogether.

First you will get out of your body at the end of your Silver Cord, and then you will find all your colour values change. You will be aware of colours which previously had no place in your knowledge. You will see that foliage is of many different hues, more colours than you knew existed. But then you may be horrified to see that there are quite unimaginable creatures gibbering at you, making obscene gestures, making obscene invitations. But do not be disheartened or frightened because here you are passing through the garbage of elementals, etc., just as in most cases to enter a great city by rail you, for some inexplicable reason, see all the backs of the slum houses first.

There is nothing at all to be afraid of, no elemental or entity can hurt you in the slightest provided that you are not afraid. If you are afraid, then you more or less attract these people. So the best thing is to carry on and realise quite fully that no one at all can hurt you unless you are afraid.

Decide that you are not going to linger in this area of elementals, but carry on—on—to the Land of the Golden Light.

Here you will see such beautiful things that it is quite impossible to describe them in words relating to a three-dimensional world, your experiences in the Land of the Golden Light have to be experienced in person not through the medium of the printed or the spoken word.

As your proficiency increases with practice you will be able to go to other worlds and to other planes, but remember you cannot intrude upon the privacy of another, you cannot harm others through astral travel because that is the crime of crimes.

Here is a happy thought for you—in the Land of the Golden Light you can only meet those with whom you are compatible, here in fact you can meet your 'twin soul', for there are such things as we shall see in our next chapter.

CHAPTER TEN

THE WORKS OF MAN

THE old Engineer smiled fondly down at the small figure resting on the bench. Straightening, he placed his hands to his
aching back and rose stiffly to greet his visitor. 'Nice of you to
come and see me,' said the Engineer, affably. 'I certainly have
a problem here.' Taking the Visitor's arm, he led him over to
the workbench. 'There he is,' he said, like a proud parent.
'The latest model. Experimental still, you know, and there are
some unexpected difficulties. I can't solve them, too close to
the subject, I suppose.' Gently he picked up the little figure
and rested it on the palm of one hand.

The Visitor glanced around. 'Quite a nice place you've got
here,' he commented. 'You seem to have some thriving
colonies even though this lot is difficult.'

'Not so thriving as you think!' replied the Engineer gloomily. 'Come and look at these.' Cradling the small figure in his
hands he led the way to a small blue-green sphere. 'There is a
viewer there, have a look—tell me what you think!'

The Visitor placed his eyes against the viewer and twisted
some knobs. For long moments he watched, and then, with a
sigh, pushed the viewer away. 'Truculent lot, aren't they?' he
asked. 'It seems to me that they are CRAZY.'

For long moments the Engineer stood in silence, idly finger-
ing the little figure in his hands. 'Crazy?' he mused. 'Crazy?
Why, yes, I suppose so. It seems to me that they have a remote
control problem or something. They do not respond correctly
to transmitted signals, nor do they return the correct information. I don't know what to do about it!' Turning, he paced up
and down, up and down, lost in deep thought, head bent in
profound contemplation of the figure in his hands. At last he
abruptly halted in front of his Visitor and asked brusquely,
'What would YOU do if you were in my position? The Board is
making difficulties over all the delay in getting them right.
What would YOU do?'

Without replying, the Visitor turned to the viewer again,
and peered through it with intense concentration. Carefully he

focused and refocused until he was quite satisfied, then for a long time he peered through the instrument. At last he turned to the impatiently waiting Engineer and said, 'You should send an Observer down. Shouldn't be impossible. It is the only way to get the results, you know. We are too far away here, we can only guess and so far we have guessed wrongly. Nothing else for it, but—on second thoughts—why not call in a Specialist Efficiency Expert?'

The Engineer shook his head doubtfully. 'No!' he replied. 'The Board would never stand for it, I don't think they would even co-operate with an Outside Specialist!'

Together, Engineer and Visitor strolled over to the workbench and sat down. 'Here,' said the Engineer, picking a figure from a box, 'is the newest model. *Homo sapiens* we call them, but they seem to have lost the "*sapiens*" for the moment.' The Visitor took the figure and examined it carefully. 'Here is another,' added the Engineer as he took another little figure from a box on the other side of the bench. The Visitor examined the second figure and compared it with the first. 'Self-reproducing,' remarked the Engineer. 'When they reach a certain age and they get together they reproduce. Actually each has just the same equipment as the other, but in more or less degree. We call one "male" and the other "female". They work by remote control, but just now the control is faulty and we don't know why.'

The Visitor pointed to another box. 'What are those?' he asked.

The Engineer made a rueful face. 'Oh! THEY are subnormal,' he said. 'They do not know Truth from Untruth; we call them PRESSMEN!'

. . . . .

Yes, humans are a bit of a mess, all right. Quite an intricate mechanism which at the present time does not seem to be functioning as well as it should.

We have to remember that in our Solar system we are composed of compounds which are rather different from those existing in other Universes, other Galaxies, etc. Here everything—everything that lives on our Earth—is composed of the same 'bricks'. There are available in this Solar system hydrogen, water, and hydrates, ammonia, methane, and various other gases. We are really composed of 'bricks' of carbon molecules and amino-acids and nucleotides. From these simple compounds are built all the species of animals, plants, and minerals upon Earth.

When that is built into human shape the resulting mechanism is subject to magnetic impulses, which we call astrological impulses, and various rays. But let us go into the matter a little more deeply and see what we can find out.

If you can get an illustration of a human body and you can see the spine and spinal nerves you will be able to follow this more accurately. The human mechanism—the controller mechanism, that is—is actually composed of nine control centres. The average occultist mentions only seven because there are seven upon the material, or mundane, plane.

The old Chinese physicians visualised all the organs of the body as being controlled and supervised by little 'men', and here in this chapter you will see an illustration adapted from one which was originally drawn in China about 7,000 years ago. You can see the little men helping the passage of food down the throat, blowing wind into the lungs, stirring up all the chemicals in the liver, and controlling various sphincters. But this dealt with merely the 'animal' part of the body, the flesh and organs. We want to go farther than that and deal with the parts which bring messages from the Overself and control the functions of the body.

We have to remember that there is very much more to the human body than meets the casual eye. If we look at a pair of wires going, let us say, past our window on telegraph poles or similar, we cannot tell by looking at those wires if any current is flowing, to us they are just copper wires. But with suitable instruments one can detect whether there be or not current flowing, and we can also determine which way it is flowing.

In the same way we can look at a body without necessarily being aware of the various centres of that body which are connected to equivalent portions of the Overself. As already stated, there are seven 'mundane' centres which are called 'chakras'. At the top of the head there is the one frequently referred to as 'the Thousand Petalled Lotus'. The actual Sanskrit name is Sahasrara Chakra. This is the 'relay', or centre, which is nearest to the spiritual and thus the one which is the more easily deranged.

Lower (we are looking at a body from the back, and we see the head, shoulders, and spine, etc.) around about the neck area is the Ajna Chakra. This is the next important, and which is actually in contact with the Overself. This is the chakra of the mind, and remember that the mind is just as an electrical function in much the same way as you can receive a telephone message, and the earpiece is just a 'function' of what is being said at the other end of the wire.

Farther down the spine we have the third chakra; this one is known as Visudha. This controls the action of the mouth, so if one has difficulty in speaking clearly it could be that this chakra is undisciplined or damaged.

To digress for a moment—just imagine that you are walking along a street and you see a telephone man messing about in one of those manholes. As you stop to look, he gets hold of a great sheathed cable and tears the insulation off it. As the insulation is removed you see thousands of tiny wires, most of them colour coated, but anyway there are thousands of wires and you wonder how on earth anyone can sort such a mess. Well, the nerves inside your spine are like that; certain nerves go down inside the spine and then branch away, so when you are thinking of chakras think of a telephone man with all those wires, and think also of little relays, or repeater stations which take an incoming signal from a distant station and amplify it (make it stronger) before sending it on to the next station in the line.

Next of our 'relays' is the Anahata Chakra which controls feel and all that we touch. Below that there is the Manipura Chakra. This one is known as the 'Fire Principle' chakra, and there is no point in going more deeply into this particular chakra because it does not greatly concern us at this stage.

Below that we have the sixth chakra, this time the Swadhishatana Chakra. This one deals with the Water Principle.

Farther down we have the seventh, or Earth Principle chakra referred to in Sanskrit as the Mooladhara. This one is the home of the Kundalini, and the Kundalini is actually the controlling, or life, force of humans. It is, let us say, the equivalent of the fire in the furnace which heats the water to raise the steam which turns the turbines to generate the electricity which lights the lamps, cools the refrigerator, etc., in civilisation. Once the fire goes out the electricity dies through want of steam, and everything comes to a standstill.

Many people who have been misinstructed, or worse, have been uninstructed, try to raise the Kundalini force by artificial

182

means, because it is a fact that if one raises the Kundalini properly one can be very much more aware, very much more intelligent. But to raise it indiscriminately without having utter purity of thought is to do immense harm to oneself, and frequently to lead to madness; to raise the Kundalini without thought of the consequences can lead to a complete mental and physical breakdown. So unless you have a Master who has been through it all and knows all about it, do not try to raise your own Kundalini. A Master will not raise the Kundalini unless he is quite sure that it is for your good.

Here it might be as well to add that people who run Correspondence Courses, etc., or offer to do small services for you for a small sum of money, do not have the power to safely supervise your development and raise your Kundalini, they can do a lot of harm instead.

Before a physical entity of the human type, that is, a person living on this world, can attain to cosmic consciousness he or she has to have certain stirrings of the Kundalini, 'stirrings' are somewhat different from actually raising the Kundalini! If one is sexually over-excited and—let me say it—lustful, it can be a bad thing indeed, because if one has sex for the sake of sex only, sex without true love, that is, it can temporarily or permanently paralyse the correct flowing of the Kundalini force. By 'permanently' I mean during this lifetime, as long as the malpractice in sex continues.

Each part of the body while upon the Earth is strongly associated and connected to its astral counterpart by way of all these chakras. No doubt you have heard of people who have had a leg amputated, and who still apparently feel pains in the amputated leg, or rather in the space which the amputated leg would have filled. This is because the physical leg which now has been removed still has certain effects upon the astral leg which, of course, has not and cannot be removed.

To refer again to astral travel, it is highly essential that we return to the physical body so that every part of the astral body fits into every part of the physical body, and so that astral and physical organs are completely compatible each with the other. The bodies must also be correctly synchronised according to the direction of current flow.

Just as all current, all electricity, must be either positive or negative—just as current can flow in one direction and return in the opposite direction, so do humans have a flow of current.

The two 'wires' of humans are known as the Ida and Pingala. Actually, of course, they are not wires but tubes in the human body. Ida is on the left side and Pingala is on the right side, and these two sources provide the energy necessary for the passive functioning of the Kundalini. We can look upon them as caretakers making sure that the Kundalini is kept in good condition, ready for use in this life if we deserve it, or if not ready for use in the next life, because when the Kundalini starts to rise under correct treatment and under correct control, Ida and Pingala are by-passed. But so long as Man (and Woman!) are bound by the operation of Ida and Pingala, that man or woman will be confined to the Earth plane, and to the theory and practice of birth, death, and rebirth. It is only when Man is able to raise his Kundalini and by-pass the caretaking energy sources of Ida and Pingala that he can progress and know that his time of release from the cycle of birth, death, and rebirth has come to an end.

It is better to regard these chakras as relay stations, or if you like, remote control spots. Remember, also, that there are other important parts of the body such as the cervical ganglion in the neck, and somewhat below it the vagus nerve. After that we have the cardiac plexus, the solar plexus, and the pelvic plexus, but these are 'sub-stations' and should not bother us unduly.

We upon Earth are affected very greatly by all sorts of outside influences. There are various rays which affect humans, and let me say at the outset that astrology is a very, very real thing indeed, and people should not sneer at it; one should only sneer at the practitioners who misrepresent astrology because to do astrology properly takes a long time and entails a lot of work, so much time and so much work that it is not a commercial proposition. Certainly you cannot get anything of a worthwhile reading by looking at the columns of the daily newspaper and reading your 'horoscope'.

The 'rays' are a form of off-shoot of cosmic rays, and according to the time of the day and your own latitude and longitude you are subject to certain rays. How the rays affect you depends upon your astrological make-up. There are, for example, the orange, the yellow, green, blue, indigo, and others, but it will be far too much to go into the principle of these rays in a book of this nature. Let us say, though, that as one gets to the red end of the spectrum one finds that one is

184

dealing with the development of individuality, and the purple is concerned with a group mind, while a green ray tends to give one an impetus to learning. The yellow ray itself is the ray of wisdom.

One of the more interesting of the rays is the blue ray which is supposed to come under the domination of Hermes. In ancient Egypt, and Chaldea, it was known as the Magicians' Ray.

Of more use to us at the moment are the Zodiac Signs. Imagine that you had a large ball-bearing on a smooth level surface, then if you arranged magnets all around, you could hold the ball-bearing in one position, and by juggling with the position of the magnets you could make the ball-bearing take up any desired position. Look upon the planets as the magnets and yourself as the ball-bearing! Our first magnet is the Sun, but it manifests in what we call the seventh plane of the Abstract Spiritual Consciousness. The result of the Sun's influence is to give life and to cause life to flourish.

Our next magnet shall be Jupiter; Jupiter is 'jovial', benevolent, kind. Here it refers to the sixth plane of Spiritual Consciousness. It is a beneficent planet and gives good balance in morals.

Everyone knows that 'jovial' people are happy people and good to know.

Our next magnet is Mercury which has the fifth plane of abstract mind. It makes people sharp-witted and 'jumpy'. It leads to astute business deals. People understand perfectly what is meant by a 'mercurial type'. Mercury, the God who delivered messages, is supposed to control this fifth plane which also gives good memory.

Our fourth position is Saturn, this is coming down to solid consciousness. Saturnine people dwell upon things, and it is often the opposite to the jovial temperament. Saturn people are limited, restricted, and stern. People who have over-abundance of this particular Sign have to get patience and stability before they can progress farther.

Now we come to Venus—our 'magnet' occupying the third plane of the abstract emotions. Everyone knows that Venus is the Goddess of Love; it is also a mildly benevolent planet. It makes people have higher ideals and emotions, it causes people to develop their own personalities and individuality. Venus people can be beautiful people unless they are too closely associated with 'malefics'.

Our second plane is Mars, it is also our sixth 'magnet'. Mars—martial, warlike—is known as the energiser. It can be a mildly bad-effect planet if its powers are not correctly used. Mars dominates the physical body, and frequently, sex desires. If correctly used Mars increases the consciousness, and increases courage, strength, and endurance.

Lastly our seventh influence is the Moon. Well, everyone knows what the Moon does, it has an extreme effect on human life, it causes the tides to rise and fall, not merely at sea, but also in the human body. Think of the woman's 'tide' every month, think of the word 'lunatic' from 'lunar'—the Moon. The Moon has no light of her own, she reflects only that which is shone upon her, thus a person who has too much Moon influence has no great personality of his own, he merely reflects the views and opinions of those around him.

Probably almost everyone has heard of 'twin souls'. There are such things, you know, but upon the Earth plane the meeting of twin souls is a very rare occurrence. You see, if you are going to get down to basics and you consider the world of anti-matter, you will appreciate that to be a complete 'battery' there must be a positive and a negative. So if you are going to have a twin soul which forms one complete entity, you have to get a person in our system of the astral and a person of the corresponding system of the anti-matter astral, and these people have to be completely compatible.

What usually happens here, however, is that in the astral there are two Overselves who are highly compatible, and they send down to Earth a puppet from each and the puppet from each is completely compatible with the other, they fit in, and if they come into close proximity with each other there is an immediate feeling of rapport, of 'belonging'. One will say, 'I know I have met that person before!' In such cases a very true friendship can develop, but as already stated, such instances are rather rare upon the Earth. Instead there is often a very great degree of compatibility between two people, and because they are so compatible, because they complement each other, they consider that they are twin souls. They may get each other's thoughts, they may know just what the other is going to say seconds before it is said.

One gets much the same sort of affair between identical

186

twins, which of course is two people from the one egg. These two will be very much in sympathy with each other, and even while miles apart will experience the emotions of the other, and they may even get married at the same time.

A man can be very much in love with a woman; they may fancy that they are twin souls, but if they are twin souls then they will have similar interests. For example, the man could not be, let us say, a confirmed atheist while the woman had very strong religious beliefs. The dissimilarity in their beliefs would cause some dissonance, some disharmony, some friction between them, and so instead of drawing closer together they would drift farther apart.

The most that can be hoped for on this world is that two highly compatible people can live together, and by their purity of thought and by their actions, draw each closer to the other. But this is difficult of attainment at the present time because it requires such utter sacrifice and selflessness. It is useless for a man to give in and give all to the woman thinking that he is doing right, just as it is useless for the woman to give all to the man and think that she is doing right. It is not enough that each give everything to the other, instead each must give exactly what the other needs, otherwise they will drift apart.

Many people think that they have met their twin soul when they meet a person who astrologically is compatible and who lives upon the same 'ray'. They can live in harmony, and they will live in harmony, but it still is not perfect harmony, it still is not a fusion of two souls to make one entity. In fact, if people were so perfect as that they could not stay upon this imperfect world any more than a piece of ice can exist when tossed into the flames of a raging furnace. Thus, humans— Man and Woman—must try to live with each other exercising tolerance, patience, and selflessness.

Quite a number of people are brought together to work out kharmic links, and the working out of these kharmic ties makes it necessary that people shall come in close contact with each other for good or for bad. If a man and a woman are brought together through kharmic ties and, for example, the man falls in love with the woman and the woman falls in love with the man, then a very great bond of love is formed which can have the effect of cancelling out many bad kharmic aspects, because no matter what we think down here, good will prevail in the end.

If one person loves another, and the other person hates the former, then a kharmic bond will still be formed, but it will be an unsatisfactory bond and they will have to come together until the hate is eradicated and love forms. It should be understood that only complete and utter indifference can possibly prevent any kharmic link being formed. If you like a person you form a kharmic tie, if you dislike a person you form a kharmic tie, if you couldn't care less about the person no link is formed. So—any reaction to any other person starts the chain which causes kharma. For example, there can be a relationship between a teacher and a student, in that case a bond of some sort is formed. It could be a lasting bond, or it may be just a temporary bond which is over almost in a flash and can then be attributed to the burning out of some kharmic link.

The worst state is that in which great love is severed by death. If a woman loses her husband while she is still in love with him she has no outlet for her love, and so that love is stored up until they come together again in some future incarnation and the conditions are right for the expression of that love. So if anyone tells you that he or she has met their twin soul, smile understandingly and hold your peace.

These wretched old bodies of ours are subject to all sorts of weird ailments, just as an intricate piece of apparatus can be jarred out of adjustment, so can human bodies be shaken somewhat out of their best condition. So, as many people desire to be healers, it might not be out of place to give a little about healing treatment here—after all, we are dealing with the works of Man!

This is the negative world, from which it follows that a negative treatment is most suitable, that, then, is the actual term which one uses in describing this particular treatment—negative treatment.

First you have to get rid of as much breath as you can from your lungs, really exhale, force the air out, and stay like that for as long as you can without too much discomfort. This enables the body to attain what we might call negative polarity because it is now deficient in prana, deficient in air.

Then breathe lightly for just a few moments (to get your breath back, so to speak!). Then repeat the whole affair by exhaling as thoroughly as possible and getting the air out of your lungs. Stay with empty lungs for as long as you can without too much discomfort or killing yourself. Then breathe again lightly, and when you have got back some breath, do this system once again so that you have done it in all three times—three times you have exhaled completely and let your body become negatively polarised.

Now you know where you are hurting, so place your hand over the skin at the site to be treated. Then withdraw the hand, the palm, so that only the forefinger and the thumb are pressed firmly upon the skin. Hold your finger and thumb firmly upon the area to be treated, and then again exhale and stop breathing. While you are thus stopped breathing vividly imagine the life-force flowing out of your left finger-tips into the part that you desire to be treated.

Soon you will have to breathe again, but breathe as shallowly as possible, taking in just enough air to sustain life, and then hold the fingers still in contact with the area being treated. You should repeat this three times, and each time you should hold your fingers in contact with the area for at least two minutes.

The best way to treat yourself really is to give this treatment every hour until you are very much recovered. These treatments do work because you are calling in outside forces.

If you are subject to colds and you get your head stuffed up you can greatly relieve the condition by giving this negative treatment. In this case you would place your finger and thumb one on each side of the nose just below the eyes. Then, again, you would hold your breath after you had expelled as much as possible. Again you would picture that life-force flowing into you, into your nose, and killing off all the bugs which are causing the trouble. Quite seriously I say to you that if you will try this you will very shortly feel a crackling in the nose as the congestion dissipates. You will find that you will then be able to breathe through your nostrils.

Asthma is a complaint which is but little understood. All sorts of nostrums are prescribed for asthma, but in many many cases asthma is caused by some nervous condition, and that nervous condition will respond to this form of treatment. In this case you put the finger and thumb on either side of the throat just above the adam's apple. That is for the ordinary type of asthma, but of course, if you have the type which causes truly harsh and painful breathing, then you will have to put your finger and thumb some three inches apart, and place them where you can feel the throat joins the chest.

Naturally enough, if you have had asthma for many years you cannot expect a cure in a few seconds. You must have patience and use common sense, but if you will persist in this treatment you will quite definitely find that the asthma will disappear. It will disappear a whole lot faster if you will do a little meditation and introspection, and reason out for yourself what it is that causes your nervous disturbance. Again, many many cases of asthma are caused by nervous worry, and the asthma just acts like a safety valve and gives you an 'out'.

Let me repeat that you must follow these instructions exactly, and you must always use your left hand. You cannot get a strong negative cure by using your right hand. Remember then—get the air out of your lungs, wait a little with empty lungs, and always use your left hand. You will find that even a severe burn will respond to treatment of this nature; in that case, of course, you use a forefinger and thumb, and place them upon the burn, and proceed with the treatment. You will appreciate, of course, that if you have a very severe burn, well, the sooner you get a doctor in, the better. But you can do your own treatment while waiting for him.

The Kundalini, as already stated, is the 'furnace' of the human body, and of course it and the brain can be regarded as the opposite poles of a magnet if you prefer the magnet theory instead of that of the furnace. But supposing you are very clairvoyant and you have a nude body before you which you can study—let us see how it would appear.

We have a wall covered preferably in black velvet; the wall is about fourteen feet square, and we place a little platform about four feet from the floor. Upon that platform a nude model stands with back to the velvet. As we stand facing the model and observing clairvoyantly we see a brilliant white streak which is the coursing current between brain and Kundalini, which as already stated is at the remote end of the spine—a bit lower than the spine actually.

You have seen these white strip lights in shops or by the side of dressing mirrors? Well, supposing you imagine that the clairvoyant sight lets you see the life-force as resembling a strip of that light. First you have that brilliant strip of light extending from the top of the brain of your subject, and descending to a few inches below the termination of the spine. You look at that for some seconds, observing how it fluctuates and pulsates, first being as a thin strip, and then as some other thought occurs to your subject, expanding until it is quite a broad band.

If you are experienced at this sort of thing you will, after seeing this, be able to see that the body is outlined with a bluish light very much like the bluish smoke of a burning cigarette. If you light a cigarette and let it burn, it gives off a bluish smoke which is quite different from the smoke which is exhaled by a smoker. This bluish light (it looks very much like luminous smoke) extends from the surface of the body, and is of a uniform thickness, the thickness depending upon the health and strength of the subject. In an elderly person it may be about half an inch in width, in a really vigorous person it may extend two or three inches, or even four. That is the etheric and is just the 'animal radiation' of a body.

The aura is superimposed over all of it. The aura extends up beyond the head, and if you are clairvoyant enough you will see from the centre of the head a play of light which looks very much like a little fountain bubbling and sparkling and changing colours, it changes colours according to the thoughts of the person. Well, around the head you will see the halo or nimbus. It looks like—well, everyone knows what a halo looks like even if they haven't really much hope of achieving one!—but perhaps we should describe the halo; it looks like a golden disc, the degree of gold, or colour or shade of gold, depends upon the spirituality and degree of evolution of the person concerned. If the person is very carnal, then the gold will be a very reddish colour. If the person is spiritual and learning to be more spiritual, the gold will have a greenish patina. The more spiritual the person the more does yellow appear in the gold.

About the body there are swirls of colours, actually there are more colours than can be described in Earth terms because these are colours, shades, hues, etc., beyond the body-encompassed range of words. They swirl about the head, the eyes, the nose, the mouth, and the throat, they swirl about the breasts, the umbilicus, and the sex organs, and then the swirlings become less intense about the knees, although there is considerable radiance from the backs of the knees. The colour becomes less and more uniform as the aura descends to the ankles and to the feet.

Our model is standing four feet, we said, from the floor, and so with the average person the bottom part of the egg-shaped

191

covering of the aura will be just touching the floor four feet below the pedal extremities of the model. The sheath is egg-shaped with the pointed end down. If you extend your arms at full length, then normally you would be just touching the outer limits of the auric sheath.

The colours of the aura flow and twirl, and intertwine with other colours, it is a constant shimmering of other colours, and although it is a remarkably poor illustration I can only say that as colours of spilled oil or petroleum shimmer upon water, so do the colours of the aura shimmer upon a person, but more so.

Every colour has meaning, every striation has meaning. Not only that, but the direction of flow has meaning too. Imagine that you have an egg and you wrap around that egg all manner of silks of different colours, you wind them backwards and forth, up and down, never using the same colour twice; that will give you a crude, a very crude idea, of what the aura looks like.

You see the aura, you see the etheric, and you see within the sharp burning light which is the life-force itself. It is rather difficult to explain, but you can see all three without one interfering with the others. Perhaps a good way to illustrate it would be this; you are sitting out in the open, and you have a big landscape in front of you. Now to your sight you have vision from a few inches from your face to limitless miles. If you want to focus on your hand you raise your hand in front of your face and you can see the lines on your palm. As you see this you can still be conscious of the view in the background, but it does not intrude on nor distract your study of your hand.

That represents, let us say, you looking at the aura and the auric sheath. Now let us go a stage farther; ten feet away from you there is a person sitting on a chair, you can look at that person and see him or her clearly. You can still be aware of your hand close to your face, and still be aware of the landscape in the distance, and neither the distant landscape nor the closeness of your hand impinges on your study of the person sitting ten feet from you. That is as looking at the etheric.

Now to look at the life-force shining so brightly between the brain and the Kundalini, one can say that we raise our eyes away from the person sitting in the chair and we survey the landscape, perhaps the setting Sun, or if you prefer and more

suitable to this illustration, the rising Sun! You can be aware of the rising Sun and you can study that landscape without being affected by the person sitting in the chair ten feet away from you, or by your hand which is a few inches from you. Thus it is clear that you can see aura, etheric, and Kundalini force depending on which way you shift or focus your clairvoyant sight.

The purpose of the black velvet background is that it avoids people becoming distracted. For example, if you have a light-switch on the wall, or a picture, or a mirror, then your sight becomes instinctively attracted by a reflection or a glittering point of light, and if your physical sight becomes so distracted it can distract your clairvoyant sight. For best results one should have a matt black background, one quite without pattern, and of course you must have a nude model because if your model has clothes then your clairvoyant sight is going to be led astray by colour-emanations from the clothes. In just the same way, if you are looking at the Sun and you pull curtains across the window, the light of the Sun undergoes an apparent change depending upon the colour of the curtains.

Another way to look at it is—you have an electric light burning, it has no shade so you see the colour actually emitted by the NAKED bulb. Now, if you are going to put a coloured shade over the bulb the apparent colour will be distorted by the intermingling of the natural colour of the unshaded bulb, and the colour of the material of the shade, and so you will be led astray. We get a similar thing in photography when, if you want to take a photograph in colour using daylight film but you take a photograph by artificial light, we get all our colour renderings wrong. So—if you are serious you must have a nude model, there is nothing wrong with the nude model, remember, but only by the thoughts of people who are led astray by something we shall deal with in Chapter Eleven in one of the questions about sex!

The old Chinese—later copied by Japanese—liked to think that all the organs of the body had little men looking after them. Well, they weren't so far wrong, you know, because all the organs of the body are connected to the brain by various nerves, and the brain is aware of what is happening to every part of every organ of the body. The functions of an organ used to be within the conscious control of the human, but now, because people neglected such things, control of the organs is

194

largely automatic. There are many Adepts who can consciously control the functioning of their organs. In India fakirs who are usually debased Adepts give demonstrations of such control. They can stick a knife through the palm of their hand, and on withdrawing the knife they can cause the wound to heal within minutes. These things are very real, but nowadays control of the organs is largely lost.

The illustration with this chapter is well worth studying because you will see that the fanciful artist has caused little monks and acolytes under the supervision of lamas to control all the functions of the body. This is much the same as the 'monitor system' which warns the brain when any damage or malfunction is about to occur. It is also worth visualising your body as being controlled by these little people, because then when you want to meditate deeply, you, by controlling these little people, can obtain complete meditation. All you have to do is, as stated in various others of my books, make the little people leave the body and congregate outside the body so that your consciousness is withdrawn. You make the little people march up your legs from your toes, and then your toes and your legs become relaxed and at peace. Make the little people leave your kidneys and your bowels and your gall bladder, etc., and you will find that you do really get complete and utter relaxation, and when you have such complete and utter relaxation you are able to do the deepest of deep meditations and obtain what are truly revelations from another world. Try it, but first of all read up about this system in others of my books. I do not want to go into it all here, or someone will say that I have nothing else to write about and I have taken to repeating myself!

CHAPTER ELEVEN

YOU WRITE THIS!

FROM Africa and India, from Australia and America, from countries all over the world—even from behind the 'Iron Curtain'—come letters. THOUSANDS of them. Questions—questions—questions. How to become a saint. How to use a mantra and win the Irish Sweepstake, how to have babies, how NOT to have babies. From Malaysia and Manchester, from Uruguay and Jugoslavia the letters come. Questions, and MORE questions. They usually fall into a certain pattern, so in this chapter I am going to reply to YOUR more common questions. Keep calm, I am most certainly not going to mention anyone by name!

QUESTION: I have read a lot of newspaper stories about you, and before buying any of your books I thought I would write and ask if your books are true.

ANSWER: I give a definite assurance that all my books are true. All that of which I write is my own experience, and I can do ALL those things of which I write. Having given that assurance, let me say something else! My books are true, yes, but surely 'doubters' cannot see the wood for the trees. What does it matter WHO I am, it is what I WRITE that is important. Throughout the years hordes of 'experts' have tried to prove me wrong. They have failed. If I am a fake, where do I get the knowledge which others are now copying? All my books contain my own personal experiences, nothing of it is the so-called 'automatic writing' beloved of the Press. I am neither possessed nor obsessed, I am just a person trying to do a very very difficult task in the face of bigotry and jealousy. There are those in 'High Places' in India and elsewhere who could help, but who prostitute their religion to politics and so, for political reasons etc., they deny the truth of what I write!

My books have done much to 'popularise' Tibet and show people that Tibet is good and spiritual, yet none of this is taken into account. A stronger leadership might have enabled Tibet to avoid Communist aggression, but no war was ever won by sitting on the fence and waiting to see 'which way the cat jumps!'

I receive thousands of letters from people who state that the truth of my books is self-evident, and I am proud indeed to be able to say that during the past ten years I have received only four unpleasant or abusive letters. To return to the first paragraph of 'ANSWER', let me add that it is most amusing to watch people squabbling over an Author's identity and missing the whole point of his books. Poor old Shakespeare must think that his Bacon is in the fire when he 'tunes-in' to some of the clever clever people who 'know' that Bacon wrote Shakespeare, and that Shakespeare was Bacon! Who wrote the Bible? The Disciples? Their descendants? A gang of monks monkeying with the original Scripts? What does it matter? Only the written word matters, not the name or identity of the author.

So to answer the question: yes, all my books are true!

QUESTION: What is Nirvana? Why do Indians just want to sit down and do nothing and hope everything will come right for them in the end?

ANSWER: The Indians do not think that at all. Nirvana is not the extinction of everything; it is utterly impossible to live in a void, in a state of vacuum. To live one has to progress and develop. Consider, for instance, a car. First of all a prototype is developed and the car is tried and tested on the works' testing track and then perhaps, if it is a good quality car, sent to the mountains of Switzerland so that it may be tested both in Switzerland and in, perhaps, South American jungles. When the car is tested certain faults develop and they can be eliminated, the purpose of testing is to find out what is wrong and how to put it right.

The same applies to humans; humans have to be tested to find their weak points, and when the weak points are discovered they can be overcome. That is being done all the time in the ordinary stages of evolution. You will agree that many new models of radios or cars, or anything else—space rockets, if you like—have faults, later models are better because the faults have been eliminated.

Nirvana is the stage in humans when faults have been eliminated. So the Indian and the erudite Easterner tries to overcome his faults, he tries to eliminate lusts and other quite interesting but harmful vices. You can say that he tries to live

197

in a state of nothingness so far as vice is concerned, he wants nothing to do with vice, he is only interested in perfection. So instead of seeking to obtain loads of nothing he tries to get rid of vice to leave more room for good.

The old idea that Nirvana is a state of nothingness where a person sits in mental and spiritual vacuity is false because there were wrong translations. Westerners think they know so much, they try to put into concrete terms that which are mere abstract whispers.

Nirvana, then, is the state wherein there is no evil, wherein one is like the three wise monkeys, who see no evil, speak no evil, and do no evil, and when there is no evil there is room for more good. Isn't that so?

QUESTION: Churches, missionaries, occultists, they are all out for money, they are all grabbers, everyone wants to take from we poor people who have to work for an honest living. Now, you tell me, why should I give, why should I bother with this old system of tithes? What's it going to do for me?

ANSWER: Well, of course, if that's how you feel about it there is little point in giving, because to give under conditions like this is much the same as going along to the local Drink Shop and trying to buy a pint of beer. You pay your money and you get a certain concrete object in return. Giving from the spiritual sense is utterly, utterly different from that, and you just cannot mix the two forms of giving any more than—it is said—you can mix your drinks. But let us look at it a bit more closely.

All Churches, all religions, realise the necessity of sacrifice, and in the very early days of Christianity the Christian Church realised that it was utterly essential to 'sacrifice' to give. In the early days of the Church, and even now in most parts of the world, the Christian Church demands a tenth of one's income. In England they call it 'a tithe', and under old English laws—ecclesiastical laws, of course—the Church was entitled to a tenth of one's possessions, and one did not escape even if one was not a church-goer because in England years ago one could actually be fined for not attending church. It was cheaper to go to church and listen to 'the words of wisdom' and then put some money in the collecting box. If you evaded 'the words of wisdom' you had to pay more by way of fine.

It was necessary that people gave a tenth of their possessions so that the Church could be financed. There were priests of various kinds who had to be able to live. Someone had to pay them, so as the Churches were in power they saw that Mr. and Mrs. Layman of the congregation did all the paying.

It is essential that a person shall give before they can receive. Giving is like opening a door, if we do not open the door we cannot admit those good things which are ready to come in to us. If we are not prepared to give, then we cannot put ourselves in a receptive frame of mind. Actually it is almost a problem in mechanics.

In ages far beyond the Christian teachings, right at the dawn of history itself, the Ancients believed in sacrifice because they did not go by the words of some self-styled 'scientist', they knew by actual experience that sacrifice was essential, and they sacrificed that which was of most value to them. They sacrificed a valuable creature, a ram, or in some instances a son. This was not done with the thought of cruelty, but with the thought of doing that which they considered would be pleasing in the sight of God. They thought that if they gave that which was of most value to them it would show God the high value which they placed upon his pleasure.

In the Far East it is the custom to give very freely to those in need. The monk with his bowl is not just a beggar who is making himself a nuisance; the housekeeper, or the woman of the house, looks forward to giving to the monk who calls at her door. She will reserve choice pieces of food for him. In many parts of India where there is extreme poverty people still keep aside food for a monk who calls and this entails very considerable sacrifice, and it means that the people of the house are always on the hunger-borderline. Yet the sacrifice is made willingly, and it is regarded as an honour if a monk calls at the door for food, the monk never has to ask, he just goes to the door and the woman of the house will see him there, will take his bowl, and will fill it with food. If she is very, very poor she will put that which she has available in the bowl, and the monk will then go to perhaps three or four houses until he has enough. But those of the neighbours who are not called upon on that day will look upon it as a sign of disfavour, because they well know the merit to be derived from giving, particularly when giving means sacrifice.

To digress again (digression is one of my vices, perhaps I shall get rid of that in Nirvana!) it is most regrettable that many people take fright at the mention of money although, actually, they love the stuff dearly. People expect to have the knowledge of ages without paying a penny for it, people expect a man to live throughout a very long life and to study all the time, and then to give away all that knowledge, all that he has gained, just for nothing, just so that he can get a good name I suppose. But what happens if you want to train to be a doctor or an undertaker (that was unfortunate, wasn't it!). Well, supposing he wants to train for anything, a man expects to have to pay for his knowledge, but when it comes to occult knowledge everyone thinks they are going to be in on it 'for free'.

People forget that even those who have occult knowledge have to live, have to eat, have to have clothing unless one is willing to be charged with indecent exposure, and if one is so busy learning and so busy teaching that one cannot earn a living, how is one to eat and to clothe oneself? Sackcloth and ashes have gone out of fashion, and there seems to be a shortage of fig leaves.

In the East hermits do not earn money because there is not much money to be earned. People do not pay money for knowledge because most times there is no money with which to pay, they pay by service instead. The student provides the food and the clothes, and the teacher provides the teaching, so they get on, each knowing and sharing the difficulties of the other and each making allowances for the difficulties of the other. But in the Western world where commerce reigns supreme and where the pound sterling or the dollar is almost as good as a God, money is all that matters. If you do not have money, then you are a fake or a failure. I will tell you that I have had some remarkable experiences in this connection; however, perhaps that will come in another book when I write of my experiences with the Press and a few jealous people in Germany and elsewhere. But now we must get back to our giving.

You must give in order that you may receive. People ask for things, people pray for things, people pray for money, for health, it does not matter what it is, people pray that they may be given something, they never say what they may give instead, and it is a definite statement of fact that if one is always asking for things one becomes as servile as a dog which merely asks for a pat from its master's hand.

There is a definite occult law which says that you cannot receive unless you are first ready to give. Imagine that you are

200

inside a room with the door and the windows shut, not locked, mind, just pushed shut. If you wish you can have the door made of thin paper, and the windows also. Outside, piled in heaps, with sacks all ready so it may be carried away, are jewels, riches worth a king's ransom or more. Outside there are all the things you have ever dreamed of and wanted. Yet if you could not push outside that paper door you could not get at all those jewels which would be yours for the taking. If you will not make the first simple move such as the symbolical pushing through the paper door, then you get nothing.

Of course this is symbolic; the act of opening the door symbolises the act of giving, because unless and until one is ready to give, and until one has actually given with a good grace, one is shutting the door on any possibility of obtaining that which one wants, not merely shutting the door but locking it and barring it, and pushing the furniture against it so that it cannot be opened. A person who is always asking for things and never giving is a dissatisfied person, a frustrated person, one who does not know his or her path in life, one who is searching, but not too energetically, for 'something', one who is expecting others to do everything for him or for her but who is not willing to give even the slightest bit of energy in order that the matter may be speeded.

Frequently a man or a woman will go to a metaphysician seeking a cure for some illness, perhaps an illness caused by an over-excited imagination. Well, in that case the person seeking aid must be willing to give—give of co-operation, for example, because a person cannot be cured until he or she co-operates, a person is wasting time in going to a metaphysician, or any other kind of physician, unless he or she is willing to co-operate. So many people say in effect, 'Well, if you cure me it will be over my dead body,' or words to that effect.

You may say as so many do, 'Well, what have I to give? I am not rich, how can I give? I work hard for all I get, I'm not going to give to somebody who just sits down and makes wise remarks.' The answer is, unless you are ready to give with good grace you are on the wrong path, you should be going backwards instead of forwards. For others who are really trying the answer is that if you have no money you can give in service, in love and care, to someone in need. If a good deed has been done to you why not give by doing a good deed to someone else? We get nothing without paying for it, and we only get that for which we pay. You would not expect a luxurious motor-car if you were prepared to only pay the price of a bicycle.

There is such a lot of misunderstanding about 'give'. People think, 'Oh, they are always begging, they always want this, they always want that, they cannot be any good if they always want money.' It is too easy to sit back and think, 'Now, what is there that I don't want, what is there that I am tired of, what can I get rid of to cut down on the load of rubbish? I know, I will give away that old so-and-so because then I shall be justified in buying a better one for myself.' That is useless, that is a waste of time and is a mockery. It is wholly useless to give that which entails no sacrifice, that which occasions no loss. Some people are born to money—then let them give money to advance some good cause, for no matter how much money a man may accrue during his lifetime he cannot take a single cent out of this world. No person has ever succeeded in taking a material object beyond that which we term the Veil of Death, but every one of us takes the learning which we have gained through our experiences on Earth, we take a distillate of all that which we have absorbed. The more we learn, and the more we learn of what is good, the richer we are when we go to that which is truly the Greater Reality, whereas those who have sought only money in this life for their own glorification, are nothing when they have no money with them.

You may have power, then with your power help others, for your power is only lent to you to see how you will use it or abuse it. The man of millions, the leader of a country—they are not always good men, they are men who are given certain things in order that they may learn. Let us remember also that here we are as actors on a stage taking the dress which suits us for the moment, in just the same way as one takes theatrical properties to enable us to live out the part which is our lot.

Remember, also, that the prince of today is the beggar of tomorrow, and the beggar of today is the prince of tomorrow. No matter how rich, how powerful one has been in past lives, when one comes to the last life in this round of existence one comes to trouble, to lack of comfort, to hardship and mis-understanding. That is because one comes to clear up the odd bits and pieces, one comes to pay all the debts that one owes. It is much the same as a person going away to a fresh house,

202

but first having to clear up all the corners, all the cellars, and the garrets of an old house. But let us deal a bit more with sacrifice.

Abraham, Moses, and others, millions and millions of others, used sacrifice. Do you know what sacrifice means? Think of 'sacrament'. Well, what does 'sacrament' mean? Sacrifice, of course; only by sacrifice could one secure the help of Higher Powers, but to sacrifice you must do without something yourself in order that someone else may benefit, in order that someone else may be helped. Sacrifice may call upon you to surrender something to which you are attached, but which would be a great blessing to a number of other people or to help another person who has not had your own good fortune.

Are you a Christian? If so you will remember that the Bible says, 'It is more blessed to give than to receive.' To give opens up the well springs of our potential for good, opens up the gates whereby we may obtain that which we want to obtain. It is useless to give in order that you may be known as a holy person of good intentions. It is useless to have your donations for charity printed in the newspapers because that would not be giving, that would be buying, you would instead, with your donations, be buying publicity for yourself.

Let us think, then, that until we give that which entails some effort, some sacrifice, some loss, then we cannot receive anything which is worth having. So—isn't it worth giving?

QUESTION: People are stated to have various faults which impede their progress on the Upward Path. What are the main faults stopping one's progress?

ANSWER: All right, let us have a look at some of these faults. Undoubtedly all of you can look at faults in a spirit of scientific detachment, because all you who are reading this are either on the way to eliminating those faults if you have not already done so. We must take a look at faults as well as at virtues. After all, doctors look at dead bodies and dissect them so that they may be enlightened and educated by the faults and the corruptions which they find in those dead bodies.

One of the worst faults is that of scandal. Scandal is the sabotage of the soul, not the victim's soul, mind, but the one who starts and continues the scandal. People love scandal, people just love to say things which will reduce to ashes the good character of another person, and if there is no truth in it then it makes them feel even better. 'I'm as good as he is!

204

Why should he get away with everything, he must have got faults somewhere!!'

It is a case that in some countries one cannot be sued for libel or slander if one is telling lies but only if one is repeating the truth! So people like scandal, they like, by words, to injure those who they have not the courage to attack physically. Scandal, lying rumour, is an insidious, evil attack on one's own soul because in repeating tittle-tattle and making up rumours and lies, the person perpetrating such things definitely injures his own electrical charges, which is the same as taking a poison which attacks one's own soul.

Perjury is another vice which injures the perjurer eventually far more than the one who is perjured. People hear a little bit of rumour, a little bit of scandal, but it is not enough, it is not dirty enough, so a little bit is added to make it worse, then it is passed on as fact to some other person who adds a bit more. That again injures the utterer's soul. Frequently jealousy— another great vice—is the cause of rumour. One man simply cannot bear the sight of another, one man is absolutely jealous of the imagined successes of another, and so he works to cut that man down to size, he starts a whispering campaign or he damns with faint praise. It is a fact, you know, that one can injure a person terribly by saying, 'Well, I suppose he did his best, after all, we must give him credit for that.' Then such a person, to the superficial hearer, gets a reputation as being a reasonable man and praising even under the most difficult circumstances.

Another vice is greed; greed is akin to jealousy. Mr. X is terribly jealous of the success of Mr. Y. Mr. X is greedy for money, money-hunger it is called in some countries, and the greed feeds the jealousy and the more jealous Mr. X becomes, the more greedy he becomes. All this is deadly poison to the soul, for the soul is a very real thing, as you should know by now. When we indulge in scandal or perjury or give way to greed or jealousy we are making opposition charges to our soul, and that really can hurt us.

Nirvana is the elimination of things like jealousy and greed, scandal, etc., and the best way to progress is to remember, 'Do unto others as you would have them do unto you.'

QUESTION: I understand that people can pick up a stone, a cigarette case, or a handkerchief, and they can obtain impressions about the owner of such things. How is this done?

ANSWER: You refer to psychometry which is receiving tactile impressions which in an occult part of the brain are transformed into pictures or visions. Now you may wonder how it is possible to pick up any impressions from an inanimate object, but let us make it clearer by giving a simple little illustration.

Supposing a person has been holding a coin in his hand, then the coin will gain warmth from the person's hand, and if that coin be placed upon a table with other coins you would have no difficulty at all in detecting which of the coins had been held. It would be the one that had some warmth to it. That is just a physical thing, but it will show you that there are impressions.

If you want to try psychometry you should first of all retire to your sanctum or meditation room. You should start off as if you were going to meditate, but then you should pick up the object whose history you desire to know; pick it up in the left hand and let it rest lightly on the palm of the left hand. Try to let your mind become blank or receptive, you may feel that you don't know what you are looking for, you do not know what to expect, you just do not know how to proceed. Well, sit there and just do nothing. Imagine that you have a big black square in front of you and you are going to see pictures appear on that big black square.

First of all you will receive impressions rather than pictures. You may receive an impression that a person is unhappy or that the person is happy, you may get vague glimpses of some particular surroundings which clearly are not your surroundings. First of all you will be inclined to doubt that you are receiving anything, but keep that article wrapped up when you are not using it so that others cannot touch it, and practise with it. You will have to make repeated attempts at that same article before you can realise how much is imagination and how much is psychometric power. Do this several times, do it every night for a week, and you will find at the end of the week that you have certain definite conclusions about the article.

If, after some minutes, you fail to get any impression at all about the article, put it either to the left or right side of your temple. If that doesn't work, put it at the back of your head just where your head joins your neck. It could easily be that you are by nature left-handed, and in that case use your right hand instead of the left. But the main thing is to experiment with different positions—left hand, right hand, left temple, right temple, or back of the head. Then you just let your mind go blank and try to draw into your mind the impressions which are being transmitted by the object.

Remember that when you see a stone in the road or a bird in the sky your eyes are not reaching up to the bird or reaching down to the stone; what you do receive is an impression or vibration transmitted by the stone or the bird. In this particular case, though, you get impressions which you call 'sight'. In psychometry, where you also receive impressions, you go deeper than the surface and so you get your visual sensations inside the occult part of the brain. It is quite a simple matter with practice.

The best way to practise is to get a person whom you truly like to pick up a stone from the beach, and wash it carefully with running water. Then the person holds the stone to his or her forehead and thinks strongly a message to you, such as, 'I picked up this stone on Monday (or whatever the day is).' Then the person carefully wraps the stone in tissue paper and gives it to you without touching it any more. If you practise things like that you will soon see that psychometry works.

QUESTION: You are not a Christian, you are not one brought up to the Bible, so what do you think of the Bible?

ANSWER: Well, you have to remember, to start with, that the Bible was written many many years after the actual events related. Further, the Bible has been translated, and mistranslated, and retranslated many many times. The Great Priest So-and-So demanded a new translation, then someone else came along with a fresh translation, and then King James I or somebody decided that he would have an authorised translation. Through all this, though, there is a great strain of truth, because the real truths never die, they can be concealed to a certain extent, but to the discerning the truths are always there. In the matter of the Bible there are strange records written in the mystery languages of prehistoric ages, but you cannot always take the Bible at its actual face value. You would not take the actual black and white letters precisely as they were written, you cannot interpret them literally, you have to use symbology.

The Bible is an esoteric book, and of course it is connected with the Indian, Chaldean, and Egyptian systems of symbology. Christ went to Tibet and after passing through India and studying Indian religions, He actually went and studied in Tibet and came back to the Western world with a religion basically of the East, but which had been altered to suit the West. If you doubt this remember that if you study the Indian systems you will find that all the glyphs and numbers are to be found in the Indian systems, and if only these wretched 'scientists' would have a correct reading of the Bible, bearing in mind anthropology, ethnology, chronology, physiology, and all that, they would have a very much greater understanding of all that there was in history, for the Bible is a most invaluable aid—if one can read it correctly—to what went on in bygone ages. Before one can read the Bible one has to know all about the Chaldean Hierophants, from which one gets the knowledge of the Quabalah.

If you will carefully study the first five books of the Old Testament you will find that they are actually legends, and they are quite a useful dissertation on philosophical phases of world cosmogony.

Everyone knows the story of Moses and how he was found in the bulrushes by the Pharaoh's daughter. Well, it may interest you to know that all this happened about 1,000 years before because there are certain tiles, known as the Babylonian Tiles, which give the story of King Sargon. He lived a long time before Moses, a very long time before Moses, about 1,000 years before actually, and this story about a baby boy being found in the bulrushes was the story of King Sargon. The book of Exodus was not written by Moses, as has been generally believed, but instead was 'made up' from various prior sources by Ezra, and in connection with this the Book of Job is the oldest in the Hebrew system and certainly dates long before Moses.

Furthermore, any of the great Bible stories such as Creation, the Fall of Man, and the Blaming of Women, the Flood and the Tower of Babel, were all written long before the time of Moses. These stories are actually rewritten versions of what archaeologists know as the Chaldean tablets.

The Jews obtained their first ideas about creation from Moses, and Moses got his ideas about creation from the Egyptians, and the whole affair, which was taken from the Chaldo–Arkadian accounts, was rewritten by Ezra. You will find that the God is the Logos. You will also find that the Bible actually starts with a mistranslation where it says, 'In the beginning God created the Heavens and the Earth.' It was not the actual physical Earth that was referred to but the upper and the lower, the visible and the invisible.

There are a lot of discrepancies in the Bible; for example consider the first part of Genesis: God said, 'Let there be firmaments,' and a second God obeyed and made the firmaments. The first God said, 'Let there be light,' and the second God made some light. From which it is clear that God commands some other God who must have been a lesser God because he did the bidding of the first.

'Let there be light.' That does not mean daylight, sunlight, or artificial light, it means instead spiritual light, it means lift the soul of Man out of darkness that he may perceive the greatness of God.

Again, Adam was not the first man created. The Bible tells us that because in Genesis 4. 16, 17 it is said that Cain went into the land of Moab with the intention of buying a wife. Now if Adam was the first man created, what was the point of Cain going into Moab in search of a wife, because there just wouldn't be any! Actually, Adam is a composite of ten Sephiroth, and of course the Father, Son, and Holy Ghost is the three of the upper triad of the archetypal world, while the second Adam is an esoteric composition who represents the seven groups of men—the seven groups of mankind, and which thus formed the first human root race.

There were the Atlanteans who made a lot of researches, and if you will read the Bible properly, esoterically, that is, you will find that the seven keys which open the mysteries of the seven great root races can be traced back to Atlantean times. So the Egyptians obtained information from the Atlanteans, the Jews obtained information from the Egyptians and altered it a bit, and then the Christians came along and they took all that information and distorted it quite considerably, and then the translators who put it into Latin softened all sorts of comments and made them fit in with the new Christian ideals and ideas, just as nowadays politicians alter history to suit their own country. I shall have something more to say about religion later in this chapter, but that is enough about the Bible for now.

QUESTION: Do you believe in the story of the Garden of Eden? Write to me and tell me what you think the Garden of Eden really means.

209

ANSWER: In the answer to the question above I blithely stated that we were finished with the Bible for the time being. Well, we have to open it again to answer this question which is, do I believe the tale about the Garden of Eden, do I believe about the Fall of Adam and Eve, and that it was caused by their new-found interest in the difference between each other's bodies. In other words, as I read the question, do I think that sex has been the ruination of mankind. No, of course I do not. I think all that is rubbish. In the time of Pope Gregory, often referred to as Pope Gregory the Great, the vast Palatine Library containing many of the original manuscripts was destroyed. Some of the manuscripts were original papyrii, and they went back to almost the date of the start of Christianity.

The Library was destroyed. The Pope of those days thought that men were learning too much, and if men learned more than the priests wanted them to know they would be a danger to the priests in that they would be asking questions which the priests found it difficult to answer.

Pope Gregory thought that men should start out again without benefit of the writings of other people. He also had an idea that the moment was opportune to rewrite the history of Christianity and edit it in such a way that the power of the priests was not diminished. So the Libraries were burned, priceless manuscripts were lost to the average man and woman. Some of those manuscripts in duplicate form had been hidden in caves in other parts of the world, but to those who can read the Akashic Record all manuscripts, all knowledge, is always available.

In the case of Adam and Eve we must remember that so-called 'original sin' was not sex, it was not anything at all to do with the physical body but was an abstract thing. The original sin was pride, false pride, an inferior people setting up as the equal of the Gods. Man and, of course, Woman, thought that they were the equal of the Gods and so they rebelled against the Gods. The Garden of Eden was the young Earth, the Earth which was only then becoming fitted to be the home of a new race, the race of Man. You will appreciate that there have been many races upon the Earth, many forms of life.

Before Man as we know him now appeared on this Earth there was another race similar to Man, not shaggy apes as has been popularly supposed, but a completely different type of person upon completely different continents of the Earth, continents which have long sunk beneath the surface of the ocean so that other continents could rise, and other nations rise with them.

These people were different. They had somewhat different anatomical features which we need not go into on this occasion. Their skin was purple, and they were rather larger and rather taller than humans of the present day. These people were intelligent, too intelligent for their own good, perhaps, and they were the ones who lived in the so-called Garden of Eden.

According to ancient records Earth is a colony, a colony which was populated by people from far beyond this Universe. At the time of the Garden of Eden some of the people—the Overseers—came to this Earth to supervise the new race of Man, the purple people, and the Overseers were giants according to Man's perceptions. They were, in fact, half as big again as the people of the Earth, and so we have a racial memory of the days when Gods, giants, walked upon the Earth.

The Overseers who, after all, were only humans of a different kind, fraternised rather too freely with the purple people of the Earth, they became altogether too friendly, and the inferior people of the Earth had inflated ideas of their own importance; they thought that if the Gods associated with them they must be wonderful. And so they were impressed with the strange, strange weapons and devices of the Gods, they were impressed with the boxes which showed pictures and produced voices and music out of the air, and they plotted and schemed whereby they could overthrow the Gods, the Overseers, and obtain those devices for themselves.

Strange vehicles known as the Chariots of the Gods flamed across the sky by day and by night. The Gods were busy seeing about the new Earth, seeing about the welfare of the people of the new Earth, but they still had time to fraternise with the people.

A scheme was concocted whereby one young lady who was particularly attractive to the Overseers should make herself even more attractive to one particular Overseer. And the plan was that while the Gods were otherwise engaged, one might say, the men would kill the Gods.

The Gods became aware of the plot, they became aware that mankind was very, very faulty, they became aware that mankind had treacherous thoughts, lusted after power, had pride, false pride. And so mankind was driven away from that particularly pleasant spot; in other words, they were driven out of the Garden of Eden by angels with flaming swords. Now just think, supposing a savage who had never seen a jet plane saw one of these things going across the sky roaring like a blowtorch, wouldn't it be a Chariot of the Gods? Supposing he saw a gun which was being fired, he saw smoke and perhaps a bit of flame coming out of the barrel, couldn't that be a flaming sword? He would have to call it something, and he wouldn't know about revolvers; a flaming sword is good enough—it got down through the history books, and all that.

In the course of time the natural evolution of the Earth caused earthquakes and tremors, caused continents to sink and continents to rise. Most of the people of the Earth were destroyed in various catastrophes and calamities, but certain people were refugees and they escaped to high land. Certain of them, in fact, live on through their racial memories. For instance, have you ever seen a native of darkest Africa who was not black but almost a purplish-black? Think of that. You will agree that there are already at least three races on this Earth, the black people, the yellow people, and the white people. They are three different races, and there is quite a lot of discord among them, a racial discord, as if each one thinks that the other one is an intruder.

So we come back to the Garden of Eden, and we find that when the Gods walked upon the Earth they were kind and considerate. They were not Gods, of course, but the Overseers from right out of this Universe. Humans tried to take advantage of them, and the original sin of humans was not sex, which is a natural function of humans, but pride and rebellion.

Of course the Church in the time of Pope Gregory and, in fact, many times in the Church's history, had a great phobia against sex. They had no phobia against pride. So because it suited their purpose, they said that the Fall of Man was through Woman, the Fall of Man was because Woman tempted him with sex, Woman was the sinner, the temptress, the offender every time.

There is nothing in the Bible, nor in true Christian belief, which supports the statement that Man's fall was through sex. Christ himself was never opposed to women, He never thought that Woman was an inferior creature to be treated as a dog or worse.

212

St. Augustine and many others took advantage of the re-writing of the Bible to preach even more and more violently against sex. Augustine was one of those who was terribly, terribly opposed to sex even in marriage. It is perhaps worth a thought here that there is no greater opponent of drink than the reformed drunkard, there is no greater opponent of vice, so-called, than the person who has been reformed from vice.

CHAPTER TWELVE

RELIGION AND SCIENCE

QUESTION: What do you think of religion?

ANSWER: Oh good gracious! I thought I had closed the Bible for the present, but of course I must say that I am 'for' religion. A short time ago I had a letter from a student priest. He took me to task, he said, 'In one of your books you refer to the Convention of Constantinople in the Year 60. I cannot find anything about it in the Bible.'

There was a convention at Constantinople in the Year 60. There is nothing in the present-day Bible about it because the Church authorities have rewritten the Bible quite a number of times. Even now there are frequent meetings in Rome to decide what shall be taught and what shall be suppressed, and what religious sect shall be recognised or ostracised. Religion is constantly in the making. It is clear that the teaching as it was 2,000 years ago would not necessarily be the most suitable now, it has to be brought up to date to deal with modern requirements. My student priest friend wrote to me in some consternation, some anger even, saying that I had misled him. I have had the pleasure of replying and saying that it was not I, but his superiors who misled him. He should consult books and papyrii and come to his own conclusion.

I am not trying to change anyone's religion. I firmly believe in a God, I may call Him by a different name than that used by a Christian, or a Jew, or a Mohammedan, but I believe in a God and I am sure that there must be religion. Religion gives mental and spiritual discipline. If more religion was taught now there would be less juvenile delinquency.

I am all for religion. I am strongly in favour of priests provided they teach the truth, provided that they recognise that all men have a right to their own belief. Some time ago in Europe I appeared in Buddhist robes and crossed the street to a taxi; a priest of a certain sect saw me and nearly collapsed as if he was looking at the Devil himself! He crossed himself several times, and hurried away quite rapidly with complete loss of dignity. I looked on in amusement. I believe that the greatest rule of all is—Do as you would be done by. It doesn't matter to me if a man wears a particular form of dress, it doesn't matter to me if he is a Christian priest or a Jewish rabbi; if he is a good man I respect him. If he is a sham in some priestly vestment, then I despise him, or sorrow that he has not the perceptions to know the harm he is doing. For the priests of any sect at all have a great, great responsibility, people look up to them and expect help and truth.

Much of that which is taught in religion, any religion, not just Christianity, any religion, or in history, is altered to suit the political powers of the time or the time itself. Consider again Sir Francis Drake—in England he is a great hero, in Spain he is regarded as a quite unmentionable pirate. Which is right?

To bring the matter closer home—how about the *Graf Spee*? The Germans thought this was a heroic ship manned by a heroic crew, but the British and the Americans thought that this was a pirate ship preying upon peaceful merchantmen. So the British destroyed the pride of Germany's navy. Which do you think was right? The German viewpoint, or the British?

In Hitler's Germany history was destroyed and rewritten. In Russia, if one would believe the current history books, most of the great inventions in the world came from Russia. I wonder if Henry Ford would be called 'Fordski' in Russia? I have read that the Russians claim they have invented the aeroplane, the telephone, the motor-car, they seem to have invented the word 'No'—niet. They also invented the cold war. However, we are not dealing with politics, but I will say that the danger is not Russia but China.

So, do not believe all that is in print, but think for yourself, and if you want something stronger than thought, if you cannot get to the great libraries of the world, get busy with your astral travelling. When you can do astral travelling you can consult the Akashic Record, and the Akashic Record cannot be tampered with, there is no way of erasing the Akashic Record, no way of concealing true knowledge. It is available for those who have eyes with which to see, and for those who have ears with which to hear.

Quite amusing about religions really—if one forgets that religion is merely a mental and spiritual discipline. Some religions say one must not eat pork, another says you must not eat meat on Friday. One religion says the body from the neck down must be covered while the face is uncovered. Another religion says one can be as naked as a boiled egg provided the face is covered.

I say—Do as you would be done by—that is the best religion of all.

QUESTION: You say some unkind things about scientists, but don't you think that only scientists can save us?

ANSWER: Well, it depends on what you mean by scientists! I believe that many of the so-called scientists are just chairpolishers. People like Royce of Rolls-Royce, Edison, and Ford, and a few like that, they were real scientists, they had not been to schools where their thought was cemented into rock-bound channels; in other words, they did not think that things were impossible, they had never been conditioned to think that a thing was impossible, so they went out and did the impossible. Many universities specialise in teaching their students that unless Professor Dogsbody or Professor Catswhisker does it no one can do it. That is all nonsense. I think the 'educated' scientist is a menace because he is 'educated' to believe that nothing can be done unless he or his fellows do it.

Some people think that in the matter of parallel worlds I should have quoted Einstein. But why should I quote Einstein? I can assure anyone who is interested that there are books about Einstein and his theories, and so anyone interested is recommended to purchase suitable books so that they may study the theories of Einstein.

Einstein dealt with theories. He theorised according to the facts available at the time, but you see, we must not always be led astray by what appears to be the obvious, because the obvious is not always so obvious. For instance, a scientist was studying the behaviour of fleas, he thought he could correlate the behaviour of fleas' psychosomatic patterns with that of humans. After all, fleas thrive exceedingly well on human blood, so our scientist went in for the study of fleas, an itching process, if I may say so.

With great care and the expenditure of much time, he trained a medium-sized flea to jump over a matchbox every time he said, 'Go.' Then when the flea had the idea, the scientist pulled off two of the flea's six legs. 'Go,' he said. The flea jumped again, and was able to repeat the performance although not so successfully as before. The scientist grunted with satisfaction, and pulled off two more of the six legs. 'Go,'

216

" Do unto others

as YOU would be

done by ! "

said the scientist. Feebly the flea did so, and the scientist nodded his approval. Reaching for the flea he pulled off the poor creature's last two legs. Unfortunately now that the flea no longer had legs the scientist could shout 'Go' endlessly and the flea would not move. The scientist, after many tries, nodded his wise old head and wrote in his report, 'A flea's hearing is in its legs. When it loses two legs it cannot hear so well and so does not jump too high. When it loses all six of its legs it becomes completely deaf!'

Let us not be in the position of the scientist who tried to study fleas, let us not blind ourselves to the obvious. If Einstein is correct, then there can never be any real space travel, it would take too long, because Einstein postulated the theory that nothing could travel faster than the speed of light, and as light from distant planets may take centuries and centuries to reach us from its source, and if Einstein is correct in his theory, we cannot hope to ever move to other planets.

Fortunately Einstein is not correct. Fortunately he is correct only on the information which he possessed at the time of his theorising.

Consider the world in 18—oh, what shall we say?—1863 instead of 1963. We are back in the year 1863 then. Scientists tell us that Man will never travel at more than thirty miles an hour, for a man to move faster than that would be to tear air from his lungs, it would not be possible for a man to travel faster. Thirty miles an hour, then, is as fast as one can ever move.

There can be no aircraft in the skies, there can only be a few hot-air balloons, and for that presumably, there will have to be a lot of speakers and lecturers and those who criticise lecturers because that would be an inexhaustible source of hot air to send balloons soaring aloft. But we are told in this year 1863 that there will never be aircraft.

As Man developed more lethal inclinations and new instruments of war, it was discovered that Man could live beyond the thirty miles an hour limit, he could even go as fast as sixty miles an hour, and when the railroads were first laid down by George Stevenson people thought that the absolute ultimate had been reached in speed. In England, in fact, motor-cars were thought to be such dangerous vehicles that they had to be preceded by a man on foot and waving a red flag! But I believe they have got beyond that stage in England now in cars, and they go a little faster, almost as fast, in fact, as they do in this part of the world.

We came up with the theory not so long ago that the absolute speed limit was that imposed by sound. We were told by reputable scientists that no man would ever travel faster than the speed of sound, it was impossible. Now there are passenger aircraft being manufactured which can exceed the speed of sound. War-craft continually travel faster than the speed of sound, leaving in their wake broken windows and furious exclamations from the owners of those broken windows. Fortunately the pilots are going beyond the speed of sound and so vituperation does not reach them until they alight at their airport and find that their commanding officer is dancing with rage at the messages he has received.

We have discovered, then, that the speed of sound does not limit us, we can travel faster. And yet not so long ago people like Einstein said Man would never travel faster than the speed of sound. If these men have been proved to be incorrect in their assumption, why should it not be that Einstein also is incorrect in his theory that light is the absolute limit of speed?

When people travel beyond the speed of light they will be able to see each other and see what lies ahead of them. The only difference is that the things that they will see will be of a different colour, which will be quite an interesting thing and which will be the same, I suppose, as looking at women's artificial faces under fluorescent lighting or sodium lamps. The whole point is that if one goes travelling in excess of the speed of light, then one will be approaching the clairvoyant's stage of seeing, and will see things in four dimensions instead of three.

I would like here to quote what the great scientists have said about the Earth. Scientists said that the Earth was flat. Ancient mythology states that the Earth was flat and strange demons lurked over the edge of the flat Earth. My own experience is that most of the demons live on this Earth. No one would seriously believe now that the Earth is flat. It is a common belief that the Earth is a more or less round contraption and people have even been out in little space craft to take a good look. Thus, we can say that the scientists have been wrong in most of their science. Unfortunately certain religious leaders made it an offence punishable by death to say that the Earth was round, and not so many years ago people were nicely toasted at the stake for saying that the Earth was round and not flat. However, I suppose we all have to die at some time, and there is always the consolation that if one is thoroughly surrounded by fire one dies of suffocation before the flames reach one—not that that would be much consolation to the victim tied at the stake.

If we are going to get some scientist's technical theory as the limits of what we might do or say or think, then we are going to put ourselves in the position of a railway locomotive which is confined to rails. People on the train pulled by that locomotive can only see a very limited amount which lies on either side of the track they traverse, they are not able to diverge to see by-ways off the main highway.

People who travel by car, or even on foot, see more and learn more. People who travel on foot are the slowest, but they learn more and more in detail and are perhaps the best off in the end, while people who travel by air may be going so fast and so high that they see nothing at all. So let us meander along, not disporting ourselves with the scientific theories of great men which may be wonderful in mathematical formula, but which do not necessarily correspond to the real facts of life and the after-life.

Western civilisation occupies much less than a tenth of a second of celestial time. If you think of the age of the Earth you will find that Man in any of his forms upon this Earth does not even occupy one minute of the twenty-four hours of the Earth's existence.

People who can do astral travelling or who are clairvoyant or telepathic can get a much better impression of what is going on, for those people know that Man upon Earth is just one manifestation of a spirit.

There have been other forms of body, there have been other forms of corporeal existence. The physical body of mankind on the Earth is just one of a long, long series of experiments to see which form will afford a spirit body the best chance of learning the most and the easiest and the quickest.

Mankind is not the ultimate, do not believe that it is. No words of religion, no scientists' theories can ever convince the celestial spirit that the little slug body it now occupies is superior to the glittering butterfly that it can become.

All this is an attempt to make you think for yourselves, an attempt to make you go into astral travelling and clairvoyance seriously. If people are going to analyse everything, and try to find fault in everything without knowing better, then they are going to stultify their own development. We must keep an open mind, we must be ready to accept, we must know what we are talking about and not say, 'Oh, that's not right, that's not what Einstein said.' Einstein and people like Einstein said that the Earth was flat; Einstein and people like Einstein said Man would never travel faster than the speed of sound; well we do, you know, some of us, and some of us travel faster than the speed of light. Astral travel is much much faster. In the astral world when we move about we really whoop it up, but I do not need to tell you all this. If you will keep an open mind, and instead of trying to criticise destructively if you will try to assimilate constructively for yourselves, then you will not find too great difficulty in doing astral travel.

Keep in mind also that approximately every 2,000 years or so a new Messiah, Saviour, or World Leader appears on Earth. This is a cycle which continues through cycles—always.

So we come to the end of another book, the twelfth chapter written in the twelfth hour of the cycle of Kali. May it be that something that I have written will help you on your way, and to conclude our remarks about religion may I add that you can have faith in what I have written because all I have written in all my books is true!

'KINDNESS TO PUBLISHERS' DEPARTMENT

THROUGHOUT the years since *The Third Eye* first appeared I have had a tremendous amount of mail, and up to the present I have always answered that mail. Now I have to say that I am no longer able to reply to any mail at all unless adequate return postage is enclosed. So please do NOT send letters to my Publisher for forwarding to me because I have asked my Publisher not to forward any letters.

People forget that they pay for a BOOK, and NOT a lifetime of free post-paid advisory service. Publishers are PUBLISHERS—not a letter forwarding service.

I have letters from all over the world, even from well behind the Iron Curtain, but not one in several thousand people encloses return postage, and the cost is so much that I can no longer undertake replies.

People ask such peculiar things, too. Here are just some:

There was a very desperate letter from Australia which reached me when I was in Ireland. The matter was (apparently) truly urgent, so at my own expense I sent a cable to Australia, and I did not even receive a note of thanks.

A certain gentleman in the U.S.A. wrote me a letter DEMANDING that I should immediately write a thesis for him and send it by return airmail. He wanted to use it as his thesis to obtain a Doctorate in Oriental Philosophy. Of course he did not enclose any postage, it was merely a somewhat threatening demand!

An Englishman wrote me a very, very haughty letter in the third person, demanding my credentials, because if they were completely satisfactory to this person he would consider placing himself under my tuition provided that there would be no charge for it. In other words, I was supposed to be honoured. (I do not think he would like my reply!)

Another one wrote to me and said that if I 'and my chums' would come from Tibet and cluster around his bed in the astral at night then he would be able to feel more happy about astral travelling.

Other people write to me and ask me everything from high esoteric things (which I can answer if I want to) to how to keep hens and one's husband! People also consider that they should write to me just whenever they think they should, and they get offensive if I do not reply by return airmail.

I will ask you NOT to bother my Publishers, in fact I have asked them not to send on any letters to me because they are in business as Publishers. For those who really do need an answer (although I do not invite letters) I have an accommodation address. It is:

Dr. T. Lobsang Rampa
BM/TLR,
London W.C.1., England.

I do not guarantee any reply, and if you use this address you will have to provide very adequate postage because the letters will be forwarded to me and I shall have to pay, so I shall not be in a sweet enough mood to reply unless you have made my expense your expense. For example, it will cost me a dollar at least by the time forwarding charges are paid.

Dr. Rampa's
Tranquilliser Touch-Stones

You are interested in the Higher Sciences or you would not be reading this book. Have you considered how your tranquillity can be nourished by a Rampa-Touch-Stone? On page 123 in *Wisdom of the Ancients* you can read about these Touch-Stones. They are available with simple instructions

AN INSTRUCTION RECORD ON MEDITATION

A large number of people wrote to Lobsang Rampa demanding a record about Meditation, so at last he has made the only special, fully authentic recording by him. Tells you how to meditate, shows you how easy it is, places peace, harmony and inner contentment within YOUR reach. Rampa-Touch-Stones Ltd. can supply this 12″ record AND THE TRANQUILLISER TOUCH STONE ANYWHERE at the prices below AIRMAIL FREE.

Price List	Record	Tranquilliser Touch-Stones	
Australia	4	4.20	dollars
Austria	110	120	schillings
Belgium	220	230	francs
Canada	5.50	5.50	dollars
Denmark	30	33.5	kroner
France	20	24	francs
Great Britain	33	37	shillings
Germany	17	18	deutsche marks
Holland	15	17	guilders
Italy	2500	2900	lires
New Zealand	4	4.20	dollars
Norway	30	32	kroner
S. Africa	3.5	3.8	rand
Sweden	20	25	kroner
U.S.A.	5	5	dollars

All other places 40 shillings or 5 dollars EACH ITEM

Rampa-Touch-Stones Ltd.
33 Ashby Road, Loughborough, Leicestershire, England.